Assessment of Adult Personality

Lewis R. Aiken, PhD, was graduated from Florida State University with B.S. and M.A. degrees in psychology. He subsequently attended Emory University and the University of North Carolina at Chapel Hill, and was graduated from the latter institution with a Ph.D. in psychology (psychometrics and experimental psychology). After receiving the doctorate, Dr. Aiken taught at the University of North Carolina at Greensboro, where he was also Director of Admissions and Placement Research. Other teaching appointments included Dana Professor of Psychology and Chairman of the Department at Guilford College, and Research Educationist at UCLA and the University for Teacher Education in Tehran, Iran. On returning to the United States, Dr. Aiken taught at the University of the Pacific for 2 years and at Pepperdine University for 13 years. Among the awards he has received are an NAS–NRC Postdoctoral Resident Research Associateship (U.S. Navy Research Laboratory and San Diego State University), a U.S.O.E. Postdoctoral Fellowship (Stanford University and the University of Georgia), and a Fulbright research/lectureship (Botswana) During his long career, Dr. Aiken has also served as a consultant for numerous educational, governmental, health, and industrial organizations. His major research interests are in psychological assessment, about which he has published several textbooks and dozens of articles. He has also published books and articles in personality theories and research, adult development and aging, death and dying, and general psychology. Dr. Aiken is a fellow in the American Psychological Association, a member of several other professional organizations, and is listed in *Who's Who in America*. He is the father of two and the grandfather of three. He and his wife, Dorothy, live in Moorpark, California.

Assessment of Adult Personality

Lewis R. Aiken, PhD

Springer Publishing Company

Springer Publishing Company, Inc.
536 Broadway
New York, NY 10012-3955

Cover design by: Margaret Dunin
Production Editor: Pamela Lankas
Acquisition Editor: Bill Tucker

97 98 99 00 01 / 5 4 3 2 1

Library of Congress Cataloging-in-Publication Data

Aiken, Lewis R., 1931-
    Assessment of adult personality / Lewis R. Aiken.
        p.   cm.
    Includes bibliographical references and indexes.
    ISBN 0-8261-9710-8
    1. Personality assessment.   I. Title.
    BF698.4.A35   1997
    155.2'8—dc21   97-12115
                                                                        CIP

Printed in the United States of America

Contents

Preface

This book is a brief survey of concepts, methods, and instruments in the field of adult personality assessment. Procedures and methods of assessment are emphasized, but because theories, research, and issues concerning human personality have influenced the measurement of stylistic characteristics and behavior, these matters are not neglected.

The term *personality assessment* refers to the measurement and appraisal of characteristic modes of thinking and acting. It is not limited to the classification and measurement of types, traits, and temperaments, but includes instruments, techniques, and methods for measuring interests, attitudes, values, perceptual styles, and other internal dynamics and behaviors characterizing the uniqueness of individuals. Both adaptive and maladaptive behaviors and cognitions, and the consistencies and changes in personality that occur with experience, disease, accidents, and aging, fall within the purview of this volume.

Each of the eight chapters in the book ends with a summary and a list of suggested readings for further study of the topic. Numerous illustrations and examples provide the reader with a background for selecting and using a variety of personality assessment devices and an understanding of the assets and limitations of such instruments and procedures. The reader is urged to scrutinize the psychometric qualities (reliability, validity, standardization, etc.) of the various instruments carefully and to become thoroughly familiar with methods by which they are administered, scored, and interpreted. The necessity for making multiple observations and measurements, depending on the goals of the psychological assessment, and integrating findings from different sources are stressed as well. Procedures for reporting assessment results to appropriate persons and subsequent follow-up and retesting are also discussed. The variety of settings (clinical, educational, industrial/organizational, judicial, military, etc.) in which personality assessments occur are considered in detail by description and illustration.

Although the book is designed primarily for use by professional psychologists and psychological assessment trainees, it should also serve well as a textbook on personality assessment at the upper undergraduate or graduate level. In addition to serving as a training manual and a textbook, the book is a useful reference source, providing coverage of a wide range of instruments and procedures, a comprehensive glossary, a list of test publishers and addresses, and complete indexes of authors, subjects, and tests.

This book consists mainly of text, but many figures and tables are also included. Statistical matters are not considered in detail; it is assumed that the reader or user of the book has had an adequate introduction to statistical and elementary mental measurement concepts.

A completed textbook is the joint product of many hands and minds, but I owe particular thanks to Bill Tucker, who encouraged and supported my efforts from the beginning, Pam Lankas, whose superb editorial work clarified and polished my writing, and Louise Farkas who shepherded the book through the editorial and production mill. As always, however, the final responsibility is mine.

Lewis R. Aiken

1

Foundations and the Contemporary Scene

In what ways and to what extent are people different from one another? Some are taller than others, some are heavier, and some are stronger, but the range of variation in such physical characteristics is not unlimited. People are also similar to each other in many respects. Of even greater interest to psychologists than similarities and differences in physical characteristics are differences and similarities in behavioral patterns and cognitive processes, and their causes and consequences.

There is a great deal of consistency and continuity in the actions and thoughts of people, so much so that we often speak of patterns or styles of cognition and behavior. We say that people are just being themselves or, alternatively, that they are beside themselves or outside themselves when they are not behaving or thinking in a familiar, expected manner. We say that they are childish or mature, smart or dumb, calm or upset, and so on. But what makes them that way? What causes a person to have one personality, temperament, or behavioral style rather than another? Of all the mysteries confronting us, this is one of the most profound—the mystery of human personality.

The term *personality* is derived from the Greek word *persona*, which was a "mask" worn by an actor when assuming a particular role in a play. As applied by contemporary psychologists, *personality* is not limited to the various roles played by a person; it encompasses all of the behaviors and thoughts that, in combination, characterize the uniqueness of the individual. There is no single agreed-on definition of personality: Gordon Allport (Super, 1990) defined it in terms of 4,000 traits and suggested

50 meanings. As a working definition, however, we may say that *personality* is the sum total of all the qualities, traits, and behaviors that characterize a person's individuality and, by which, together with his or her physical attributes, the person is recognized as unique. This is a broad definition, including not only affective characteristics, such as temperament traits, attitudes, and values, but cognitive characteristics (abilities, achievements, etc.) and even psychomotor variables, such as the characteristic ways in which people walk, talk, and express themselves nonverbally.

As in all scientific investigations, the study of personality begins with observation and measurement. This book is concerned with the measurement of personality in adulthood, or, more generally, personality assessment. *Personality assessment* is the description and analysis of personality by means of various instruments and procedures, including the following:

Ability tests
Attitude scales
Biographical and autobiographical writings
Checklists
Content analysis of diaries
Dream analysis
First memories
Interest inventories
Interviews
Observations
Perceptual measures
Physiological measures
Projective techniques
Rating scales
Values scales

These methods and procedures are not nearly as precise as those for measuring the physical characteristics of objects, but they are still interesting and valuable.

Like physical measurement, personality assessment helps psychologists and other human service professionals to understand and predict things. The "things" in this case are the behaviors of human beings and the outcomes of those behaviors. Thus, if we conclude by applying selected personality assessment procedures that a particular individual has certain tendencies or characteristics, it may help us to understand why that person behaves as he or she does, and even to predict how he or she will behave at some future time.

The accuracy with which we are able to understand and predict the behavior of a person depends on the quality of our assessment instruments and procedures. In other words, how reliably and validly do they measure what we want them to measure? Although a personality assessment instrument administered at one time and in one situation may be a valid measure of a certain characteristic at that time and in that situation, because of changes in the individual and the situation in which measurements are made, it may not be as valid at some other time or in some other situation.

Unlike many physical objects, human beings are dynamic, ever-changing entities. They have new experiences and are exposed to a variety of environmental conditions that shape or modify their behavior in different ways and consequently change them both physically and mentally over the life span. Nevertheless, there is a core of consistency in human personality from the cradle to the grave, a set of inborn temperamental dispositions that cause people to seek out different situations and react to them in a different manner from other people. In addition, external pressures and controls restrict the environments to which different people are exposed and thereby delimit their experiences. Thus, behavior and personality are shaped in a complex manner by heredity and environment, the interaction between the physicochemical structures inherited by a person and the experiences or circumstances with which he or she comes in contact before and after birth.

PSEUDOSCIENTIFIC PRECURSORS
AND MODERN HISTORY

The analysis and evaluation of people is probably as old as humanity itself. Descriptions of character and personality are found in many ancient writings and memorabilia, dating back thousands of years before the common era. Myths, stories, religious texts, philosophical treatises from ancient Greece, China, and even before abound with descriptions of the personalities and abilities of heroes and other famous persons. Many of the descriptions were based on pseudoscientific systems, such as astrology, numerology, palmistry, physiognomy, phrenology, and graphology. Several of these pseudosciences (e.g., astrology, numerology, palmistry) were concerned primarily with divination, or soothsaying, that is, prophesying or foretelling future events. Other examples of pseudosciences applied for purposes of divination were hydromancy—divination by reading the airs, winds, and waters; geomancy—divination by geographical features, figures, or lines; haruspicy—divination from reading the entrails of animals killed in sacrifice; and necromancy—

divination by communication with the dead. Even alchemists, who were concerned principally with discovering a method for changing baser metals into gold and with finding a universal solvent and an elixir of life, attempted to foretell the future by reading the shapes formed by a thin stream of molten lead poured into a bowl of water.

Astrology and Palmistry

Although the efforts made by diviners to foretell the future and to analyze human personality were not successful, astrologers in particular had (and occasionally still have) a significant influence on the decisions of political and military leaders and their consorts. Astrology is based on the notion that the relative positions of the sun, moon, and planets at a particular time, such as a person's birth date, affect his or her personality and future. As shown in Table 1.1, each of the 12 constellations that make up the zodiac is said to be associated with a particular sign and cluster of personality characteristics.[1]

Similar to astrology in attempting to relate character and personality to heavenly bodies is *palmistry* or *chiromancy*. Palmists (chiromancers) pay particular attention to the seven mounts (Jupiter, Saturn, the Sun, Mercury, Mars, the Moon, and Venus) at the bases of the thumb and fingers and on the sides of the hand. Illustrative of the characteristics said to be associated with the development of each of these mounts are the following:

Jupiter. Ambition, concern for honor, interest in religion; overdevelopment reveals pride and superstition.
Mars. High development indicates bravery and a martial character; low development suggests cowardice.
Saturn. Related to luck and wisdom.
Sun (Apollo). Related to intelligence.
Venus. Related to amorousness.

Palmists also examine the relative lengths and depth of the lines of the palm (head, heart, life, and fortune). For example, the head line is said to be related to intelligence, the heart line to affection, the fortune line to success and failure, and a short or broken life line to early death or serious illness.

Phrenology, Physiognomy, and Graphology

Phrenology, a theory and method of analysis first propounded around 1800 by J. Gall and J. Spurtzheim, is based on the belief that certain

TABLE 1.1 Personality Characteristics and the Zodiac

Birthday	Constellation	Planet	Personality characteristics
December 21–January 20	Capricorn	Saturn	Ambitious, cautious, work oriented
January 21–February 19	Aquarius	Uranus	Humane, unconventional, high/low spirits
February 20–March 20	Pisces	Neptune	Inspiration, easily influenced, dreaming
March 21–April 20	Aries	Mars	Impulsiveness, adventure, disputes
April 21–May 21	Taurus	Venus	Endurance, obstination, labor
May 22–June 21	Gemini	Mercury	Skill, versatility, good relationships
June 22–July 23	Cancer	Moon	Appreciates home life, imagination, indecision
July 24–August 23	Leo	Sun	Generality, pride, desire for power
August 24–September 23	Virgo	Mercury	Analytical, studious, modest
September 24–October 23	Libra	Venus	Justice, artistic sense, sensitivity
October 24–November 22	Scorpio	Mars	Critical sense, secrecy, fights
November 23–December 20	Sagittarius	Jupiter	Idealism, open-mindedness, mobility

mental faculties and character traits are indicated by the configurations of the skull. According to phrenologists, abstract mental qualities, such as acquisitiveness, agreeableness, artistic talent, courage, greed, and pride, are associated with the overdevelopment of one or more brain "organs," resulting in a protuberance (bump) on the skull over the corresponding site of the organ. If this is correct, it should be possible to interpret personality and character by feeling the configuration of bumps on the top of the head. For example, it was reported that the heads of courageous people were thick and full just behind the top of the ear, whereas the heads of cowardly people were thin and depressed in that particular region (Fowler, 1890, p. 1). Subsequent research in neurophysiology showed, however, that the methods and beliefs of the phrenologists were misguided.

Similar to palmistry and phrenology in the belief that certain physical features of the body reveal mental qualities is *physiognomy*. Physiognomists analyze the personal characteristics of an individual from the form or features of the body, especially the face. Actually, the English language is replete with physiognomic descriptions (e.g., a disarming smile, an honest expression, a poker face, or shifty eyes). Many actors pride themselves on being able to make facial expressions that connote certain feelings or attitudes. But these are dynamic, changing expressions rather than static, structural features.

Although physiognomy is not entirely without foundation, it has been carried too far in psychometric instruments, such as the Szondi Test. In taking this test, the examinee selects the two pictures he or she likes most, and the two he or she likes least from each of six sets of eight pictures of mental patients with different psychiatric diagnoses (catatonia, depression, hysteria, mania, etc.). The assumption on which the Szondi Test is based is that the examinee is most like the patients depicted in the photographs that he or she likes most, and least like the patients in the photographs that he or she likes least. Perpetuation of the belief that facial features reveal personality is also found in the requirement of submitting a photograph with a educational or employment application.

Perhaps more reputable than either phrenology or physiognomy is *graphology*, the analysis of handwriting to ascertain the character, personality, and abilities of the writer. Graphologists may employ the "global" technique of attempting to interpreting handwriting intuitively on the basis of overall impressions or analytically by emphasizing certain signs or cues, such as how the writer dots *i*s or slants letters. To be fair, graphology is not considered to be as unscientific as astrology or phrenology. In fact, many prominent psychologists (e.g., Alfred Binet) have shown an interest in graphology. At a fairly elementary level, there is evidence that the size and shape of a signature are related to certain psychosocial characteristics of the person (Aiken & Zweigenhaft, 1978). However, handwriting is affected by drugs, aging, disease, and many other factors than personality (Kelly, 1987). For this and other reasons, studies have found that the reliability and validity of graphologists' interpretations of handwriting samples are not high (Neter & Ben-Shakhar et al., 1989). Computers, unfortunately, have proved no better than graphologists in analyzing personality from handwriting samples (Rothenberg, 1990).

Modern History of Personality Assessment

The modern history of personality assessment began with the study of individual differences in abilities, temperament, and other characteristics. The first pioneering researches on individual differences were conducted by a Victorian gentleman-scientist, Sir Francis Galton. Galton, who was stimulated by his cousin Charles Darwin's writings on the evolution of species differences, was especially interested in the hereditary origins of general mental ability. To measure and investigate the variability of intelligence in the general population, Galton devised a set of sensorimotor tests (of reaction time, sensory discrimination, etc.). He administered these simple tests to over 9,000 people ranging in age from 5 to 80 years, but, unfortunately, they did not prove to be good predictors of performance in school work and other tasks that presumably require intelligence. Galton also proposed to measure emotions by means of changes in heart and pulse rate and to measure optimism, good temper, and other character traits by means of rating scales and observations of people in various social situations. Another technique devised by Galton was the *word association test*, in which examinees were asked to respond to a series of stimulus words with the first words that occurred to them. This technique was developed further for clinical assessment purposes by Emil Kraepelin (1892) and Carl Jung (1905). The work of Kraepelin and other psychiatrists during the late 19th and early 20th centuries also contributed to the design of additional instruments and procedures for the assessment of personality.

Despite their potential and the interest shown by certain psychologists and psychiatrists in the development of measures of personality characteristics and mental disorders, even more significant in the early years of psychological assessment was construction of a practical, standardized intelligence test. The first edition of this test, the Binet–Simon Intelligence Scale, was published in 1905 and revised in 1908 and 1911. It consisted of a series of age-scaled school-type tasks presented to a child for the purpose of determining the child's mental age and judging whether he or she was below average, average, or above average in mental ability.

Many translations and revisions of the Binet–Simon Scale were made, the most prominent of which—the Stanford–Binet Intelligence Scale— has been used extensively for testing the mental abilities of children and adults throughout this century. Another series of intelligence tests, which ultimately proved to be even more popular than the Stanford– Binet, were the tests devised by David Wechsler for measuring the mental abilities of preschool children (Wechsler Preschool and Primary Scale of Intelligence), school-age children (Wechsler Intelligence Scale for Children), and adults (Wechsler Adult Intelligence Scale). As we shall see, a revision of the last of these tests has been used extensively in research on adult personality and for clinical diagnosis of psychological disorders in adults. Intelligence tests, such as the Wechsler Adult Intelligence Scale-Revised, have been used extensively in clinical and educational/developmental contexts to identify mental retardation and to determine the presence of other cognitive disorders and (sometimes incidentally) personality characteristics and adjustment problems.

Many of the significant events in the history of personality assessment are listed in Table 1.2. Prominent among these are the development and use of the first personality inventory, the Woodworth Personal Data Sheet, for military selection in World War I. This paper-and-pencil inventory consisted of a series of 116 statements concerned with psychoneurotic symptoms; respondents were told to check yes or no to each statement, depending on whether it was true or false about them. Examples are the following (Hollingworth, 1920, pp. 120–126):

Do you feel sad and low spirited most of the time?
Are you often frightened in the middle of the night?
Do you think you have hurt yourself by going too much with women?
Have you ever lost your memory for a time?
Do you usually feel well and strong?
Do you ever walk in your sleep?
Do you ever feel an awful pressure in or about your head?
Are you troubled with the idea that people are watching you on the street?
Do you make friends easily?
Are you troubled by shyness?
Did you have a happy childhood?
Are you ever bothered by feeling that things are not real?

The Personal Data Sheet was designed as a psychiatric screening device for soldiers during World War I, but it appeared too late to be used in that conflict. It was important less for its use than for the fact that it was the first practical personality inventory: it led the way in the development of more popular instruments, such as the Minnesota Multiphasic Personality Inventory (MMPI) and the Sixteen Personality Factor Questionnaire (16 PF). Unlike the Personal Data Sheet, which yielded a single score, inventories such as the MMPI and the 16 PF were multiscore instruments that could be scored on numerous variables or scales. Although single-score inventories of normal and pathological characteristics continued to be developed in the context of particular research investigations or for particular clinical/diagnostic purposes, multiscore instruments greatly exceeded them in popularity. In addition to instruments specifically designated as personality inventories, measures of interests, attitudes, values, and other psychosocial characteristics that are reflective of personality have been constructed over the years. More personality assessment instruments are listed than tests in any other category in *Books in Print IV* (Murphy, Conoley, & Impara,

TABLE 1.2 Selected Events in the History of Personality Assessment

4th century B.C.—Descriptions of 30 personality/character types made by Theophrastus.

A.D. 2nd century—Galen relates Hippocrates's theory of body humors to temperament.

1800—Pseudoscience of phrenology, relating bumps on the skull to personality, established by J. Gall and F. Spurzheim.

1884—Methods for measuring character described by F. Galton, including word associations and behavior-sampling techniques.

1892—Word-association technique first used in clinical contexts by E. Kraepelin.

1896—New classification of mental disorders described by E. Kraepelin.

1905—Word-association test used by C. Jung for analysis of mental complexes. First practical intelligence test, the Binet–Simon Scale, by A. Binet and T. Simon, published.

1906—List of symptoms indicative of psychopathology developed by Heymans and Wiersma.

1910—Word lists published by Kent and Rosanoff.

1919—First standardized personality inventory, the Woodworth Personal Data Sheet, used in military selection. S. Pressey's X-O Test published.

1920—Rorschach Psychodiagnostic Test first published.

1925—Observations on the relationships of body build to personality and mental disorders described by E. Kretschmer.

1926—F. Goodenough's Draw-a-Man Test published.

1927—First edition of E. K. Strong's Vocational Interest Blank for Men published.

1928—Studies of character reported by H. Hartshorne and M. May.

1935—H. Murray and collaborators develop the Thematic Apperception Test. Humm-Wadsworth Temperament Scale published.

1938—*Explorations in Personality*, describing the theoretical foundations of the Thematic Apperception Test, published by H. Murray. Bender Visual–Motor Gestalt Test for assessing personality and organic brain damage published. First edition of *Mental Measurements Yearbook* published.

1939—Kuder Preference Record published. Wechsler-Bellevue Intelligence Scale published.

1940—J. P. Guilford applies factor analysis to the construction of a personality inventory.

1941–45—Office of Strategic Services develops situational tests for selection of espionage agents.

1942—Research on the relationships between body build and temperament reported by W. Sheldon and S. Stevens.

1943—Minnesota Multiphasic Personality Inventory published.

1949—Sixteen Personality Factor Questionnaire published by R. B. Cattell.

1953—W. Stephenson develops Q-sort technique.

1954—*Clinical Versus Statistical Prediction* published by P. Meehl.

1955—*Psychology of Personal Constructs* published by G. Kelly.

1958—First version of Moral Judgment Scale published by L. Kohlberg.

1970–90—Digital computers increasingly used in the design, administration, scoring, and interpretation of personality assessment instruments and procedures.

1972—The Self-Directed Search, a measure of interests and personality, published by J. Holland. Model Penal Code rule for legal insanity published and widely adopted in the U.S.

(Continued)

TABLE 1.2 (Continued)

1985—American Psychological Association publishes *Standards for Educational and Psychological Testing.*
1987—California Psychological Inventory–Revised published.
1989—Minnesota Multiphasic Personality Inventory–II published.
1994—Fourth edition of the *Diagnostic and Statistical Manual–IV* published.
1995—Twelfth edition of *The Mental Measurements Yearbook* published.

1994). The most widely referenced personality tests are listed in Table 1.3.

Equal in importance to personality inventories in the history of personality assessment is the use of relatively unstructured stimulus materials, such as cloud pictures or incomplete sentences, to analyze personality characteristics and problems. Although Emil Kraepelin, Alfred Binet, Hermann Ebbinghaus, and certain other psychologists had experimented with these procedures earlier, not until the 20th century did such projective techniques become popular in psychological examinations. The two most widely used projective techniques have been the Rorschach Inkblot Test and the Thematic Apperception Test (TAT). Other projectives, such as the Draw-a-Man Test, the Bender Visual-Motor Gestalt Test, and several standardized word association tests, also had their supporters, but not to the same extent as the Rorschach and the TAT.

In addition to personality inventories and projective techniques, checklists, rating scales, attitude scales, and various physiologically oriented instruments and procedures (polygraph, perceptual tests, etc.) have been developed to provide information on personality. Some of these instruments were designed to diagnose psychopathological conditions, whereas others were designed to measure personality characteristics and adjustment in relatively normal individuals. Even more basic than the construction of personality assessment instruments have been refinements in observational and interviewing procedures that can yield a wealth of information on behavior and mental functioning.

The construction and use of personality assessment instruments and procedures has accompanied applications and research on psychological topics in various contexts—clinical, developmental, educational, industrial/organizational, military, legal—during this century. Clinical/counseling, educational/school, industrial/organizational, and other areas of applied psychology have grown extensively during the past half-century, a growth that has been accompanied and in some measure stimulated by the development of psychological assessment methods and procedures. The increased speed, economy, and flexibility of digital

TABLE 1.3 Reference Frequencies for Personality Tests Cited in *Tests in Print IV*

	No. of references
Adjective Check List (The)	92
Beck Depression Inventory (1993, rev.)	660
Bem Sex-Role Inventory	204
Brief Symptom Inventory	59
Child Behavior Checklist	135
Children's Depression Inventory	71
Coopersmith Self-Esteem Inventories	106
Depression Adjective Check Lists	79
Eysenck Personality Inventory	226
Eysenck Personality Questionnaire (rev.)	190
Jenkins Activity Survey	146
Millon Clinical Multiaxial Inventory–II	104
Minnesota Multiphasic Personality Inventory–II	504
Multiple Affective Adjective Check List (rev.)	96
Piers-Harris Children's Self-Concept Scale	123
Profile of Mood States	191
Present State Examination	237
Rorschach	273
Schedule for Affective Disorders and Schizophrenia (3rd ed.)	152
Shipley Institute of Living Scale	63
Sixteen Personality Factor Questionnaire (5th ed.)	140
State-Trait Anxiety Inventory	646
Symptom Checklist–90 (rev.)	318
Thematic Apperception Test	107

computers in administering and scoring tests and other assessments, and in analyzing the findings, has led to broader and more effective applications of psychological assessment. Of particular interest has been the assessment of children to determine how their behavior and mental characteristics develop and function. This book is concerned mainly with the personality assessment of adults, but, as emphasized by Sigmund Freud, "the child is father to the man." Because the roots of adult personality are found in childhood, as we consider the identification and measurement of personality in adulthood we shall refer frequently to its beginnings in childhood.

PROFESSIONAL ORGANIZATIONS AND ISSUES

Research and practice in adult personality assessment is pursued by members of many professional organizations, such as the Society for

Personality Assessment, the American Psychological Association, the American Psychiatric Association, and the American Personnel and Guidance Association. Journals containing research reports, theoretical and discussion papers, and reviews of specific personality assessment instruments and procedures are published by many professional organizations. The most prominent English-language periodicals in this category are listed in Table 1.4.

The first personality assessment instruments were developed principally to facilitate the identification and diagnosis of psychopathology, and many contemporary personality inventories, rating scales, and projective techniques that focus on personality disorders are still administered for this purpose. Foremost among the psychometric instruments administered in clinical situations are the MMPI-II, the Thematic Apperception Test, the Rorschach, the Bender-Gestalt, the Beck Depression Inventory, the Millon Clinical Multiaxial Inventory–II, the Symptom Checklist–90R, and various sentence completion and projective drawing tests (Watkins, Campbell, Nieberding, & Hallmark, 1995). Information obtained from administering these instruments assists in diagnosing the characteristics and causes of personal problems and mental disorders. In addition, it contributes to the planning of psychological and physical treatments or interventions and evaluating the effectiveness of these procedures.

People who refer themselves or are referred by others to clinical psychologists and psychiatrists usually have some fairly serious problem(s) with which they are unable to cope. Among the many problems that prompt adults to seek psychological or psychiatric help are the following:

Aches and pains
Addiction to smoking, alcohol, drugs, gambling, etc.
Anxiety
Chronic anger (aggression)
Chronic fatigue
Compulsions
Depression
Disorganized or strange thoughts and behaviors
Failure (in school, on a job, in marriage, etc.)
Impulsivity
Inability to get along with acquaintances, coworkers, or colleagues
Inability to hold down a job
Marital difficulties
Memory problems
Sexual disorders

TABLE 1.4 Some Journals Publishing Articles on Adult Personality Assessment

Advances in Personality Assessment
British Journal of Projective Psychology
Journal of Clinical Psychology
Journal of Counseling Psychology
Journal of Personality
Journal of Personality and Clinical Studies
Journal of Personality and Social Psychology
Journal of Personality Assessment
Journal of Psychopathology and Behavioral Assessment
Journal of Research in Personality
Journal of Social Behavior and Personality
Journal of Vocational Behavior
Personality and Clinical Psychology
Personality and Individual Differences
Personality, Psychopathology, and Psychotherapy
Personality and Social Psychology Bulletin
Psychological Assessment: A Journal of Consulting and Clinical Psychology

Stress
Suicidal thoughts
Uncontrollable fears
Unemployment

The presenting problem, as stated by the patient or the referral source, is, however, usually not the total problem and may even be only a superficial symptom of a more complex, deep-seated difficulty. It is not always necessary to understand the causes of a person's problems before attempting to help him or her, but identifying and understanding the problem is the first step in most cases. This process may be facilitated by the use of psychological tests and other assessment procedures. To select tests that will contribute to an understanding of the patient and the problem(s), a psychological examiner must know what psychometric instruments are appropriate, how to administer, score, and interpret them, and what their strengths and weaknesses are.

In addition to their uses in clinical or psychiatric diagnoses, paper-and-pencil inventories and scales and other personality assessment devices are used for purposes of selection, classification, placement, promotion, dismissal, and the rotation of employees and trainees (students) in industrial/organizations, military and government, educational, and health contexts. Illustrative of instruments administered for these purposes are the Sixteen Personality Factor Questionnaire, the

Myers-Briggs Type Indicator, the California Psychological Inventory, and the Edwards Personal Preference Schedule. Personality assessment instruments can also be helpful in law enforcement contexts, as in predicting violence or recidivism in criminal defendants, and as aids in understanding and dealing with marital, family, and health problems. Examples of instruments used in marital and family assessment, legal/law enforcement contexts, and health contexts are given in Table 1.5.

In addition to describing and analyzing individual characteristics, psychological assessment instruments and procedures are used to assess the psychological environments or climate of organizations, such as schools, hospitals, and factories. Illustrative of instruments of this type are the Social Climate Scales, the Environmental Response Inventory, and the Organizational Climate Index.

Sources of Information on Personality Tests

There are literally thousands of published and unpublished personality assessment instruments and procedures. Commercially available instru-

TABLE 1.5 Representative Personality Assessment Instruments for Various Applied Contexts

Marriage and family
  California Marriage Readiness Evaluation
  Family Apperception Test
  Family Environment Scale
  Marriage Adjustment Inventory
  Marital Attitude Evaluation
  Marital Satisfaction Inventory

Health
  Attributional Styles Questionnaire
  Health Attribution Test
  Health Locus of Control Scale
  Millon Behavioral Health Inventory

Legal/Law Enforcement
  Clarke Sex History Questionnaire for Males
  Competency Assessment Instrument
  Competency Screening Test
  Custody Quotient
  Georgetown Screening Interview for Competency to Stand Trial
  Georgia Court Competency Test
  Rogers Criminal Responsibility Scales

ments are described and reviewed in various sources, including *Tests in Print IV* (Murphy, Conoley, & Impara, 1994), *The Mental Measurements Yearbooks* (Buros, 1978 and earlier editions; Conoley & Impara, 1995; Conoley & Kramer, 1989; Kramer & Conoley, 1992; Mitchell, 1985), *Personality Tests and Reviews* (Buros, 1970), *Tests* (Sweetland & Keyser, 1991), and *Test Critiques* (Keyser & Sweetland, 1984–94). Additional information on personality assessment instruments for adults can be found in *Testing Adults* (Swiercinsky, 1985), and in the catalogs provided by the publishers and distributors listed in the appendix. Corcoran and Fischer's (1987) sourcebook of measures for clinical practices contains dozens of scales and inventories for use with adults, couples, and families.

Information on numerous unpublished measures of adult personality can be found in *Dissertation Abstracts*, the several volumes of the *Directory of Unpublished Experimental Mental Measures* (Goldman & Busch, 1978, 1982; Goldman & Mitchell, 1990; Goldman & Osborne, 1985; Goldman & Saunders, 1974), *Measures for Psychological Assessment* (Chun, Cobb, & French, 1976), *A Consumer's Guide to Tests in Print* (Hammill, Brown, & Bryant, 1992), and *Index to Tests Used in Educational Dissertations* (Fabiano, 1989).

Both published and unpublished measures designed for clinical/diagnostic purposes are referenced in *A Source Book for Mental Health Measures* (Comrey, Bacher, & Glaser, 1973) and the *Handbook of Psychiatric Rating Scales* (2nd ed.) (Lyerly, 1978). Information on unpublished measures of attitudes can be found in the series of volumes from the University of Michigan's Institute for Social Research (Robinson, Athanasiou, & Head, 1974; Robinson, Rush, & Head, 1974; Robinson, Shaver, & Wrightsman, 1991), and volume 5 of *The ETS Test Collection Catalog* (1991). Other informative sources concerned with unpublished psychometric instruments are The Health and Psychosocial Instruments and PsychINFO databases.

Although personality assessment instruments are not used as extensively as achievement tests, their development and marketing is a fairly lucrative business. Psychologists of all stripes (clinical, counseling, industrial/organizational, military, forensic, educational) conduct personality assessments for applied and research purposes. Extensive usage does not guarantee proper usage. Awareness of this truism has led to increasing concern about ethical issues and standards in psychological testing during the past few decades.

Standards and Ethics

Like all psychological tests, personality assessment instruments are far from completely objective or free from bias. They have been criticized as being biased toward gender and race, of being based on faulty models and assumptions about human behavior, of having low reliability and validity, of being easily faked and misinterpreted, and even as suggesting immoral and irreverent behavior. Realizing that such allegations often contain an element of truth, many years ago the American Psychological Association developed a set of *Standards for Educational and Psychological Testing* (American Educational Research Association et al., 1985), the *Guidelines for Computer-Based Tests and Interpretation* (American Psychological Association, 1993), and "Ethical Principles of Psychologists and Code of Conduct" (American Psychological Association, 1992). Central to the Code is standard 202 concerning competence and appropriate use of assessments and interventions:

(a) Psychologists who develop, administer, score, interpret, or use psychological assessment techniques, interviews, tests, or instruments do so in a manner and for purposes that are appropriate in light of the research on or evidence of the usefulness and proper application of the techniques.

(b) Psychologists refrain from misuse of assessment techniques, interventions, results, and interpretations and take reasonable steps to prevent others from misusing the information these techniques provide. This includes refraining from releasing raw test results or raw data to persons, other than to patients or clients as appropriate, who are not qualified to use such information.

Because many of the problems and shortcomings associated with psychological tests stem from their use by unqualified persons, commercial organizations that market tests should adhere to the standards and guidelines of the American Psychological Association by demanding that their customers fulfill certain requirements. These requirements depend on the nature of the psychometric instrument and the training and experience needed to administer it. A good example is the three-level qualification system of The Psychological Corporation. Although tests at Level A can be purchased by any school, organization, or person certified or licensed to administer them, purchasers of tests at Level B must have a master's degree in psychology or education, equivalent training relevant to assessment, or membership in a professional association that requires appropriate training in assessment of its members. Purchasers of Level C tests—the highest level—must have a PhD in psychology or education, the equivalent in training in assessment, or verification of licensure or certification requiring appropriate training and experience in psychological assessment.

With respect to the ethics of assessment, the American Psychological Association and the American Personnel and Guidance Association have ethical codes pertaining to test administration and usage. In addition to stressing the importance of the recommendations concerning test administration, standardization, reliability, and validity made in the *Standards for Educational and Psychological Testing*, both of these codes emphasize the need to consider the welfare of examinees and to guard against the misuse of psychological assessment instruments. According to the "Ethical Principles of Psychologists and Code of Conduct" (American Psychological Association, 1992), evaluation and psychodiagnosis should be carried out only by professionals who are trained and competent in the administration of appropriate tests. The "Ethical Principles" also emphasize that scientific procedures should be applied in the design and selection of tests and techniques that are appropriate for the specified individuals, and that the results should be interpreted judiciously, used cautiously, and kept secure.

A set of standards and a code of ethics for assessment are only as effective as the skills and ethical awareness of the people to whom they apply. Unfortunately, many people who administer, score, and interpret psychological tests are not adequately trained to do so. Neither are they especially conscientious or sensitive to the needs and welfare of examinees or the institutions they serve. For these reasons, continuing emphasis must be placed on extensive training of psychological examiners, making certain that they meet the highest professional standards before allowing them to purchase or administer specified tests, and emphasizing the necessity of relying on other professionals and up-to-date sources of information for assistance.

Informed Consent and Confidentiality

Related to the matter of the ethics of psychological assessment are informed consent and confidentially. These concepts are concerned with the ethical issue of improper disclosure of psychological assessment information, particularly when identified by the name of the examinee. In law, *confidentiality* refers to the fact that certain information is not secret but rather is restricted in terms of its accessibility to individuals who need to be familiar with it and have a right to know. With respect to psychometric information, those who have a legal right of access to the information include the person who was assessed and his (her) legal guardians or representatives. The related concept of *informed consent* refers to a formal agreement made by an individual, or the individual's guardian or legal representative, with an agency or another person to permit use of the individual's name or personal information (test scores and the like) for a specified purpose. Before administering any psychometric instrument or procedure, it is wise to have the examinee or his or her legal representative read and sign an informed consent form such as the one in Figure 1.1. This form requires that, before conducting any psychometric procedures, the examinee must be informed of the nature and purpose of the examination, why he or she was evaluated, to whom the information will be made available, and how it will be used.

As is true of certain information shared by the attorney and client in a legal dispute, data obtained from a psychological examination are considered to be *privileged communication*. Similar to the concept of confidentiality, this implies that the data will be shared with other people only on a legal, need-to-know basis. Even when an informed consent form has been signed, psychometric information may still be *privileged*, in that only the client (examinee), his or her parent or guardian, or the client's attorney, physician, or psychologist may have access to it. A person's rights to informed consent and privileged communication are honored in all but the most extreme circumstances, as, for example, when he or she is considered dangerous to himself (herself) or other people.

I, _____ voluntarily give my consent to serve as a participant in a psychological examination conducted by _____. I have received a clear and complete explanation of the general nature and purposes(s) of the examination and the specific reason(s) why I am being examined. I have also been informed of the kinds of tests and other procedures to be administered and how the results will be used.

I realize that it may not be possible for the examiner to explain all aspects of the examination to me until it has been completed. It is also my understanding that I may terminate my participation in the examination at any time without penalty. I further understand that I will be informed of the results and that the results will be reported to no one else without my permission. At this time, I request that a copy of the results of this examination be sent to:

_____

_____

| _____ | _____ |
| Examinee's Name | Signature of Examinee |

| _____ | _____ |
| Date | Signature of Examiner |

FIGURE 1.1 Form for obtaining informed consent for a psychological examination.

SUMMARY

This chapter has provided a brief introduction to the historical foundations of adult personality assessment and its current professional status. We have discussed the pseudoscientific precursors and the scientific beginnings of psychological assessment, as well as its uses in research and applied contexts. The need for extensive training and a sense of ethical responsibility to conduct psychological examinations—topics to which we shall return frequently in this book—were emphasized.

The largest portion of the book is concerned with specific personality assessment procedures and instruments, but applications of these techniques to specific purposes in clinical, counseling, employment, educational, military, and other applied contexts are discussed at length. First, however, an overview of theories and research on adult personality is presented. It is hoped that this overview serves as a foundation for further study and for the judicious selection, administration, and interpretation of specific assessment instruments and procedures for various applied and research purposes.

NOTES

1. Associations between the calendar and personality characteristics are also described in the following poem of unknown authorship:

> Monday's child is fair of face,
> Tuesday's child is full of grace,
> Wednesday's child is full of woe,
> Thursday's child has far to go,
> Friday's child is loving and giving,
> Saturday's child works hard for its living,
> And a child that's born on the Sabbath day
> Is fair and wise and good and gay.

SUGGESTED READINGS

Ben-Porath, Y. S., & Butcher, J. N. (1991). The historical development of personality assessment. In C. E. Walker (Ed.), *Clinical psychology: Historical and research foundations* (pp. 121–156). New York: Plenum.

Butcher, J. N. (1995). Clinical personality assessment: An overview. In J. N. Butcher (Ed.), *Clinical personality assessment: Practical approaches* (pp. 3–9). New York: Oxford University Press.

Exner, J. E., Jr. (1995). Why use personality tests: A brief historical view. In J. N. Butcher (Ed.), *Clinical personality assessment: Practical approaches* (pp. 10–18). New York: Oxford University Press.

Goldstein, G., & Hersen, R. L. (1990). Historical perspectives. In G. Goldstein & M. Hersen (Eds.), *Handbook of psychological assessment* (2nd ed., pp. 3–17). New York: Pergamon.

Megargee, E. L., & Spielberger, C. D. (1992). Reflections on fifty years of personality assessment and future directions for the field. In E. I. Megargee & C. D. Spielberger (Eds.), *Personality assessment in America: A retrospective on the occasion of the fiftieth anniversary of the Society for Personality Assessment* (pp. 170–186). Hillsdale, NJ: Erlbaum.

Weiner, I. B. (1995). How to anticipate ethical and legal challenges in personality assessments. In J. N. Butcher (Ed.), *Clinical personality assessment: Practical approaches* (pp. 95–103). New York: Oxford University Press.

2

Personality Theories and Research Methods

Measurement, research, and theory go hand in hand, because all three are concerned with variables. *Variables* constitute the shorthand of science, the real or hypothetical features of objects and events that are observed and manipulated in the game of science making. Dependent, independent, control, extraneous, and concomitant are all adjectives used to characterize variables that are measured and whose causes, effects, and correlates are studied in observational, correlational, and experimental investigations. Judgments as to which variables are potentially worthwhile examining in scientific research are usually made on the basis of hypotheses or theories pertaining to how people and things function in various contexts. These variables must be measured or assessed in some way—no matter how crudely—to test the hypothesis or theory of interest to an investigator.

The word "theory" may conjure up visions of something that is speculative or fanciful, highly impractical, and that has little or nothing to do with the "real world." Except for some procedures and products developed by painstaking trial-and-error, however, most research investigations and instruments are based on theory—albeit often not an elaborate theory and perhaps not far from common sense. This is as true of psychology as it is of other sciences, and within psychology it is as true of the study of personality as it is of the study of learning, perception, or other "tough-minded" topics.

Rather than being useless speculation, there is actually nothing so practical as a good theory. Without some theoretical or conceptual assumptions, some basic framework for their activities, scientists might find themselves wasting time with few guideposts or directions. By providing a tentative map of an area of study, a good theory can lead to predictions concerning what is likely to happen if the variables constituting the language of the theory are changed or manipulated in some way.

Fundamentally, a theory consists of a set of statements concerning the relationships among the variables of interest to researchers in an area of concern. Temperature, weight, luminosity, amperes, and ergs are among the variables with which physicists work. Psychologists are also cognizant of these variables, but they prefer to concentrate more on such variables as reinforcement, anxiety, aggression, depression, dependency, and the like. As with physical variables, the relationships among psychological variables may be complex and baffling but are seldom specifiable in precise, mathematical terms. In any event, the statements of relationships among the variables in a theory frequently take the form of hypotheses—educated guesses about those relationships and what might happen if and when the magnitude or direction of the variables change. Information concerning the correctness of these hypotheses can often be obtained by detailed observation and experimentation. But, even when one is careful in controlling for possible contaminating factors in the research investigations, seldom does this end the matter. The findings of a research study or experiment usually lead to other questions and the recognition of a need to redefine the variables, change the hypothesis, or even scrap the theory altogether.

Most people have heard something about the many theories in the natural sciences, for example, relativity theory, quantum theory, superstring theory, the theory of evolution, and the kinetic theory of gases. Many of these theories have become familiar because they can be used to explain and predict certain events in the natural world with a high degree of accuracy. Unfortunately, psychology has not been able to match the successes of the natural sciences. Psychologists have their share of theories, including psychoanalytic theory, behavior theories, self-theories, attribution theory, cognitive theories, and so forth. However, they are still a long way from being able to explain precisely how and why people become what they are or to predict accurately how they will behave under certain conditions. Psychological theories are frequently informal, but even psychologists who pride themselves on being empiricists and not merely armchair theoreticians make certain assumptions or harbor certain notions about human behavior and cognition.

Rather than viewing themselves as pure empiricists who appreciate only facts and evidence or as believers in comprehensive theories of learning and personality, most psychologists are eclectic: They select and use what they consider the most reasonable or applicable parts of a theory in interpreting and explaining why people behave as they do. To them, theories serve as frames of reference for suggesting and guiding research. Theories are, however, not to be accepted as invariably true and are always subject to modification if the facts fail to confirm the predictions.

THEORIES OF PERSONALITY

Theories of personality and individual differences are given a tall order. Ideally, they should be able to explain how personality develops and changes with age, what factors (e.g., heredity and experience) influence personality and how they do so, what role personality plays in determining behavior and influencing social acceptance and success, how and why personality becomes disordered, and how it might be changed by treatment or intervention.

Many theories of personality are based on everyday observation and common sense, but one must be careful about accepting the truth of theories propounded by "the man in the street." Old clichés about human nature and activities are almost never true for all people all of the time. Absence may make the heart grow fonder, but sometimes out of sight is out of mind. Some women become furious when they are scorned, but others merely become depressed. Sparing the rod may spoil the child, but it may also make him less fractious and more considerate. Stereotypes or overgeneralizations concerning human behavior and personality may make us smile and even appear to have a ring of truth, but valid descriptions and accurate predictions of behavior cannot be made from them.

For convenience, theories of personality may be classified into five groups: type theories, trait theories, psychoanalytic theories, phenomenological theories, and social learning theories. These five groups of theories have different origins and emphasize different variables. The oldest among them, and the ones that have had the most influence on the development of personality assessment instruments, are the type and trait theories. The most comprehensive and influential theories, although not necessarily the most successful, in attempting to explain the origins, development, and problems of human personality are psychodynamic, or psychoanalytic, theories. Another group of theories—phenomenological, including *self-theory*—developed, like psychoanalysis, from observations of patients or clients undergoing treatment. The last group of theories—social learning theories and their predeces-

24

sor, behavior theories—began from observations made in laboratory research contexts and were later extended to clinical situations.

Our major purpose in introducing these five groups of theories is not to give a detailed, in-depth descriptions of them but rather to provide a background for a discussion of adult personality assessment. All of the theories that we shall consider have contributed to the growth of personality assessment, but trait/type and psychoanalytic theories have been especially influential in this regard. A list of personality theorists and representative assessment instruments and methods based on their efforts is given in Table 2.1. Of this company, Freud, Adler, Jung, and Erikson are psychoanalytic theorists; Allport, Buss, Plomin, Cattell, and Murray are trait theorists; Sheldon is a type theorist, Maslow and Rogers are phenomenological theorists, and Rotter and Kelly are social learning theorists. The remaining individuals—Kelly, McClelland, and Witkin— were eclectics whose ideas about personality and the assessment instruments developed from them were influenced by one or more theories as well as by the results of empirical research.

Type Theories

Conceptualizations of personality in terms of traits or types are known as dispositional theories, in that they focus on temperaments, inclinations, or orientations to behave in a certain manner. These dispositions are usually considered to be—at least to some extent—natural or inborn and rather pervasive and general in their influences on how people behave and think. Dispositional theories are more descriptive than explanatory, in that they do not provide adequate explanations of the origins of particular dispositions or how they regulate specific behaviors. However, such descriptive theories have some predictive value and have stimulated the development of more personality assessment instruments than any other theories considered in this chapter.

The characterization of personality in terms of types is one of the oldest simplifications for understanding and dealing with people. Capsule descriptions of "types of people" are found in everyday speech, literature, and, more systematically but not necessarily more accurately, in scientific studies. Many of the characters found in the plays of Shakespeare, the novels of Dickens, and other classical and contemporary writings are "personality types" in this sense. More systematic typologies are represented in the descriptive observations of philosophers and scientists, such as Theophrastus and Hippocrates in ancient times, and Cesare Lombroso, Ernst Kretschmer, and William Sheldon in the present century.

TABLE 2.1 Personality Assessment Methods Associated with Specific Theorists

Alfred Adler	Analysis of birth order, early recollections, dream analysis, social interest (Crandall, 1975)
Gordon Allport	Idiographic content analyses of letters and diaries; Dominance-Submission Test, Study of Values
Arnold Buss and Robert Plomin	EASI Temperament Survey, EASI Temperament Survey for Adults
Raymond Cattell	Factor analysis (I-data, Q-data, T-data), psychological tests (16 Personality Factor Questionnaire and other personality inventories)
Erik Erikson	Psychohistorical analysis
Sigmund Freud	Free association, dream analysis, analysis of transference, analysis of resistance
Carl Jung	Word associations, method of amplification, symptom analysis, dream analysis, painting therapy
George Kelly	Role Construct Repertory Test
Abraham Maslow	Personal Orientation Inventory: A Measure of Self Actualization (Shostrom, 1974)
David McClelland	Projective measures of need for achievement and need for power
Henry Murray	Thematic Apperception Test, situational tests (Office of Strategic Services, 1948); concept of *needs* also used in Edwards Personal Preference Schedule and Adjective Check List
Carl Rogers	Q-Sort (Stephenson, 1953), Experience Inventory (Coan, 1972), Experiencing Scale (Gendlin & Tomlinson, 1967; Klein et al., 1969)
Julian Rotter	I-E Scale, Interpersonal Trust Scale
William Sheldon	Somatotyping and temperament typing
Herman Witkin	Body Adjustment Test, Rod and Frame Test, Embedded Figures Test

Typologies are not merely a topic for idle discussion: some have had strong supporters and exerted a great deal of influence on intellectual thought and scientific investigations. For example, the 30 descriptive sketches, such as "The Garrulous Man" and "The Penurious Man," provided by Theophrastus (372–287 B.C.) were detailed, if often amusing, characterizations:

> The Garrulous man is one that will sit down close beside somebody he does not know, and begin talk with a eulogy of his own life, and then relate a dream he had the night before, and after that tell dish by dish what he had for supper. As he warms up to his work he will remark that we are by no means the men we were, and the price of wheat has gone down, and there's a ship of strangers in town.... Next he will surmise that the

crops would be all the better for some more rain, and tell him what he is going to grow on his own farm next year, adding that it is difficult to make both ends meet . . . and "I vomited yesterday" and "What day is it today?" . . . And if you let him go on he will never stop. (Edmonds, 1929, pp. 48–49)

Another influential Greek in ancient times was Hippocrates (460–377 B.C.). Based on an explanation of natural things in terms of four elements (earth, air, fire, water), Hippocrates propounded the doctrine of four bodily humors (yellow bile, black bile, blood, and phlegm) and the four temperament types (choleric, melancholic, sanguine, and phlegmatic) corresponding to an excess of each humor. This doctrine was believed in by physicians for centuries and continues to intrigue researchers even today (see Figure 2.1).

Among the more modern type theories of personality are characterizations in terms of the physical structure of the human body. In act I, scene II of Shakespeare's *Julius Caesar*, Caesar states:

Let me have men about me that are fat,
Sleek-headed men, and such as sleep a-nights.
Yond Cassius has a lean and hungry look;
He thinks too much, such men are dangerous.

A somewhat more systematic analysis of the relationships of personality to physique was undertaken by Cesare Lombroso (1836–1909). Lombroso believed that the bodies of criminals represented a lower stage of human evolution than noncriminals. He pointed to the large jaws, receding foreheads, and other primitive physical characteristics that are presumably earmarks of criminals. However, not all criminals possess the features delineated by Lombroso and many noncriminals do. The psychiatrist Ernst Kretschmer opted to study mental patients rather than criminals and found what he believed was evidence for three types of body builds associated with specific mental disorders. Kretschmer concluded from his observations that both a thin, lanky, angular (asthenic) physique and a muscular (athletic) physique are associated with a schizoid (withdrawing) temperament. Conversely, a rotund, stock (pyknic) physique is, according to Kretschmer, associated with cycloid (emotionally unstable) temperament.[1]

Even more influential than the body type theories of Lombroso and Kretschmer was William Sheldon's somatotypology. Careful observations and measurements of a large sample of people led Sheldon to classify human physiques in terms of three components: endomorphy (fatness), mesomorphy (muscularity), and ectomorphy (thinness). From photographs of individuals in various orientations, body builds

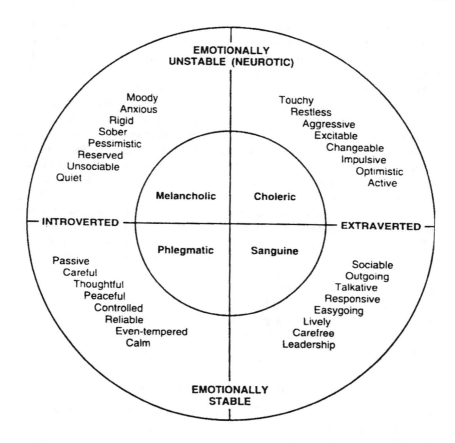

FIGURE 2.1 A two-dimensional classification of personality. The diagram depicts the relationships of Eysenck's supertraits of introversion/extraversion and emotional stability/instability to the four humors of Hippocrates and Galen. (From *Personality and Individual Differences*, by H. J. Eysenck & M. W. Eysenck, 1958, New York: Plenum. Reprinted by permission.)

were rated on a scale of 1 to 7 on each of these three components. The results were designations, such as 7-1-1 (extreme endomorph), 1-7-1 (extreme mesomorph), 1-1-7 (extreme ectomorph), or a possible 343 somatotypic combinations in all. The next step was to relate body build to three dimensions of temperament: viscerotonia, somatotonia, and cerebrotonia. A person's score (1 to 7) on each temperament dimension was obtained on the basis of questionnaires and observations of 20 personality traits. High scorers on viscerotonia are jolly, sociable, and lovers of comfort and eating. High scorers on somatotonia are assertive, dominating, noisy, callous, youth oriented, and lovers of physical adventure and exercise. High scorers on cerebrotonia are restrained, fast reacting, introversive individuals who are oversensitive to pain, have difficulty sleeping, and are oriented toward later periods of life. Although a viscerotonic temperament is moderately related to an endomorphic physique, a somatotonic temperament is related to an endomorphic physique, and a cerebrotonic temperament is related to an ectomorphic physique, the direction of causation is far from clear: Does physique cause temperament, or does temperament cause physique? Furthermore, there are many exceptions to the presumed relationships between physique and temperament.

Although typologies have had some influence on the development of personality assessment instruments, such as the Myers–Briggs Type Indicator and the Singer–Loomis Inventory of Personality, typological approaches have generally met with strong opposition. Most modern psychologists consider human personality too complex to be described in terms of a small number of types. In addition, labeling people as particular "types" overemphasizes internal causation of behavior. It may lead to a self-fulfilling prophecy in which an individual tends to become whatever he or she is labeled as being—an introvert, extrovert, or type A personality.

Allport's Trait Theory

Personality "types" are usually conceived of as fairly discrete rather than as existing in different quantities or measurable on continua. A particular person represents a certain type and not a certain amount or degree of that type. Personality types are also seen as fairly wide ranging in their effects, influencing the ways in which people act in a broad spectrum of situations. Personality traits, conversely, are much more likely to be viewed as measurable on continua: Although a person may "have" a specific trait, it is likely that he has it to a certain degree or in a certain amount rather than to an all-or-none extent.

One of the first psychologists to identify himself as a "trait theorist" was Gordon Allport. Allport's theoretical and empirical research on personality traits began with the identification and analysis of almost 18,000 English words referring to traits. He combined and classified these words according to their order of pervasiveness or the generality of their influences on behavior across different situations. According to the resulting scheme, three major groups of traits, from most to least pervasive, are cardinal traits, central traits, and secondary traits. Examples of *cardinal traits*, which are so pervasive in a person's life that they are expressed in almost all of his or her behavior, are authoritarianism, humanitarianism, Machiavellianism (striving for power), sadism, and narcissism (self-love). Next in order of their pervasiveness are *central traits*, tendencies such as affectionateness, assertiveness, distractibility, honestly, kindness, reliability, and sociability that affect behavior in various situations but not so generally as cardinal traits. Last in order of pervasiveness are *secondary traits*, such as preferences for foods or music. Most people have few cardinal traits, more central traits, and many secondary traits.

In addition to classifying traits according to their pervasiveness across different situations, Allport differentiated among three classes of traits in terms of the extent to which they are shared by different people: *common traits*, *individual traits*, and *personal dispositions*. Although common traits, such as anxiety or aggression, and even traits that are more specific to the individual, can be measured by standardized assessment instruments, Allport maintained that the assessment of personal dispositions requires the careful study of a person.

Another distinction made by Allport was between the idiographic and the nomothetic approaches to the study of people. The *nomothetic approach* consists of the search for general laws of behavior and personality that apply to all people, whereas the idiographic approach views the individual as a lawful, integrated system in his or her own right. Allport believed that personality researchers should follow the idiographic approach of attempting to understand the uniqueness or individuality of a person by means of an the in-depth study of his or her personality.

Factor Theories

Many researchers who follow a trait model or theory of personality have employed the statistical techniques of factor analysis. *Factor analysis* is a set of mathematical procedures for analyzing a matrix of correlations among measurements of many variables made on many people. The purpose of factor analysis is to isolate the constructs or factors that are sufficient to explain the pattern of correlations among the variables. In personality research, the factors extracted by factor analysis are viewed as basic dimensions, characteristics, or traits of personality.

Two representative trait theories based on the results of factor analysis are Hans Eysenck's supertrait theory and Raymond Cattell's multifactor theory. The three supertraits in Eysenck's theory are *introversion* versus *extraversion*, *emotional stability* versus *emotional instability* (neuroticism), and *psychoticism*. Figure 2.1 provides a graphical representation of the first two of these supertraits; the particular characteristics manifested by a person depend on where he or she falls on this two-dimensional surface. Note the overlap between the four quadrants of this two-dimensional surface and the four humors of Hippocrates. Much of Eysenck's research, and that of many other investigators as well, has been conducted on the first of these dimensions—introversion/extroversion.[2] Eysenck describes an *introvert* as "a quiet, retiring sort of person, introspective, fond of books rather than people, reserved and distant except to intimate friends." A typical *extravert*, conversely, is "sociable, likes parties, has many friends, needs to have people to talk to, and does not like reading or studying by himself" (Eysenck & Eysenck, 1975, p. 5). Individuals closer to the "emotional instability" pole of the first supertrait dimension are anxious, moody, restless, touchy, emotionally responsive; those closer to the "emotional stability" pole are calm, careful, and even-tempered.

Raymond Cattell's multifactor theory stemmed from his extensive factor analytic research and the development of numerous assessment instruments, such as the 16 Personality Factor Questionnaire (16 PF). The 16 traits measured by this questionnaire are the following:

A	Cool, reserved versus warm, easygoing
B	Concrete thinking versus abstract thinking
C	Easily upset versus calm, stable
D	Not assertive versus dominant
E	Sober, serious versus enthusiastic
F	Expedient versus conscientious
G	Shy, timid versus venturesome
H	Tough-minded versus sensitive
I	Trusting versus suspicious
J	Practical versus imaginative
K	Forthright versus shrewd
L	Self-assured versus self-doubting
Q_1	Conservative versus experimenting
Q_2	Group oriented versus self-sufficient
Q_3	Undisciplined versus self-disciplined
Q_4	Relaxed versus tense, driven

Some of the so-called source traits measured by the 16 PF and other personality inventories are labeled *environmental-mold* traits, whereas others are labeled *constitutional* traits. The former are thought to be due more to environment, and the latter to heredity. Cattell also distinguished between *general* and *specific* source traits, the former influencing behavior in more situations than the latter. Like Allport, Cattell differentiated *common traits*, which characterize all people, and *unique* (individual) *traits*, which are peculiar to the individual. Another distinction is between *dynamic traits*, which motivate the person toward a goal, *ability traits*, which determine the ability to achieve a goal, and *temperament traits*, which pertain to the emotional aspects of goal-directed activity. All three of these may be further subdivided, for example, dynamic traits into attitudes, sentiments, and ergs.

The Big Five

Trait/factor theories of personality have been roundly and continuously criticized for their lack of explanatory power and their limited ability to predict behavior across various situations (e.g., Mischel, 1968). Recently, however, there has been some consensus that personality can be efficiently described in terms of the following five basic factors (Costa & McCrae, 1986).

Neuroticism

Worrying versus calm, insecure versus secure, self-pitying versus self-satisfied. High scorers feel generally anxious, cope poorly with stress, have unrealistic self-assessments, and readily experience negative emotions.

Extraversion

Sociable versus retiring, fun loving versus sober, affectionate versus reserved. Extroverts are active, assertive, cheerful, optimistic people who enjoy social gatherings; introverts are the opposite.

Openness

Imaginative versus down to earth, preference for variety versus preference for routine, independent versus conforming. High scorers feel emotions keenly, are intellectually sensitive, and are attuned to external sights and sounds and internal experiences. Low scorers are conventional, down-to-earth people with narrow interests and low aesthetic appreciation.

Agreeableness

Soft hearted versus ruthless, trusting versus suspicious, helpful versus uncooperative. High scorers are eager to help other people and expect to be treated similarly; low scorers are cynical, suspicious, and uncooperative.

Conscientiousness

Well organized versus disorganized, careful versus careless, self-disciplined versus weak willed. High scorers are persistent, consistent, reliable, and frequently puritanical in their attitudes; low scorers are aimless, lax, and unreliable.

The five-factor model of personality has stimulated a great deal of empirical research, and some studies have found the factors to be highly consistent across different cultures and nationalities (Angleitner & Ostendorf, 1994; Goldberg, 1994; McCrae & Costa, 1987). Block (1995), conversely, questioned the conceptual and methodological assumptions of the five-factor model and concluded that there are serious uncertainties concerning the model and the substantive meanings of the factors.

Classical Psychoanalysis

Psychoanalysis began with Sigmund Freud and his followers during the late 19th century and arguably has had more influence on 20th-century thought than any other psychological system. In addition to being a theory of personality, psychoanalysis is a method of conducting psychotherapy and a methodology for research on personality and behavior. As a theory of personality, psychoanalysis was conceptualized by Freud as dynamic, intrapsychic, and developmental. It is *dynamic* because it deals with motives—both unconscious and conscious, *developmental* because it views personality as changing in response to biological and environmental forces, and *intrapsychic* in that the interactions among the various motives occur in the mind and lead to conflicts. These intrapsychic conflicts occur between the three components of personality: id, ego, and superego. The *id*, or animalistic, instinctive nature of man, acts according to the *pleasure principle*. The *ego*, or rational (I or me) aspect of the mind, acts according to the *reality principle*. The *superego*, a composite of the "conscience" and the ego ideal, acts according to the *moral principle*. The id is natural, inborn, whereas the ego develops as a result of the interplay between the id and the external world. It serves as the mediator between the unrelenting counterpressures of the id and superego, coming into conflict with the id and superego as well as the external world. To Freud, anxiety produced by these intrapsychic conflicts leads the ego to construct *defense mechanisms* (rationalization, projection, sublimation, etc.) to keep the anxiety under control. These defense mechanisms, when expressed in behavior, can produce seemingly bizarre and frequently self-defeating actions on the part of the individual.

Among the most controversial of the many psychoanalytic concepts are the doctrine of the unconscious, the notion of childhood sexuality, and the theory of psychosexual stages in development. To Freud, the mind was like an iceberg, most of it below the surface, or *unconscious*, with smaller parts being in the preconscious or conscious. Desires and conflicts that are unacceptable to the ego are repressed into the unconscious, but they continue to be expressed in thoughts and behaviors in disguised ways. The purpose of psychoanalytic therapy, as practiced by Freud and other classical psychoanalysts, is to assist the patient in bringing these repressed impulses into conscious awareness so they can be dealt with in more realistic and effective ways.

According to Freud, children normally pass through a series of *psychosexual stages*—oral, anal, phallic, latency, and genital—in their development of mature sexuality. This notion, an important aspect of which is the occurrence and resolution of the Oedipus complex in males, has also been a target of unrelenting criticism. Freud maintained that adult character and personality are determined to a large extent by the individual's success in resolving the problems and conflicts during different psychosexual stages. People who are unable to resolve them, in whole or in part, are said to be *fixated* at a particular stage or may *regress* (in whole or in part) to an earlier stage when sufficiently frustrated. Fixation at the *oral stage* leads to an orally oriented, dependent character in adulthood, whereas fixation at the *anal stage* leads to the three *p*s of the anal personality: parsimony, petulance, and pedantry. Parsimony is stinginess, petulance is irritability, and pedantry is overattention to details.

The principal assessment techniques employed in classical psychoanalysis are clinical observations, interviews, and dream analysis. However, several projective techniques, which aspire to get at deeper, less conscious needs, feelings, and conflicts, have been developed for both clinical practice and research. These include associations to words, inkblots, and other fairly nonstructured material. The development of certain rating scales and inventories has also been stimulated by classical psychoanalytic theory, but these have not proved to be popular.

Other Psychoanalytic Theories

Although the original "big three" of psychoanalysis during the early years of this century were Sigmund Freud, Carl Jung, and Alfred Adler, Jung and Adler broke away from Freud and established their own theories and psychotherapeutic methods. Jung's system, which he designated *analytic psychology*, downplayed the importance of sexual factors in personality development. Jung emphasized the concept of the *collective unconscious* (inherited racial memories) and the importance of *ar-*

chetypes and other inherited propensities. Examples of archetypes are the hero, the earth mother, the shadow, God, and the devil. In addition to being a psychoanalytic psychologist, Jung's interest in certain personality dimensions (introversion versus extroversion, sensing versus intuition, thinking versus feeling, and judging versus perception) suggest that he was, at least to some extent, also a trait/factor or type theorist.

Like Jung, Adler differed with Freud on the importance of repressed sexual impulses in the development of personality. Adler made *strivings for power* and resulting feelings of inferiority (the *inferiority complex*) a cornerstone of his individual psychology. He also emphasis the mechanism of *compensation* as a way of coping with feelings of inferiority. In his later writings Adler stressed the concept of *social interest* as particularly important in understanding the development of personality. A fairly reliable measure of this concept is the Social Interest Scale (Crandall, 1975), which consists of 15 pairs of items. Each item pair contains one trait closely related to social interest (helpful, sympathetic, tolerant, etc.) and one trait not relevant to social interest (quick-witted, neat, capable, etc.). Respondents are asked to choose the trait in each pair that they would rather have.

Many other psychiatrists and psychologists also deviated from orthodox Freudian theory and procedures; a group of these individuals became known as neoanalysts or *ego psychologists*. They placed greater emphasis than Freud on the ego rather than the id, and greater emphasis on sociocultural rather than biological factors as determinants of personality. A prominent representative of the group is Erik Erikson, whose conception of crises and goals in human psychosocial (rather than "psychosexual") development had a great influence on developmental psychology. According to Erikson, there are eight stages in the psychological development of a person: infancy, early childhood, play age, school age, adolescence, young adulthood, middle age, and old age. At each stage there is a crisis or conflict that the individual must resolve if he or she is to progress to the next stage. In infancy, that crisis is trust versus mistrust; in early childhood, it is autonomy versus doubt; in the play age (preschool age), it is initiative versus guilt; in the school age, it is industry versus inferiority; and in adolescence, it is identity versus role confusion. The crises and goals or the three stages in adult development are listed in Table 2.2. Domino and Affonso (1990) designed a self-report inventory, the Inventory of Psychosocial Balance (IPB), to assess an individual's standing on all eight stages, including the intimacy, generativity, and ego integrity stages of adulthood.

Levinson's Theory

Transition theorists, such as Daniel Levinson (1978), emphasize the fact that a person's psychological needs are not satisfied once and for all;

TABLE 2.2 Erikson's Stages of Psychosocial Development in Adulthood

Young adulthood

Crisis (conflict). Intimacy versus isolation.
Goal (resolution). To become intimate with someone.
Outcome. The fusing of one's identity with that of another person leads to intimacy. Competitive and combative relations with others may lead to isolation.

Middle age

Crisis (conflict). Generativity versus self-absorption.
Goal (resolution). To develop an interest in future generations.
Outcome. Establishing and guiding the next generation produces a sense of generativity. A concern primarily with the self leads to self-absorption.

Old age

Crisis (conflict). Integrity versus despair.
Goal (resolution). To become an integrated and self-accepting person.
Outcome. Acceptance of one's life leads to a sense of integrity. Feeling that it is too late to make up for missed opportunities leads to despair.

Source: Adapted from Erikson (1963).

they change with experience and must be continually renegotiated. These needs, including control over one's life, enthusiasm for activities and commitments to other people and values, and a feeling that one matters to others, must be satisfied in different ways as the individual passes through the age-graded social structure and the demands and expectations of social situation change. Changes in behaviors that are socially expected at different ages lead the individual to acquire new attitudes, roles, and beliefs.

Levinson's theory of adult development is actually both a stage and a transition theory. According to the theory, there is an external, socio-cultural side and an internal, personal side to development in adulthood. The development of the two sides occurs in a series of stable stages (6–8 years long), which alternate with five transition periods (4–5 years long) (see Table 2.3). During each transition period, the individual reexamines his or her life and prepares for the next stage.

Phenomenological Theories

The *phenomenal world*, as distinguished from the *real world*, is the world as it is perceived by the experiencing observer. Consequently,

TABLE 2.3 Levinson's Stages and Transitions in Adult Development

---

Early adult transition (ages 17–22). Goal is to terminate adolescent life structure and form a basis for living in the adult world.

Entrance into the adult world (ages 22–28). Form and test out preliminary life structures and provide a link between the self and adult society.

Age 30 transition (ages 30–33). Revise life structure of previous period and form a basis for more satisfactory life structure to be created in the settling-down stage.

Settling-down stage (ages 33–40). Establish one's niche in society ("early settling down"), work at advancement, and strive for further success ("become one's own person").

Midlife transition (ages 40–45). Evaluate success in attaining goals of settling-down stage, take steps toward initiating midlife, and deal with relationships between oneself and the external world (*individuation*).

Entrance into middle adulthood (ages 50–55).

Age 50 transition (ages 50–55).

Building of a second middle adult structure (ages 55–60). Analogous to settling-down stage of young adulthood.

Late adult transition (ages 60–65). Changing mental and physical capacities intensify one's own aging and sense of mortality.

Source: Adapted from Levinson (1978).

phenomenological theories of personality are concerned with the individual's perception of objects and events, and how they affect and are affected by his or her past experiences, attitudes, values, beliefs, and personality in general. The part of the phenomenal world that is concerned with the individual himself (herself) is known as the *self*, and the individual's evaluation of that self is the *self-concept*.

The most prominent phenomenological theorist was Carl Rogers, whose theory of personality stemmed from his findings in client-centered therapy. In *client-centered therapy*, clients (patients) are encouraged to take the lead and say whatever they wish to tell the therapist, who, in turn, is accepting, noncritical, and fairly neutral. Unlike psychoanalytic therapy, in which interpretations (of the patient's free associations, dreams, and resistance) provided by the analyst play a major role, the therapist or counselor in client-centered therapy offers few interpretations. Rather, the therapist usually limits himself (herself) to such nondirective procedures as simple acceptance and reflecting the feeling tone in the client's statements. By being nondirective, the therapist aims to encourage the client to assume the responsibility for facing up to his or her own problems and working out solutions to them in a permissive, nonpunitive atmosphere. Regardless of his or her background, beliefs, or current situation, the client is given *unconditional positive regard* by the therapist: The therapist projects an accepting, sincere attitude, regardless of the feelings or actions revealed by the client. Rogers believed that only under these conditions can the client find the will and strength to formulate solutions with which he or she can live.

Like Abraham Maslow, Rogers believed that people strive to attain a condition of *self-actualization*, a state of complete congruence between the *real self*—what a person is now—and the *ideal self*—what the person is capable of becoming. Rogers felt that people want to achieve self-actualization and maintain pleasant relations with others, but for various reasons they are unable to do so. By treating children as objects of *conditional positive regard*, placing certain conditions on their worth and accepting their behavior only if it conforms to expected standards, children become unable to accept the full range of their experiences. Consequently, they are capable of recognizing only a portion of their experiences and thereby cannot be wholly functioning individuals. This situation can be reversed only when they receive unconditional positive regard from other people, and are accepted regardless of what they are or do.

Although Rogers and many other client-centered therapists have preferred observations and interviews to personality inventories and projectives as methods of assessing personality, several assessment instruments have been constructed along the lines of phenomenological theory. Examples are the Coopersmith Self-Esteem Inventories, the Piers-Harris Children's Self-Concept Scale, and the Tennessee Self-Concept Scale.

Social Learning Theory

Traditional behaviorists, such as B. F. Skinner, emphasized the importance of reinforcement in shaping behavior; to Skinner, behavior is controlled by its consequences—especially when those consequences involve positive reinforcement. According to Albert Bandura, however, reinforcement may be necessary for performance, but learning can occur without reinforcement. People learn by observing and modeling the behavior of others, but it may not become apparent until they are reinforced for demonstrating the learned behavior.

To Bandura, Julian Rotter, Walter Mischel, and other social learning theorists, it is important to attend not only to the learner's actions but also to his or her cognitive processes. Among those cognitive processes are expectancies, values, plans, and strategies for governing behavior. Rotter's concept of *expectancy* refers to a kind of "bet" made by the individual that when a certain behavior occurs in a specific situation it will lead to reinforcement. Some expectancies, such as locus of control and interpersonal trust, are *generalized expectancies*, in that they apply generally to a wide range of situations. Examples are locus of control and interpersonal trust. *Locus of control* refers to the direction from which people perceive their behavior as being controlled—either internally (within the person) or externally (outside the person). Another instrument designed to measure a generalized expectancy is the Interpersonal Trust Scale. Rotter defined *interpersonal trust* as an expectancy on the part of an individual or group "that the word, promise, verbal or written statement of another individual or group can be relied upon" (Rotter, 1967, p. 651).

Bandura's social learning theory, which has developed over the years in response to the results of his researches on the modeling of aggression, fears, and other behaviors and cognitions, incorporates several processes (attentional, retention, motor reproduction, motivational) that are important to an explanation of learning and behavior. Like Mischel, who distinguishes between *person* and *situational* variables as interactive determinants of behavior, Bandura (1977b, 1986) has studied several "person" (or personality) variables that he views as significant. Among these are *self-efficacy*, or the expectations of a person that he or she can learn or perform certain behaviors that will result in desirable outcomes in particular situations. Many variables affect self-efficacy, including the person's history of reinforcement (successes and failures), vicarious experiences, verbal persuasion, and emotional arousal. Another important concept in Bandura's theory is the *self-system*, an internal frame of reference for perceiving, evaluating, and regulating one's behavior. Self-efficacy is a part of the self-system, as are *performance standards* acquired in the process of growing up. Several measures, both performance and paper-and-pencil, have been devised to measure self-efficacy, but most of them are unstandardized.

RESEARCH ON PERSONALITY

Personality assessment instruments are administered for various purposes: in academic and employment contexts for personnel and student selection, in clinical contexts for assessing psychological disorders and measuring the effects of interventions, in business/industrial contexts for assuring employee integrity, in counseling situations for determining the causes of marital or familial difficulties, in court cases for identifying child molesters and proneness to violence, and in social situations for assigning people to groups. Many such instruments have been developed in clinical and research contexts to study specific psychological variables. Two prominent illustrations are the research of the Harvard personologists that resulted in the Thematic Apperception Test (Murray, 1938) and the research conducted at the University of California (MacKinnon, 1962), which produced the Omnibus Personality Inventory. Other examples are the researches on achievement motivation (McClelland, 1961), the authoritarian personality (Adorno et al., 1950), on morality (Kohlberg, 1974), cognitive styles (Witkin et al., 1974) and reflectivity/impulsivity (Kagan, 1966), and sensation seeking (Zuckerman, 1994). The development of specific instruments and their refinement has also accompanied many investigations of the role of heredity in personality, the continuity of personality across the life span, as well as the relationships of personality to criminal behavior, gender, ethnicity, social class, culture, ordinal position (in the family), and parenting style.

Personality Variables

Among the many personality variables that have been measured by standardized or nonstandardized instruments are the following:

achievement motivation	impulsivity
affiliation motivation	introversion/extroversion
aggression	learned helplessness
anxiety	level of aspiration
attachment	locus of control
attributions	needs
compulsivity	obedience
conformity	power motivation
dependency	self-efficacy
depression	self-actualization
fear	self-concept
hardiness	shyness
hostility	stress

Measures of these concepts (or constructs) have served as dependent, control, and moderator variables in numerous psychological research investigations. When such personality measures are used as dependent variables, the researcher is interested in determining how certain independent (or experimenter-manipulated) variables affect scores on the measures. When measures of personality are used as control variables, the researcher is interested in holding certain aspects of personality constant while determining the effects of an independent variable on some other measure of behavior. When personality measures are used as moderator variables, the researcher wants to determine whether the effect of a particular independent variable on a specified dependent variable is different for people with different personalities. Finally, when measures of personality are used along with other variables in correlational studies, the researcher wants to determine the relative contribution of the personality variables to the prediction of some criterion variable when the overlap of the personality variables with other variables is considered.

Observational Studies

To understand human nature, it helps to be a good observer. This is not a quotation, but it is a fact. Attaining insight into the motivations and behaviors of other people requires acute observational skills and patience, abilities that can be assumed to have been possessed by Sigmund Freud, Carl Rogers, and other personality theorists whom we have considered. All of these theorists actually began with uncontrolled, and often indirect, observations of the behaviors of their fellow human beings—in classrooms, in clinics, on the street, on the playground, or wherever they found themselves. They observed both the nonverbal and verbal behavior of their patients, clients, or "subjects," often spending hours just looking, listening, and thinking about what they saw and heard.

Careful observation is the foundation of both theory and research. In research, observation may be *uncontrolled*, as in watching how people behave when they are alone as well as interacting with others in naturally occurring situations. It is best if the observations are as objective as possible—if what is observed is separated from the interpretation placed on it, and if the observer is aware of his preconceptions or biases and tries not to let them influence the report of the observations or the interpretations placed on them. Some observers go to great lengths not to be obtrusive, that is, to make certain that they do not influence what is observed. To accomplish this aim, they may even become participants, so-called participant observers, in an ongoing human drama. But uncontrolled observation is time-consuming, many variables are left uncontrolled, and the person or persons being observed may never get around to demonstrating the behaviors in which the observer is interested. For reasons of both efficiency and control, observational situations are often planned or contrived by the researcher. In such *controlled observation*, people are exposed to a prearranged situation and their behavior is observed unobtrusively through a one-way mirror or a hidden camera or microphone. The subjects presumably do not realize that they are being watched; hence, they are more apt to behave normally rather than playing a role as one would when "on stage."

Developmental Studies

In addition to their uses in observational correlational, and experimental studies, personality variables have been measured in many developmental studies to determine changes in personality over time (Caspi & Herbener, 1989). Traditionally, the designs of developmental studies have been either cross-sectional or longitudinal. In a *longitudinal study*, a group of individuals of the same age is followed up and periodically retested over several years. In a *cross-sectional study*, several age groups are examined at a certain time. The purpose of both kinds of studies is to determine how personality (or some other characteristic) changes with chronological age. However, there are methodological problems with both types of studies. Cross-sectional studies are subject to *cohort effects*, in which differences in personality between different age groups occur because of the sociocultural climate of the times when they grew up rather than to changes in chronological age per se. A major shortcoming of the longitudinal design, however, is that it involves reexamining the same individuals—who may respond differently on successive examinations because of having been administered the same instruments on previous occasions. In addition, the dropout rate in longitudinal studies is often substantial, and those who do not drop out may not be typical of all people with whom the study began. To some extent, the problems with the longitudinal and cross-sectional approaches to developmental research can be reduced by using both approaches, as in the time-lag design in which several cohorts are examined, each at a different period (Schaie, 1967).

Reliability, Validity, and Standardization

According to classical psychometric theory, a good measuring instrument is reliable, valid, and standardized. *Reliability* is concerned with the extent to which the instrument is free from errors of measure. A reliable instrument measures consistently, being relatively uninfluenced by time of testing or by the sample of items or tasks composing it. In general, *objective tests*—which yield the same scores when scored by any competent person—are more reliable than instruments on which the scoring is more subjective. Checklists, rating scales, and personality inventories are more likely than projective tests and certain other measures of performance to be scored objectively. This does not mean that psychometric information obtained by administrating projectives is any less valuable than that obtained from paper-and-pencil instruments, but the lack of objectivity and the suspected low reliability of the former may cast doubt on their value (or validity).

Three methods of evaluating the reliability of a psychometric instrument are the *method of stability* (*test–retest method*), the *method of equivalence* (equivalent or *parallel forms method*), and the *method of internal consistency*. The test–retest procedure provides information on the effects of time of testing on scores, and the parallel-forms procedure provides information on the effects of different item samples on scores. The method of internal consistency, employing Spearman's split-half (or odd-even) method, Kuder and Richardson's formulas, and Cronbach's alpha coefficient, provides information on the extent to which the items constituting a test measure the same variable. The internal consistency procedure, which yields a kind of shortcut parallel forms coefficient, is efficient but inappropriate with tests that are highly speeded.

Reliability is a necessary but not a sufficient condition for validity. A measuring instrument can be reliable (i.e., measure consistently) without being valid (i.e., measure what it is supposed to measure). Both the reliability and validity of a measuring instrument can vary with the situation in which the measurements occur and the individuals on whom they are made. In other words, a test may be fairly reliable and valid in one situation or with one group but not necessarily with another. In any case, depending on the nature and purposes of the measuring instrument, information on its *validity* may be determined by the following procedures:

1. A thorough analysis of the content of the instrument (*content validity*)
2. An analysis of the extent to which scores on the instrument are related to measures on a criterion of whatever the instrument is supposed to measure obtained at the same time as the scores on the instrument are obtained (*concurrent or congruent validity*) or sometime in the future (*predictive validity*)
3. A series of investigations employing various procedures to determine whether the instrument measures the psychological variable, or construct, that it was designed to measure (*construct validity*)

Data on all three types of validity—content, criterion related, and construct—are of interest in evaluating a personality assessment instrument. For example, if scores on a personality test are to be used for predicting performance, then its predictive validity will be of great interest. However, construct validity has been of particular interest with respect to personality assessment instruments administered in clinical contexts and for diagnostic purposes. It is important in evaluating the construct validity of an instrument to look at the results of investigations designed to examine both its convergent and discriminant validity. This entails comparing two types of correlation coefficients:

1. The correlation between scores on the instrument and scores on the same or a different variable (or trait) measured by the same method.
2. The correlation between scores on the instrument and scores on the same variable (or trait) measured by the same or a different method.

The instrument is said to possess construct validity when the correlations between the same variable measured by the same and different methods are higher than correlations between different variables measured by the same and different methods, respectively.

A third quality of a well-constructed assessment instrument is *standardization*. This means that it has been administered to a sample of individuals who are representative of the population for which the instrument is intended. *Norms* (percentile ranks, standard scores, etc.) computed from the raw scores of the standardization group are then used as a frame of reference for interpreting the scores of people to whom the instrument is administered in the future. Not all personality assessment instruments are standardized, and even those that are have not necessarily been standardized on a representative sample of the intended (target) population. Consequently, scores on these instruments are often interpreted subjectively—without an objective frame of reference for making sense of them.

SUMMARY

The construction of many personality assessment instruments has been stimulated by the ideas of psychoanalysts, trait/factor theorists, and other psychologists specializing in the study of personality development and behavior disorders. Research concerned with child development, the biological bases of personality, criminal behavior, mental disorders, and adjustment to school, work, marriage, and other interpersonal situations has also led to the construction and improvement of personality assessment devices. Most of these instruments have been devised by a combination of rational (theory, logic, etc.) and empirical (research, trial-and-error, etc.) approaches.

Personality assessment instruments are usually not as reliable nor as valid as tests of ability. Personality tests and other affective instruments usually contribute less than tests of intelligence and special aptitudes to the prediction of behavior in academic and employment situations and other contexts. Because personality assessment instruments are typically less well standardized than tests of ability, they pose greater problems of score interpretation. Be that as it may, it is recognized that adjustment and success in a wide range of life situations depend as much or more on interpersonal or socioemotional factors as on cognitive and physical abilities. The need for personality assessments and their potential utility are well recognized, so efforts to develop better instruments and methods to facilitate our understanding of human personality will undoubtedly continue.

NOTES

1. Modern psychiatry classifies the mental disorder characterized by mood swings from mania to depression as *bipolar disorder*. This condition has been found to have a substantial genetic component.
2. Most psychologists spell the word "extroversion," but Eysenck prefers "extraversion." We shall use the first spelling except when quoting Eysenck or describing the personality inventories devised by him and his associates.

SUGGESTED READINGS

Caspi, A., & Bem, D. J. (1990). Personality continuity and change across the life course. In L. A. Pervin (Ed.), *Handbook of personality theory and research* (pp. 549–575). New York: Guilford Press.

Harkness, A. R., & Hogan, R. (1995). The theory and measurement of traits: Two views. In J. N. Butcher (Ed.), *Clinical personality assessment: Practical approaches* (pp. 28–41). New York: Oxford University Press.

McCrae, R. R., & Costa, P. T., Jr. (1990). *Personality in adulthood.* New York: Guilford Press.

Pervin, L. A. (1990). A brief history of modern personality theory. In L. A. Pervin (Ed.), *Handbook of personality theory and research* (pp. 21–65). New York: Guilford Press.

Pervin, L. A. (1990). Personality theory and research: Prospects for the future. In L. A. Pervin (Ed.), *Handbook of personality theory and research* (pp. 723–727). New York: Guilford Press.

Westen, D. (1990). Psychoanalytic approaches to personality. In L. A. Pervin (Ed.), *Handbook of personality theory and research* (pp. 21–65). New York: Guilford Press.

3

Observations and Interviews

People are gregarious creatures who are fond of observing, interacting with, and thinking about other people. Like Desmond Morris (1967), they may simply "hang out" on street corners watching various specimens of "the naked ape" go by. Alternatively, longing for security, acceptance, human companionship, or whatever else the association with members of one's species may provide, they may decide to introduce themselves and try to establish friendships.

Rarely, however, does one attempt to become intimate with everyone. We watch and wait, pick and choose, approach and withdraw, depending on our perceptions of the personal characteristics of others and how they respond to us. Our observations can sometimes lead us astray. We may observe other people in unusual circumstances and overgeneralize from what is for them unrepresentative or atypical behavior. Our first impressions, although important and often valid, may be wrong and lead us to prematurely accept or reject another person who is actually not at all like what we surmise. Many people have been deceived by glad-handed salesmen and poker-faced gamblers, as well as by stern-faced and gruff-mannered people of character.

Keenness of observation is not limited to psychologists, psychiatrists, detectives, or other professional people watchers. In fact, some people are apparently born to be good observers or at least they learn how to be observant at an early age. Many famous writers have revealed a perceptiveness that goes beyond the brief attention most of us give to

45

our social encounters. For example, both perspicacity and eloquent writing are seen in the following description by Henry James:

> I saw her but four times, though I remember them vividly. She made an impression on me. Close upon thirty, by every presumption, she was made almost like a little girl and had the complexion of a child. She was artistic, I suspected. Her eyes were perhaps too round and too inveterately surprised, but her lips had a mild decision, and her teeth, when she showed them, were charming. (Fadiman, 1945, pp. 3–4 passim)

OBSERVATIONS OF BEHAVIOR

As with laymen, psychologists and other trained observers are not infallible in their judgments of people. They see and evaluate others through the clouded lenses of their personal experiences, needs, and attitudes. They are also apt to observe students, patients, parents, or others who come to them for help in a narrowly defined situation. Consequently, they are often surprised when the "Jane" or "Joe" described by another observer turns out to be different from the "Jane" or "Joe" whom they know. Their evaluations of Jane and Joe are not only different from those of others; they are different from reality. But despite the problems of reliability and validity that accompany behavioral observations, laymen and professional people watchers alike depend on their perceptions and memories in making judgments about other people.

Situational Testing

As indicated in chapter 2, direct observations may be controlled or uncontrolled. Most observations are uncontrolled and naturalistic: Behavior is evaluated "on the wing" and in a naturally occurring setting rather than in a contrived, circumscribed context. In conducting research on personality and social behavior, however, psychologists frequently arrange a situation—a so-called situational test—to control for the effects of unwanted variables and to compare the responses of a collection of people. Such was the case in the Office of Strategic Services (OSS) (1948) Assessment Program during World War II. The examinees in this program, who were candidates for espionage training, were asked to perform certain tasks under prearranged conditions. Three such test tasks designed to assess the social relations skills of the OSS recruits were construction, recruitment, and improvisation. On the construction test, the recruit was asked to build a simple structure with the help of two assistants; on the recruitment test, the recruit played the role of a recruiter interviewing an applicant; and on the third test, the recruit played the role of a certain character in a defined interactive situation. For example, on one of the construction tests (the "wall problem"), three men, only one of whom was a genuine candidate, were assigned the task of crossing a "canyon." Unknown to the candidate, the other two men were confederates of the assessment staff rather than bona fide candidates. The two confederates were consistently argumentative, ineffective, and uncooperative. One of them made unrealistic suggestions and insulting or worrisome remarks, whereas the other pretended not to understand the directions and passively resisted them.

The assessment staff and the candidates' peers observed and evaluated the efforts of each candidate in these and other tests, interviews, and exercises over a 3-day period. Evaluations were made in terms of 10 variables: effective intelligence, emotional stability, energy and initiative, leadership, motivation for assignment, observing and reporting, physical ability, propaganda skills, security, and social relations. One product of the assessment was a written report describing the candidate's personality and how he could be expected to function as a member of the organization. Although the OSS staff found little concrete evidence for the predictive validity of the situational tests (OSS, 1948), after reanalyzing the data Wiggins (1973) concluded that the OSS assessment procedures improved decisions regarding the candidates to a modest extent.

Situational tests have also been administered in several other programs, for example, in the selection of clinical psychologists (Kelly & Fiske, 1951) and in the *leaderless group discussion test* (LGD). In administering an LGD, six or so candidates for an administrative position are asked to discuss a given topic for 30 minutes or so. The examiners observe the interactions among the group members during this time and rate their performances on variables such as participation activity, organizational skills, and decision-making ability.

Though appealing for their seeming realism, situational tests are expensive and time-consuming, and examinees frequently realize that the situations are contrived. Moreover, examinees' responses to the situations are often difficult to evaluate. For these reasons, the reliabilities and validities of situational tests are not high.

Participant Observation

Related to both situational testing and naturalistic observation is *participant observation*. It might seem as if an observer could not participate unobtrusively in the situation that he or she is observing, but many cultural anthropologists maintain that this is the only way in which authentic data on other cultures and societies can be obtained. They believe that to keep the persons who are being observed from behaving unnaturally—in other words, from feeling as if they were "on stage" and, hence, playing a role—researchers become participants in the human drama that they are observing. Participant observation is not always successful, but it can produce volumes of data.

Participant observation has also been applied in educational, clinical, and work situations for assessment and diagnostic purposes. For example, to learn more about the personalities of particular employees and how they function is specific work groups, a psychologist/observer may become a member of the group. Again, however, if the other employees are informed that the "new worker" is an assessor or researcher, they may behave differently. If they do not know, it can result in an uncomfortable (and even painful!) situation if and when they eventually discover the truth.

Clinical Observations

Behavioral observations of adults by psychologists and psychiatrists frequently occur in a private office, a clinic, a hospital, or other institution. Many principles and theories of personality dynamics and behavior disorders have been derived from observations made in clinical situations. Alert clinical observers note a variety of details: the patient's manner of dress and grooming; whether the patient will shake hands and look at the therapist (examiner); how the patient sits, stands, walks, and his or her facial expressions, body movements, and voice tones. These observations serve multiple purposes, including diagnosis, psychotherapy, evaluation of treatment effectiveness, and the prediction of future behavior.

Unless both the clinician and the patient are deaf mutes, the observed behaviors consist not only of body movements but also speech. If the patient answers a question posed by the therapist or otherwise interacts verbally with him, an interview is being conducted. In reality, both nonverbal and verbal behaviors are observed in most clinical situations, and the observer's judgments and evaluations are shaped by both kinds of responses. Some observers are more acute or sensitive to the information communicated by verbal and nonverbal social interactions. A classic example is the following vignette related by the psychiatrist Theodore Reik (1948, pp. 263–264):

> After a few sentences about the eventful day, the patient fell into a long silence. She assured me that nothing was in her thoughts. Silence from

me. After many minutes she complained about a toothache. She told me that she had been to the dentist yesterday. He had given her an injection and then had pulled a wisdom tooth. The spot was hurting again. New and longer silence. She pointed to my bookcase in the corner and said, "There's a book standing on its head."

Without the slightest hesitation and in a reproachful voice I said, "But why did you not tell me that you had an abortion?" I had said it without an inkling of what I would say and why I would say it. It felt as if, not I, but something in me had said that. The patient jumped up and looked at me as if I were a ghost. Nobody knew or could know that her love, the physician, had performed an abortion on her. The operation, especially dangerous because of the advanced stage of her pregnancy, was, of course, kept very secret because abortion in the case of gentiles was punishable by death in Germany. To protect the man she still loved, she had decided to tell me all except the secret.

Not all clinicians are as observant or as lucky as Reik, but close contact with a patient, a spouse, or even a business partner can increase one's sensitivity to certain behaviors and their meanings. I once knew a psychiatrist who said that he could "smell" a schizophrenia. A patient would enter the psychiatrist's office, and, by noting the patient's stance, gaze, and general demeanor, the psychiatrist quickly arrived at a diagnosis of schizophrenia without administering any tests or asking any questions. This is not "smelling" in the usual sense. The psychiatrist had become so sensitive to the mannerisms of certain schizophrenics that it seemed to him as if he could almost smell them. One might also interpret the psychiatrist's behavior as indicative of a long association with dogs or other animals having keen olfactory senses.

Nonverbal Behavior

Most people possess something of the ability of our psychiatrist friend to detect and interpret nonverbal behavior. They realize that what is said can mean different things, depending on the speaker's tone of voice and body language. Nonverbal signals or cues are common. For example, looking connotes interest, a rigid posture suggest defensiveness, and unconscious hand movements indicate nervousness. In an investigation by Mehrabian and Weiner (1967), it was estimated that 65 to 90 percent of the meaning in interpersonal communications came from nonverbal cues. According to Freud (1905, p. 94):

He that has eyes to see and ears to hear may convince himself that no mortal can keep a secret. If his lips are silent, he chatters with his fingertips; betrayal oozes out of him at every pore.

The three types of nonverbals to which most of us are somewhat sensitive are kinesics, proximics, and paralinguistics. *Kinesics* are movements of the face, arms, legs, or any part of the body. Small movements are referred to as *microkinesics* and large movements as *macrokinesics*. Movements of the face and hands are most commonly interpreted as messages. The eyes, lips, and fingertips all can communicate emotions and feelings that may or may not belie what we are actually saying. For example, research has found that dependent individuals use eye contact to communicate and elicit positive attitudes. Dominant people and deceivers look less, whereas extroverts and lovers look more often and longer at the person with whom they are interacting (Bernard & Huckins, 1978). Some other facial/head patterns, posture patterns, and gestures used—in this case by flirting women—are listed in Box 3.1.

The messages communicated by movements of the eyes and eyebrows ("eyebrow flash") are, however, not always clear. Depending on the context or situation, an eyebrow flash may be interpreted as flirting, agreement, surprise, fear, disbelief, disapproval, or a silent greeting. Like many other nonverbals, the meaning of an eyebrow flash also varies with the culture. For example, it may indicate agreement among Samoans, disagreement among Greeks, or disapproval among other Europeans and Americans. According to psychologist Dane Archer, the eyebrows and forehead are more authentic than the lower face, which is used for polite smiling and other things. Because the upper face is under less control than the lower face, masking of feelings is usually done with the lower face (Kelleher, 1996).

A second class of nonverbals, *proximics*, has to do with how close you stand to someone. According to Hall's (1969) classification scheme, *intimate distance* is between 0 and 18 inches, *personal distance* between 18 inches to 4 feet, *social distance* between 4 to 12 feet, and *public distance* between 12 feet or more (Hall, 1969). Most of the time spent interacting with other people is at a social distance, which varies with age, sex, culture, and the strength of the relationship.

When two people become intimate, they move closer, and when they do not desire to interact at all they remain at a public distance of 12 feet or more. In any event, the physical distance maintained between two people communicates not only something about their feelings toward each other but also their culture. It is interesting, for example, to watch the kind of "dance" that an American businessman and his counterpart in a Middle Eastern country do when they are conversing. The American moves away, the Middle-Easterner moves closer, the American moves back, and so on in a kind of pas de deux.

A third type of nonverbal communication, *paralinguistics*, consists of tone of voice, rate, rhythm, and modulation of speech, and other nonver-

BOX 3.1 Fifty-Two Ways That Women Flirt

Monica Moore and teams of graduate students spent hundreds of hours in bars and student centers covertly watching women and men court. The following is a list of 52 gestures they found that women use to signal their interest in men (Baum, 1994):

Facial/Head Patterns

Coy smile

Eyebrow flash

Face to face

Fixed gaze

Giggle

Hair flip

Head toss

Head nod

Kiss

Laugh

Lip lick

Lipstick application

Neck presentation

Pout

Room-compassing glance

Short, darting glance

Smile

Whisper

Posture Patterns

Aid solicitation

Approach

Breast touch

Brush

Dance (acceptance)

Foot to foot

Frontal body contact

Hang

Hug

Knee touch

Lateral body contact

Lean

Parade

Placement

Play

Point

Request dance

Shoulder hug

Solitary dance

Thigh touch

Gestures

Arm flexion

Buttock pat

Caress (arm)

Caress (back)

Caress (face/hair)

Caress (leg)

Caress (object)

Caress (torso)

Gesticulation

Hand hold

Hike skirt

Palm

Primp

Tap

bal aspects of vocalization. Variations in loudness and pitch from moderate to extreme, down to up contour, low to high pitch level, and slow to fast tempo all communicate certain emotions.[1]

The meaning of particular voice tones, movements, or postures is almost never universal: It depends on the person, the circumstances in which it is expressed, and the culture. The kind and frequency of kinesics, proximics, and paralinguistics also vary with the culture. Head and hand movements, for example, are different in magnitude, manner, and meaning in different cultures. But culture also influences communication in other ways. Mode of dress, manner of eating, posture (squatting, etc.)—all convey specific messages to those who are familiar with the culture. These culturally determined nonverbals are referred to collectively as *culturics*. Finally, it should be noted that nonverbal behaviors are not limited to human beings. Many animal species possess a rich repertoire of kinesics, proximics, and paralinguistics that serve to maintain order and encourage survival.

Behavior Modification

Psychotherapeutic procedures based on learning theory and research findings and designed to change inappropriate behaviors to more personally and socially acceptable behaviors are referred to collectively as *behavior modification*. Unlike psychoanalysis and more depth-oriented psychotherapies, behavior modification procedures focus on current behavior rather than its underlying, historical causes. The emphasis is on changing maladaptive behavior directly without the necessity of the patient's achieving insight into the causes of those behaviors. In addition to the maladaptive behaviors (the *B*s) themselves, efforts are also made to determine their antecedents (the *A*s) and consequences (the *C*s). This *A-B-C* sequence is a symbolic representation of the principle that behavior is precipitated by certain stimuli in the immediate environment and sustained by its reinforcing consequences. The antecedents and consequences may be either overt, objectively observable conditions or covert mental events. Behavior modifiers attempt to disrupt the *A-B-C* sequence by controlling the antecedents and consequences of the behaviors.

Among the types of maladaptive behaviors that have been successfully treated by behavior modification procedures are alcoholism, anorexia, bed-wetting, chronic tension, chronic pain, drug addiction, fears or phobias, overeating, sexual inadequacy, smoking, and underassertiveness. Such procedures include reinforcement, extinction, systematic desensitization, counterconditioning, and self-monitoring. Perhaps the simplest behavior modification technique is simply to positively reinforce the person for adaptive or appropriate behavior and not reinforce him or her for maladaptive or inappropriate behavior. This is the technique employed in *contingency management*, in which the behaviors of institutionalized persons are controlled by giving them token reinforcements and privileges for socially approved behaviors (keeping neat and clean, eating properly, socially interacting with other persons, etc.). Contingency management involves both positive reinforcement and *extinction*—withdrawing reinforcement, such as not nodding, not smiling, or in other ways failing to show approval of disruptive behavior. *Systematic desensitization*, which has proved especially effective in the treatment of unreasonable fears and anxieties, involves exposing the patient to a real or imagined hierarchy of anxiety-provoking situations directly while encouraging him or her to relax. *Counterconditioning* (or *reciprocal inhibition*), which is often employed in conjunction with systematic desensitization, consists of extinguishing an undesirable response to a stimulus by introducing a more desirable, often incompatible response. In this procedure, the patient is exposed to a conditioned stimulus for anxiety while he or she is making responses (relaxing, eating, or otherwise doing something enjoyable) that are incompatible with anxiety.

Applications of most behavior modification procedures entail some preliminary assessment of the antecedent conditions that precipitate the behavior or at least make it more likely to occur. Observations, interviews, checklists, rating scales, and questionnaires may be completed by the patient or people who are familiar with him or her. The observational procedures consist of noting the frequency and duration of the target behaviors, what triggers the behavior (*antecedents*), and what effect the behavior has (*consequences*). These observations are made by family members, associates, nurses, psychiatric aids, and other people who have watched the patient for a sustained period. The recording of observations of aggressive, communicative, cooperative, and other behaviors expressed by patients may be facilitated by psychometric instruments, such as the Nurses' Observation Scale for Inpatient Evaluation (Honigfeld & Klett, 1965) or the Ward Behavior Inventory (Burdock et al., 1968). In addition to observing and interviewing the patient and other significant people, various questionnaires, rating scales, and personality inventories may be administered.

Self-Monitoring

People are frequent observers of their own behavior. Some people (*high self-monitors*) are more sensitive to situational cues for socially appropriate behavior and act accordingly. Other people (*low self-monitors*) are less sensitive to situational cues for socially acceptable behavior;

by attending more to their own internal attitudes and feelings, low self-monitors behave more consistently than high self-monitors across different situations. A special Self-Monitoring Scale (Snyder, 1974, 1979) has been constructed to measure the extent to which people are high or low self-monitors.

The term *self-monitoring* also refers to an informational/therapeutic procedure in which people observe and record their own behaviors. A patient with an addictive habit may carry a notepad around with him or her and keep a record of when, where, and under what circumstances the addictive need is felt. Alternatively, a patient with maladaptive thought processes (fears, depression, etc.) may keep a diary of daily experiences and thoughts (pleasant or unpleasant) and then discuss them with the therapist once a week. Other self-observers may carry index cards, wrist counters, and timers to record the occurrence of target behaviors and the time, place, and circumstances under which they occurred. Sometimes the very process of observing and monitoring oneself has a therapeutic effect. For example, heavy smokers may smoke less when they are required to keep track of how often, how long, and under what conditions they feel an urge to smoke.

Training Observers

Because of its economy and provision of a means of obtaining information on private mental events, self-observation is an appealing method. However, probably no one is completely objective in describing his or her thoughts and behaviors, and self-observations are even more likely to be biased than observations made by others. Rather than providing an exact report of what they thought, felt, or did, observers typically reconstruct or filter the actual happenings through their own personalities, attitudes, and desires.

Self- and other observers often find it difficult to separate themselves from their own backgrounds, needs, and personalities, but with proper training they can be taught to make more objective and perceptive observations. They can be told in specific, behavioral terms

What to look for and how to record their observations clearly, objectively, and unobtrusively

How to distinguish between what they observe and how they interpret it

How to be more aware of the effects of their personal biases and other factors on what they reportedly observe

When combined with feedback, extensive practice will usually produce improvements in the observer's ability to make valid observations.

Other suggestions for improving the accuracy of observations are observing a few specific behaviors, which are defined beforehand; using an objective system for coding what is observed; making an immediate record of observations; periodically reviewing and recalibrating the observers' recorded responses; using more than one observer and determining the interobserver reliability; and combining (aggregating) the observations of two or more observers. Videotaping the observed scene, at least in the beginning, can also serve as a check on the accuracy of what observers report having seen and heard. Because certain nuances of the observed scene are not picked up by videotape, written notes of what human observers see and hear are also helpful in interpreting an electronic recording. But training cannot work miracles, and some people never become good observers. Conversely, certain individuals appear to be "born observers" or to have had personal experiences that promote greater perceptivity, empathy, and objectivity in observing people, events, and things.

PERSONAL DOCUMENTS

As a way of making an ongoing record of their experiences and thoughts, many people keep diaries, write long letters, prepare autobiographies, make drawings, and keep other personal documents. These materials may provide a wealth of information on the thoughts, behavior, and personality of the writer, but they are seldom easy to interpret. Despite the interest of Gordon Allport (1942, 1965) and certain other psychologists, the complexity and laboriousness of a *content analysis* of written documents has limited their use in clinical diagnosis. A brief review of the psychological uses and shortcomings of various kinds of personal documents, and autobiography in particular, is provided by Wrightsman (1994b).

In addition to their potential uses in clinical diagnosis, personal documents provide information for psychobiographers. Psychobiography is actually a subcategory of psychohistory, in that both employ psychological concepts and theories to reconstruct and interpret happenings that occurred in the past. More specifically, *psychohistory* is concerned with the analysis, by means of history and psychology, of events, such as the Salem witchcraft trials or the rise of Nazi Germany. The term *psychobiography*, conversely, refers to the psychological exploration of a person's life (Wrightsman, 1994a). Psychobiographical studies of many famous people, including political leaders such as Adolf Hitler (Binion, 1976; Langer, 1972), Mohandas Gandhi (Erikson, 1969), and several American presidents (Brodie, 1983; Freud & Bullitt, 1967; Glad, 1980;

Kearns, 1976; Mazlish, 1973), have been conducted for both theoretical and practical purposes. Among the practical reasons are providing opposition leaders or others who must deal with certain political figures with insights into the personalities and behaviors of those leaders and predictions as to what they might do under certain circumstances. These were the motives behind Freud and Bullitt's (1967) psychobiography of Woodrow Wilson and Langer's (1972) psychobiography of Adolf Hitler.

Psychobiography has been criticized for several errors—factual, theoretical, cultural, and logical. Wrightsman's (1994a) review is critical of the approach, but critics, such as Elms (1976) and Cocks and Crosby (1987), have made suggestions for improving psychobiographical procedures. To begin with, a psychobiographical analysis should not be made unless sufficient information is available on the person's life or at least on those areas or periods that are being analyzed. Furthermore, other psychological theories than just classical psychoanalysis should be applied to the analysis. Finally, the preconceptions and biases of psychobiographers should be acknowledged.

In addition to autobiographies and other personal documents, the biographical information that is recorded on application blanks, in letters of recommendation, and in the answers given to biographical (biodata) inventories may provide insights into personality characteristics. These sources are used extensively in employment and admissions decisions, but they may also prove valuable in personality assessment and in the diagnosis of behavioral disorders and their causes (Stokes, Mumford, & Owens, 1994).

ASSESSMENT INTERVIEWING

Next to observations of behavior, interviewing is the oldest and most widely used of all psychological assessment methods. Although diagnostic interviewing for the purpose of determining the mental status of a patient was formally introduced into psychiatry by Adolf Meyer in 1902, personal interviews were conducted extensively in school, work, medical, and service contexts long before then. Today, interviewing is the most frequently used evaluation procedure in employee selection and clinical practice. A personal interview is usually the first step in a comprehensive assessment of personality, to be followed by the administration of several tests, inventories, or other psychometric devices, and perhaps culminating in another (posttesting) interview.

An interview is similar to but more purposeful or focused than a typical conversation. Its flexibility is indicated by the fact that it may be conducted anywhere, face to face or over the telephone, and typically requires no special apparatus or materials. When designed to encourage the interviewee to engage in self-exploration, an interview yields information not only on the experiences of the interviewee but also on how he or she responded to those experiences and what long-term effects they may have had. Details concerning the background and life history of the interviewee and other factual data, as well as expressions of feelings, attitudes, perceptions, and expectations are revealed. Not only what is said, but how it is said and the accompanying body language of the interviewee become grist for the interviewer's analytic mill.

Interviews are conducted in many different contexts, principally for academic, occupational, clinical, and research purposes. In academic contexts, they are used to select students, award scholarships, and for other educational purposes. In occupational situations, they are used in the selection and placement of employees, in performance appraisal, and in transfer and termination decisions. In clinical situations, patients and their relatives are interviewed to obtain case history data for purposes of medical and psychological diagnoses, to determine treatment and to evaluate its effectiveness, and for discharge purposes. In research contexts, interviews are used in polling, surveying, and collecting personality data to test a specific hypothesis or theory.

Interviewing is as much of an art as a science: Sensitivity and skill in dealing with people and insight into their feelings and problems are needed to conduct an open-ended, free-response interview. These abilities can be learned to some extent, but certain individuals appear to be naturally more capable than others in putting people at ease, encouraging them to "open up," and understanding what makes them "tick." Furthermore, effective interviewing is a dynamic interaction of two personalities, in that the appearance, manner, and responses of both parties affect the other.

Interviewing Techniques and Procedures

Whatever their theoretical orientation may be—behavioral, client centered, psychoanalytic, or eclectic—experienced interviews of all stripes follow many of the same rules or procedures (see Table 3.1). A psychological assessment interview typically begins with introductions and a brief get-acquainted period. A successful professional interviewer attempts to establish *rapport*—a warm relationship that encourages the interviewee to be comfortable, trusting, and open. The interviewer waits for the interviewee to answer, encourages clarification and elaboration, and attends to the content, feeling tone, and manner of the interviewee's responses. In short, a successful interviewer conveys to an interviewee

TABLE 3.1 Suggestions for Conducting an Assessment Interview

The Interviewer

Assures the interviewee of the confidentiality of the interview
Conveys feelings of interest and warmth (rapport)
Tries to put the interviewee at ease
Tries to "get in touch" with how the interviewee feels (empathy)
Is courteous, patient, and accepting
Encourages the interviewee to express his or her thoughts and feelings freely
Adjusts the questions to the cultural and educational background of the inter-
    viewee
Avoids psychological or psychiatric jargon
Avoids leading questions (e.g., "Do you still beat your wife?")
Shares personal information and experiences with the interviewee (self-disclo-
    sure) if appropriate and timed accurately
Uses humor sparingly, and only if appropriate and not insulting
Listens without overreacting emotionally
Attends not only to what is said but also to how it is said
Takes notes or makes a recording as inconspicuously as possible

---

a feeling of genuine interest and a desire to learn more about the latter's
life, problems, and aspirations.

The approach followed by the interviewer will vary with the personality and purposes of the interview. The questions are usually fairly general and nonthreatening at first, becoming more focused or specific as
the interview progresses.

Degree of Structure

Traditionally, interviews conducted for the purposes of psychiatric/
psychological diagnosis have been fairly *unstructured*. That is, the questions to be asked were not explicitly prepared beforehand but rather
were allowed to vary with the interviewee, the interviewer, the purposes
of the interview and the flow of topics. In a highly *structured interview*,
conversely, a list or guide containing a series of questions to be asked,
with space for recording the interviewee's responses, is used. When
administered in an employment setting—in which it is more popular—a
structured interview form is similar to a detailed application blank.

Unstructured interviewing has the potential for providing information
in greater depth and of greater relevance to the interviewee, but it has
several drawbacks. Among these are that (a) it demands greater skill
and longer training time, (b) a narrower range of topics is usually covered, and (c) its objectivity and, hence, lower reliability are lower than
that of structured interviewing.

Though most clinicians show a preference for unstructured interviewing, *semistructured interviewing* has become more commonplace in recent years. In this approach, the interviewer is provided with a list of questions to ask, but he or she can also ask other questions that offer the promise of opening up interesting leads or providing insight into the interviewee's circumstances or problems. The advent of microcomputers and associated software for interviewing has attracted more clinicians to structured or semistructured interviewing. In general, interviews with more structure are preferable when answers to many specific questions, as in employment settings, are needed. But less structure is required when the goal of the interview is to provide insight or understanding into the personality and problems of the interviewee as well as their causes and solutions.

Topics and Questions

An outline of the information that it is desirable to obtain in a detailed personality assessment interview is given in Table 3.2. This is an outline of a complete life-history interview, and it is seldom necessary or possible to obtain all the information listed. The interviewer can pick and choose those topics that are most relevant to the purposes of the interview, concentrating on some of them and omitting others altogether. In any case, questions for a structured or semistructured interview can be prepared beforehand from this outline.

Employee and Student Interviews

Most common of all types of interviews are those conducted with applicants for employment or admission to educational institutions. The purpose of such interviews is not simply to determine the ability of the applicant to perform the activities or duties of the position or program for which he (she) is being considered, but also to assess the interpersonal skills, character, and other personality traits of the applicant. Whether a person succeeds or fails on a job or in an educational course or program depends not only on the ability to do the required work but also on temperament, motivation, interests, and other affective factors.

Much of the objective information needed about applicants can be obtained by means of an application blank, questionnaire, resume, letters of recommendation, samples of productive work, and other materials. Interviewers typically have access to much of this information at the time of the interview, and there may be no need for the applicant to report or review it at length. Rather, the interviewer's main task is to confirm questionable or unclear biographical data, to integrate all

TABLE 3.2 Information to Obtain in an Assessment Interview

Identifying data. Name, age, sex, education, ethnic group, nationality, address, date of birth, marital status, date of interview, and so forth

Purpose(s) of interview. Employment, psychiatric intake, psychodiagnostic, problem solving or troubleshooting, performance evaluation, termination or exit

Physical appearance. Clothing, grooming, physical description (attractiveness, unusual features, etc.), obvious or apparent physical disorders or disabilities

Behavior. Attitudes and emotions (cooperative, outgoing or reserved, friendly or hostile, defensive, etc.); motoric behavior (active versus passive, posture, gait, carriage); level of intellectual functioning (bright, average, retarded—estimated from vocabulary, immediate and long-term memory, judgment, abstract thinking); signs of mental disorder (distorted thought processes—bizarre constructions, thought blocking, etc.; distorted perceptions—delusions, hallucinations, disorientation in time or space, etc.; inappropriate or extreme emotional reactions—depression, mania; unusual mannerisms, postures, or facial expressions)

Family. Parents, siblings, other family members; sociocultural group; attitude(s) toward family members

Medical history. Present health, health history, physical problems

Developmental history. Physical, intellectual, language, emotional, and social development; irregularities or problem of development

Education and training. Schools attended, performance level, adjustment to school, plans for further education and training

Employment. Nature and number of jobs or positions held, military service (rank and duties), job performance level(s), job problems

Legal problems. Arrests and convictions, nature of misdemeanors or felonies

Sexual and marital history. Sexual activities and problems, marriages, marital problems, separations and divorce(s), children

Interests and attitudes. Hobbies, recreational activities, social activities and attitude(s) toward others, level of self-acceptance and satisfaction, aspirations or goals

Current problems. Details of current problems and plans for solving them

the data on the applicant obtained from various sources, to explain certain factual and procedural matters to the applicant, and to encourage him or her to elaborate, provide any missing information, and ask questions. Depending on the purposes of the interview and the role and status of the interviewer, details pertaining to duties, benefits, and other technical matters may be discussed. Employment interviewers must be cautious, however, not to ask questions pertaining to age, sex, race, marital/family situation, or other personal or private matters that are not directly related to the applicant's ability to perform the tasks for which he or she is being considered. It is illegal to require job or student applicants to answer questions concerning demographic or personal matters that are not directly related to the job or program for which they are applying.

In addition to their uses in selection and screening, interviews are conducted in business/industrial and other organizational contexts for purposes of placement, performance appraisal, transfer, promotion, retention, and other personnel decisions. Postappraisal interviews designed to integrate information on employee performance evaluation and to communicate it to the employee are particularly commonplace, albeit not popular with either employees or supervisors.

Clinical Interviews

Second in frequency to employment interviews are diagnostic and therapeutic interviews conducted in clinical situations. Many of the same procedures recommended for interviews conducted in other contexts apply to clinical interviews as well. Rapport and active listening are important, as is the ability of the interviewer to ask questions without appearing perfunctory, prying, or pedantic. However, clinical interviewing is typically more open-ended or unstructured than interviewing in organizational or research situations.

The purpose of a *diagnostic interview* is to determine the precise nature, causes, and correlates of the patient's problem(s). The purpose of a *therapeutic interview* is much the same, but with a greater emphasis on patient exploration and a focus on procedures for improving the patient's condition. These procedures depend to some extent on the interviewer's theoretical persuasion. Psychoanalytic therapists, for example, tend to be fairly active and directive—emphasizing the attainment of patient insight by means of free association, the analysis of dreams, the analysis of transference, the analysis of resistance, and direct interpretation. Behavior therapists are similarly active and directive, but they focus more on determining the antecedents and consequences of maladaptive behavior(s) so a program of behavior modification can be constructed. Client-centered therapists are less active than either psychoanalytic or behavior therapists, emphasizing extensive client involvement, whereas the counselor is limited to simple acceptance, restatement of content, reflection of feeling, and similar nondirective activities. Regardless of the theory they espouse, experienced therapeutic interviewers do many of the same things: They are all accepting, uncritical, interested listeners who provide emotional support and helpful suggestions.

A properly conducted diagnostic or therapeutic interview provides a substantial amount of information about a person, including the following:

Nature, duration, and severity of the patient's problem(s)
Ways in which the problem(s) are demonstrated (inward, outward)
Past influences related to the present difficulties of the patient
Patient's resources for coping with the problem(s)
Types of psychological assistance that have already been obtained
    by the patient
Types of psychological assistance that are expected by the patient
    and that might be helpful

A special kind of diagnostic interview referred to as a *mental status interview* is conducted to determine, for clinical or legal purposes, a person's mental competencies. In-depth information is elicited on the person's

Emotional state (affect and mood)
Intellectual and perceptual functioning (attention, concentration,
    memory, intelligence, judgment)
Style and content of thought processes and speech
Level of insight into his or her mental state and personality problems
Psychomotor activity
General appearance
Attitude

Much of this information can be obtained more efficiently and reliably by administering appropriate psychological assessment instruments rather than by extensive interviewing. Interview and observation schedules, such as the Schedule for Affective Disorders and Schizophrenia (3rd ed.)[2] can also assist in the process of conducting a mental status examination.

Stress Interview

Despite the interviewer's efforts to maintain a cordial, calm, supportive atmosphere, an interview is often a stressful experience. This is particularly true when the rule of cordiality is suspended, and the interviewer applies more pressure by becoming confrontational. Such is the case in a *stress interview*. Designed to determine the interviewee's ability to cope or solve problems under emotionally stressful conditions, a stress interview may be used when time is short, and the interviewee is defensive, emotionally unresponsive, or repetitious. The aim of a stress interview is to remove the superficial social mask of the interviewee by asking probing and challenging questions, in a police interrogation-like atmosphere.

Defensiveness and resistance are common in clinical interviews that deal with sensitive areas and prompt the need to protect oneself. Consider the following vignette from a case study:

> During the intake interview, Mr. D was sullen, argumentative, and difficult for the examiner to relate to. He took a long time to answer questions that were asked, was reluctant to discuss his present legal problems, and tended to change the subject when his charges were discussed with him. (Courtesy of James N. Butcher, personal communication)

Stress interviewing should be used sparingly and only by interviewers who are thoroughly trained in the technique. A great deal of professional expertise is needed to make the interview seem realistic and not let things get out of hand or to lose control of the situation.

Computer-Based Interviewing

Structured interview instruments, such as the Psychiatric Diagnostic Interview–Revised (E. Othmer and coauthors; Western Psychological Services) and the Structured Clinical Interview for the *Diagnostic and Statistical Manual of Mental Disorders* (3rd ed., rev.) (DSM-III-R) (SCID)[2] have been available for many years but administered primarily for research purposes. These schedules contain both objective and open-ended questions and require the examiner to make clinical judgments at various decision points in the interview. One such instrument, the Structured Interview of Reported Symptoms (by R. Rogers, R. M. Bagby, & S. E. Dickens; available from Psychological Assessment Resources), was designed specifically to detect malingering and other forms of feigning of psychological symptoms.

The widespread availability of microcomputers has increased interest in and usage of structured interview forms and procedures. Krug (1993) lists dozens of computer-based interviewing programs, primarily for administration in clinical contexts. Among the advantages ascribed to these programs are that they save professional time, permit a broad coverage of topics, and are more flexible than questions posed by human interviewers. Some computer-based interviewing packages are broad-spectrum instruments that provide a range of diagnoses, whereas others focus on specific disorders or symptoms.

Two examples of computer-based interviewing packages that have seen a substantial amount of use are the Giannetti On-Line Psychosocial History and the Quickview Social History, both of which are available from NCS Assessments. These programs summarize routine psychosocial history information entered by the patient into the computer and print out the results in the form of a clinical report. The "branching" facility of the programs allows the interview to be tailored to the responses made to previous questions. Other illustrative computer packages permit users to construct their own interviews (Q-Fast; from StatSoft) or to modifying existing interviews (Psychosocial History Report; from Psychometric Software).

The results of computer-based interviewing are highly correlated with those from standard structured interviews and are no less reliable. Furthermore, most people do not object to being interviewed by a computer, and, in fact, they may reveal even more personal information to a computer than to a live interviewer (Farrell, 1993; Rosenfeld et al., 1989). A major disadvantage of computers is their inability to handle anything other than structured verbal information. Unlike unstructured or semistructured interviewing in a person-to-person situation, the wording of computer-presented questions is not tailored to the person and the context. Be that as it may, the development of computer programs for assisting in psychiatric/psychological diagnosis will undoubtedly continue. The programs of the future promise to have a greater ability to combine interview data with psychological test results and to contribute even more to psychodiagnosis and treatment planning in clinical contexts.

Reliability and Validity

The problems of reliability and validity that plague observational procedures are shared with interviewing. Structured interviews are more reliable than unstructured ones, but the results obtained with the former are still not completely consistent. The verbal information supplied by an interviewee depends not only on the actual state of things, but also on how well those matters are remembered and how they are interpreted by the interviewee. In addition, the personality and behavior of the interviewer can have an effect on the information reported by an interviewee.

The interrater reliabilities of structured interviews, computed as the correlation between the ratings given by two or more raters to interviewees' responses, are, under the best of circumstances, no higher than .80. Validity depends on reliability, so it is not surprising that the validities of structured interviews are higher than those of unstructured ones. It can be argued, however, that there is a trade-off in that the greater validity of structured interviews is obtained by sacrificing the depth or richness of the information obtained from unstructured interviews.

SUMMARY

Observing and interviewing are the two most common methods of assessing personality. Widely used in clinical, education, employment, and research contexts, observations may be controlled or uncontrolled, and interviews may be structured or unstructured. In general, controlled observational procedures are more objective, and consequently the results more reliable, than those of uncontrolled observations. Likewise, structured interviews are more objective, and the results more reliable, than those obtained with unstructured interviews. It is possible, however, that the greater objectivity and reliability of controlled observation and structured interviewing are obtained at the expense of greater breadth and depth of information.

Other observational procedures include naturalistic observation, in which behavior is observed in naturally occurring situations, and participant observation—becoming a part of the observational scene to better understand what is occurring.

Interviews are conducted in both educational and employment situations for purposes of applicant selection and placement, and, at least in the latter context, for promotion, transfer, and performance appraisal. Two types of clinical interviewing are diagnostic and therapeutic. A mental status interview is a particular kind of diagnostic interview designed to assess the interviewee's competency.

Regardless of their theoretical persuasion, successful clinical interviewers all employ many of the same techniques and procedures. The diagnostic and therapeutic interviewers conducted by most clinicians are fairly unstructured, though structured and semistructured interviewing are becoming increasingly popular. A number of forms and computer programs are available for conducting structured interviews.

Situational testing involves observing a person in a contrived, presumably life-like, situation to determine his or her abilities and personality characteristics. Illustrative of situational testing are the assessment programs of the OSS and the Kelly and Fiske (1951) studies of clinical psychology trainees. Another contrived situation is stress interviewing, in which the interviewee's ability to give acceptable answers to questions posed by a confrontational, stress-provoking interviewer is evaluated.

In addition to verbal responses, nonverbal behaviors—kinesics, proximics, paralinguistics, culturics—reveal data concerning thoughts and personality. The content analysis of personal documents—autobiographies, diaries, letters, and so on—can also yield valuable information for the assessment of personality.

NOTES

1. A test of the ability to understand nonverbal cues conveyed by the face, body, and tone of voice was designed by Robert Rosenthal and his associates. Available from Irvington Publishers, Inc., this Profile of Nonverbal Sensitivity is appropriate for grades 3 to 16 and adults. It requires examinees to match facial expressions, body movements, and tone of voice to situations.
2. Available from Department of Research Assessment and Training, New York State Psychiatric Institute, 722 West 168th Street, New York, NY 10032.

SUGGESTED READINGS

Beutler, L. E. (1995). The clinical interview. In L. E. Beutler & M. R. Berren (Eds.), *Integrative assessment of adult personality* (pp. 94–120). New York: Guilford Press.

Craik, K. H. (1988). Assessing the personalities of historical figures. In W. M. Kunyan (Ed.), *Psychology and historical interpretation* (pp. 196–218). New York: Oxford University Press.

Haynes, S. N. (1990). Behavioral assessment of adults. In G. Goldstein & M. Hersen (Eds.), *Handbook of psychological assessment* (2nd ed., pp. 403–422). New York: Pergamon.

Leichtman, M. (1995). Behavioral observations. In J. N. Butcher (Ed.), *Clinical personality assessment: Practical approaches* (pp. 251–266). New York: Oxford University Press.

Phares, E. J. (1992). The assessment interview. In *Clinical psychology: Concepts, methods, & profession* (4th ed., pp. 150–178). Belmont, CA: Wadsworth.

Wiens, A. N. (1990). Structured clinical interviews for adults. In G. Goldstein & M. Hersen (Eds.), *Handbook of psychological assessment* (2nd ed., pp. 324–344). New York: Pergamon.

Wrightsman, L. S. (1994). *Adult personality development* (Vol. 1, pp. 85–108; Vol. 2, pp. 145–173). Newbury Park, CA: Sage.

4

Checklists and Rating Scales

The results of controlled or uncontrolled observations or a structured or unstructured interview can be summarized and made more objective by recording them on a well-constructed checklist or rating scale. Rating scales and checklists may also be used independently of the results of observational or interview sessions by having them completed by the individuals to be evaluated or by others who are well acquainted with those individuals.

Checklists and rating scales are the most popular, economical, convenient, and versatile of all methods of personality assessment. Their popularity is attested to by the fact that, next to achievement tests, more rating scales and checklists are administered than any other kind of psychometric instrument. They are economical in that they are fairly easy and cheap to construct. They are convenient in that only paper and pencil and good observational skills are needed to use them. They are versatile in that they can be used alone or in combination with other methods of evaluating a wide range of characteristics of people, objects, and events. Hundreds of rating scales and checklists are commercially available, and for almost any need that exists.

As applied to the assessment of personality, a *checklist* is a list of words, phrases, or statements that describe the personal characteristics of the person being evaluated. Respondents check, underline, or in some other way indicate which word(s) or phrases are descriptive of themselves (self-checking) or another designated ratee. Responses to checklist items are usually dichotomous (check/not check or yes/

no), but some lists provide for three responses (check yes, check no, or do not check).

A *rating scale* is actually a generalized checklist, in that there may be several response categories. The numbers, letters, or words designating the possible responses to a rating scale item may be arranged in the form of a continuous line divided into sections corresponding to degrees of the characteristic to be evaluated. As on a checklist, the rater indicates judgments of either his or her own behavior and traits or the behavior and traits of another person. If the characteristic of interest is naturally dichotomous (male/female, graduated high school/did not graduate high school, etc.), then it can be phrased as an item or a checklist. However, many human characteristics can be evaluated in terms of 2 to 5, or any number of response categories. Examples are intelligence (high/low or high/average/low, or very high/high/average/ low/very low), and aggressiveness (aggressive/submissive, very aggressive/aggressive/submissive/very submissive). In this case, the instrument designer can choose between a checklist and a rating scale format. Although a rating scale may give the appearance of greater precision and may actually yield a more reliable measure of a characteristic(s) or behavior, in many cases a checklist format is perfectly satisfactory in supplying the information needed to make judgments or decisions. Because they require judgments concerning the quality, frequency, or intensity of behaviors and personality characteristics, rating scales require more time to complete than checklists. Both types of instruments have increased in popularity since the 1960s, owing, in large measure, to heightened demand for periodic evaluation of the effectiveness of governmentally or privately sponsored programs in education, public health, and other social organizations. Rating scales and checklists are used extensively to evaluate people for purposes of employment and educational selection and placement, and to determine the effects of training, psychotherapy, and other treatments.

CHECKLISTS

Because responding to checklist items is fairly simple and efficient, many characteristics or behaviors may be evaluated using this format. Most checklists are homemade instruments that have not been adequately standardized and are of uncertain reliability and validity. In this case, convenience outweighs psychometric rigor in importance, though "homemade" need not imply "makeshift" or "shoddy." An example is the Social Readjustment Scale (SRS) (Holmes & Rahe, 1967). This checklist was designed to study the effects of life changes, both negative and positive, on behavior and physiological reactions to the stress precipitated by such change. According to the theory on which the SRS is based, the greater the degree of readjustment in a given year, the greater the person's chances of developing a stress-related illness. Each of the 43 items on the SRS is weighted from 0 to 100, depending on the degree of readjustment necessitated by the event referred to in the item. Another stress-related instrument, based on research conducted by the author with college students, is presented in Figure 4.1. List I consists of 25 worries or sources of stress, in rank order according to the frequency with which they were reported (checked) by the sample of students. List II consists of 41 stress reactions, in rank order according to the frequency with which they were checked. List III consists of 28 stress-coping techniques, in order of the frequency with which they were checked by the students.

A final example of a nonstandardized checklist is the Behavioral Checklist for Performance Anxiety shown in Figure 4.2. This instrument is not commercially available, but it has proved valuable in assessing the effects of desensitization (a type of behavior therapy) on anxiety. As noted previously, one advantage of a checklist is that it can be filled out repeatedly to determine changes in behavior over several periods or sessions. This feature is illustrated by the eight boxes opposite each of the observed behaviors listed in Figure 4.2; a check mark is made in a box to indicate that the specified behavior is observed during the designated period.

A representative list of commercially distributed checklists in a variety of categories is given in Appendix 4.1. Some of these instruments focus on specific behaviors or clinical symptoms, whereas others are more general information-gathering devices concerned with personal history, problems, and personality traits. Most checklists are designed to detect behavioral and developmental problems in children. Checklists are available for assessing adaptive behavior, school difficulties, learning disabilities, neuropsychological disorders, and many other characteristics and problems of children. However, all of the instruments listed in Appendix 4.1 are appropriate for adults (age 18 years and older). There are checklists for anxiety, depression, hostility, psychopathy, and mental status, as well as marital, sexual, and interpersonal relations in adults. Unfortunately, the standardization, reliability, and validity data on many such checklists are inadequate. Consequently, interested purchasers would do well to examine the manual of administration, scoring, and interpretation accompanying a specific instrument before committing themselves to it. In particular, the following questions should be considered in selecting any checklist or rating scale:

(Continued on page 73)

FIGURE 4.1 Three checklists for studying the epidemiology of stress in college students.

List I. Check each of the following that is a cause of worry or stress for you at this time in your life:

_____ 1. Grades (marks)
_____ 2. Tests or examinations
_____ 3. Finances (money and bills)
_____ 4. Course paper assignments
_____ 5. Too much homework
_____ 6. Uncertainty about my future
_____ 7. Job prospects after graduation
_____ 8. My parents or other family members
_____ 9. Lack of exercise
_____ 10. Relationship with my boyfriend or girlfriend
_____ 11. Dieting
_____ 12. Friend ships (other than romantic)
_____ 13. Living conditions (room, roommate, etc.)
_____ 14. Participation in an athletic team
_____ 15. My health
_____ 16. Overeating
_____ 17. Deciding on a major
_____ 18. Marital plans
_____ 19. Transportation
_____ 20. Meetings
_____ 21. Fear of AIDS
_____ 22. Boredom
_____ 23. Poor class schedule
_____ 24. Problems with my present job
_____ 25. My neighbors

List II. Check each of the following that you have experienced during times of stress:

_____ 1. Anxiety
_____ 2. Feelings of frustration
_____ 3. Anger
_____ 4. Irritability
_____ 5. Extreme fatigue
_____ 6. Depression
_____ 7. Tension headaches
_____ 8. Crying
_____ 9. Biting my fingernails or lips
_____ 10. Neckaches
_____ 11. Acne flare-ups
_____ 12. Upset stomach
_____ 13. Insomnia (trouble sleeping)
_____ 14. Backache
_____ 15. Loss of appetite
_____ 16. Muscle tension or spasms
_____ 17. Oversleeping
_____ 18. Indigestion

_____ 19. Colds or other respiratory problems
_____ 20. Shouting or screaming
_____ 21. Menstrual irregularities
_____ 22. Panic attacks
_____ 23. Increased blood pressure
_____ 24. Lightheadedness
_____ 25. Migraine headaches
_____ 26. Irregular heartbeat
_____ 27. Heavy perspiration
_____ 28. Dizziness
_____ 29. Shortness of breath
_____ 30. Diarrhea
_____ 31. Vomiting
_____ 32. Uncontrollable trembling
_____ 33. Tightness in throat or chest
_____ 34. Itching skin
_____ 35. Dermatitis (skin inflammation)
_____ 36. Constipation
_____ 37. Blurred vision
_____ 38. Allergy flare-ups
_____ 39. Skin rashes (other than acne)
_____ 40. Hyperventilation (excessively rapid and deep breathing)
_____ 41. Dandruff flare-ups

List III. Check each of the following techniques that you typically use to cope with stress:

_____ 1. Analyze the situation
_____ 2. Talk with someone about it
_____ 3. Make a list of what I have to do
_____ 4. Go to sleep
_____ 5. Listen to music
_____ 6. Rest
_____ 7. Get away from the source of stress
_____ 8. Reevaluate and reorganize things
_____ 9. Exercise more
_____ 10. Buy something to cheer myself up
_____ 11. Pray or read the Bible, the Koran, or other inspirational text
_____ 12. Try to remain calm
_____ 13. Do something constructive about the stress
_____ 14. Withdraw into myself
_____ 15. Go to a movie
_____ 16. Drink coffee or soda, or eat something good
_____ 17. Go to a party
_____ 18. Drink beer or another alcoholic beverage
_____ 19. Cook, construct, or design something
_____ 20. Write in my journal or diary
_____ 21. Take deep breaths
_____ 22. Put it out of my mind
_____ 23. Bury myself in work
_____ 24. Talk myself out of it

(Continued)

FIGURE 4.1 *(Continued)*

—————— 25. Smoke cigarettes
—————— 26. Hit something or somebody
—————— 27. Read a good book or something inspiring
—————— 28. Take tranquilizers or other drugs

FIGURE 4.2 A behavioral checklist for performance anxiety. (Reprinted from INSIGHT VS. DESENSITIZATION IN PSYCHOTHERAPY by Gordon L. Paul with the permission of the publishers, Stanford University Press. © 1966 by the Board of Trustees of the Leland Stanford Junior University.)

Behavior Observed	Time Period							
	1	2	3	4	5	6	7	8
1 Paces								
2 Sways								
3 Shuffles feet								
4 Knees tremble								
5 Extraneous arm & hand movement (swings, scratches, toys, etc.)								
6 Arms rigid								
7 Hands restrained (in pockets, behind back, clasped)								
8 Hand tremors								
9 No eye contact								
10 Face muscles tense (drawn, tics, grimaces)								
11 Face "deadpan"								
12 Face pale								
13 Face flushed (blushes)								

Behavior Observed	Time Period							
	1	2	3	4	5	6	7	8
14 Moistens lips								
15 Swallows								
16 Clears throat								
17 Breathes heavily								
18 Perspires (face, hands, arm-pits)								
19 Voice quivers								
20 Speech blocks or stammers								

1. What variables (constructs) are purportedly measured by the instrument, and how are they defined?
2. What is the rationale on which the instrument is based (a specific theory of personality or behavior, previous research findings, etc.)?
3. What special training or specific conditions are required for using the instrument? By whom and under what conditions (environmental context, materials, etc.) can it be used?
4. How is the instrument scored, and what materials are needed to score it? Can it be scored quickly and accurately by hand, or is a computer or other scoring machine needed?
5. Has the instrument been standardized? If so, was the standardization group representative of the people who will be evaluated with the instrument?
6. What kinds of evidence are presented for the reliability (test–retest, parallel forms, internal consistency, etc.) of the instrument?
7. What kinds of evidence for the validity (content, criterion-related, construct) of the instrument is presented or available from other sources?

Scoring Checklist Responses

In scoring responses to checklist items, 1 point is usually given to each checked item, and no points to unchecked items. However, numerical weights other than 0 and 1, including negative weights, may be assigned to responses. As with other types of test items, differential weighting of responses to checklist items has little effect on the reliability or validity of a sum of weights on many items. Rather than simple counts of the number of items checked, if one is interested primarily in comparing the responses of n different people, scores consisting of the percentage overlap in the responses of each pair of persons to all items may be more appropriate. The n by n matrix of these scores can then be subjected to further analysis.

A problem that occurs in scoring the responses to checklist items is that different people have a tendency (response set) to check different numbers of items regardless of the content of those items. Because this *frequency response set* can have an effect on composite scores on the checklist, some kind of statistical procedure is often employed as a control. For example, the frequency distribution of scores on the "number checked" variable of the Adjective Check List (ACL) is divided into five groups, and standard scores on the other variables have been determined separately for each group. So when converting a person's raw score on one of the ACL content scales to a standard score, the table of norms for the subgroup of the standardization sample having a number-checked interval in which the respondent's number-checked score falls is referred to.

Another way of controlling for the frequency response set is appropriate when total scores on a checklist variable (Y) are linearly related to the total number of items checked (X). In this circumstance, a reasonable measure of a person's standing on the variable is the difference between his or her actual Y score and the Y score predicted from his or her X score (i.e., $Y\text{-}Y_{pred}$). Finally, when the relationships of scores on the content scales of a checklist to an external criterion are of interest, the frequency with which items on the checklist as a whole are checked may be controlled statistically by means of partial or semipartial correlational procedures.

Adjective Checklists

One of the most popular kinds of checklists in personality research and clinical practice consists of a series of adjectives, such as the following:

Achievement oriented	Explosive
Aggressive	Impatient
Ambitious	Irritable
Competitive	Restless
Efficient	Tense

You are probably acquainted with one or more individuals who fit the description provided by these adjectives, commonly designated as a *type A personality*. In addition to unstandardized adjective checklists like this one, which are designed to measure a single variable or construct, many standardized checklists measure several variables. Two examples are the Adjective Check List and the Multiple Affect Adjective Check List.

Adjective Check List (ACL)

This instrument consists of 300 adjectives arranged in alphabetical order from absent-minded to zany. The examinee is instructed to mark those adjectives that he or she considers to be self-descriptive. The ACL takes 15 to 20 minutes to complete, and it can be scored on the 37 variables or scales listed in Table 4.1. The four Modus Operandi Scales (scales 1–4) are concerned with the manner in which respondents deal with the checklist. The 15 Need Scales (scales 5–19) are based on descriptions given by Allen Edwards (1954) of the 15 needs in Henry Murray's (1938) need-press personality theory. The nine Topical Scales (scales 20–28) assess different topics or components of interpersonal behavior. The five Transactional Analysis Scales (scales 29–33) are measures of the five ego functions in Eric Berne's (1966) theory of transactional analysis. Lastly, the four Origence-Intellectence Scales (scales 34–37) are measures of George Welsh's (1977) origence-intellectence creativity and intelligence dimensions of personality.

Raw scores on the 37 ACL scales are converted to standard T scores for purposes of interpretation and counseling. As an illustration, consider the T scores in Table 4.1 and the associated personality description in Report 4.1. Clearly, these scores provide useful information, but they do not provide a complete picture of this woman's personality. Additional psychometric data, coupled with detailed observations in a variety of situations and an in-depth interview, are required for a comprehensive portrait of her personality and behavior. As shown in Report 4.1, much of the information included in a psychological report comes from observational and interview data rather than directly from the results of the psychometric instruments administered.

The internal consistency reliabilities of most of the ACL scales are reasonably high, although the test-retest reliabilities are substantially lower. Teeter (1985) and Zarske (1985) concluded that the instrument is well developed, but the scales have significant correlations with each other and should, therefore, not be interpreted as independent variables. Many research studies have been conducted with the ACL, particularly studies of the self-concept in normal adolescents and adults.

TABLE 4.1 Scales and Sample T Scores on the Adjective Check List

Scale Name and Designation	T Scores for Case in Report 4.1
Modus Operandi Scales	
Total number of adjectives checked (No Ckd)	53
Number of favorable adjectives checked	53
Number of unfavorable adjectives checked (Unfav)	48
Communality (Com)	57
Need Scales	
Achievement (Ach)	52
Dominance (Dom)	47
Endurance (End)	41
Order (Ord)	40
Intraception (Int)	48
Nurturance (Nur)	49
Affiliation (Aff)	54
Heterosexuality (Het)	64
Exhibition (Exh)	43
Autonomy (Aut)	47
Aggression (Agg)	45
Change (Cha)	52
Succorance (Suc)	44
Abasement (Aba)	58
Deference (Def)	58
Topical Scales	
Counseling Readiness (Crs)	56
Self-control (S-Cn)	57
Self-Confidence (S-Cfd)	55
Personal Adjustment (P-Adj)	55
Ideal Self (Iss)	47
Creative Personality (Cps)	46
Military Leadership (Mls)	52
Masculine Attributes (Mas)	45
Feminine Attributes (Fem)	68
Transactional Analysis Scales	
Critical Parent (CP)	46
Nurturing Parent (NP)	43
Adult (A)	39
Free Child (FC)	49
Adapted Child (AC)	53
Origence-Intellectence Scales	
High Origence, Low Intellectence (A-1)	64
High Origence, High Intellectence (A-2)	49

(Continued)

TABLE 4.1 *(Continued)*

Low Origence, Low Intellectence (A-3)	56
Low Origence, High Intellectence (A-4)	48

REPORT 4.1 Case Description Accompanying Adjective Check List Scores in Table 4.1

This profile was obtained from a 34-year-old homemaker, married to a skilled tradesman, and the mother of two children. She completed 12 years of education. She had previously worked as a secretary and intended to resume working outside their home when her children were older. In the life-history interview, she described herself as "ridiculously dependable" and as quiet except in the company of close friends and family. She had a depressive episode about 10 years before the time of testing, but was in good physical and psychological health when interviewed. Marital adjustment appeared to be good, and she reported satisfaction with sexual life including orgasm about 90 percent of the time. When asked about women's role in modern life, she replied, "I think it's important to have a choice of working or not, and equal pay for equal work is important, too. However, I get turned off by women who do masculine things—like climbing telephone poles—just because men do. But maybe that's because I'm not very physical myself and wouldn't be able to do it. My husband likes the idea of coming home and finding me there and knowing that the kids are properly looked after." She was adamantly opposed to capital punishment, thought there may be a life hereafter but was not personally religious, had ambivalent feelings about abortion, liked modern art, and thought children should be raised as permissively as possible.

Her ACL profile had three scores of 60 or higher: heterosexuality, femininity, and A-1 (high origence, low intellectence). Only order and adult scores were at 40 or below. Moderately elevated scores of 58 were noted on abasement and deference, and the scale for endurance was moderately low at 41. The high score on Fem suggests a need for intimacy and mutuality in relationships, along with a considerate and sympathetic social manner. Her heterosexual drive is strong. She is neither analytic nor intellectual, but responds with feelings and intuition, and she is uncomfortable in dealing with the logical, problem-solving demands of adult life. She is at her best in interdependent relationships with others, particularly with her husband and children.

However, it has not been used extensively in psychodiagnosis and treatment planning.

Multiple Affect Adjective Check List–Revised (MAACL-R)

This instrument consists of 132 adjectives descriptive of personal feelings. Respondents check the adjectives that are indicative of how they generally feel (General Form), or how they feel today or at present (Today Form). Either form can be completed in approximately 5 minutes and yields scores on five variables: anxiety (A), depression (D), hostility (H), positive affect (PA), and sensation seeking (SS). Summary scores are also computed on dysphoria (Dys = A + D + H) and positive affect and sensation seeking (PASS = PA + SS). All seven scores may be converted to standard T scores for interpretation purposes.

The General (Trait) Form of the MAACL-R was standardized on a national sample of 1,491 18-year-olds, and the Today (State) Form on a (nonrepresentative) sample of 538 students in a midwestern college. Except for the Sensation Seeking scale, internal-consistency reliabilities are adequate for both forms; test–retest coefficients are satisfactory for the trait scales but low for the state scales. The MAACL-R manual contains the results of validity studies conducted on samples of normal adolescents and adults, counseling clients, and patients from clinics and state hospitals (Zuckerman & Lubin, 1985). The standardized scales have been shown to differentiate patients with affective disorders from other types of patients and nonpatients. Validity evidence is also found in the significant correlations of the MAACL-R scales with scores on the Minnesota Multiphasic Personality Inventory and the Profile of Mood States, as well as peer ratings, self-ratings, and psychiatric diagnoses.

Templer's (1985) review of the MAACL-R concluded that it is definitely superior to its predecessor (MAACL) and possesses several advantages. These include brevity and ease of administration, the provision of both state and trait measures, the assessment of five affect dimensions, sensitivity to changes over time, and good reliability. MAACL-R scores are also relatively independent of response sets. This instrument has commendable construct validity, and it can be applied in a wide range of research problems in normal and abnormal populations. One of these is in the assessment of temporal changes because of psychotherapy and other intervention procedures.

Problem Checklists

Checklists consisting of a series of problems in different areas are a common method of detecting adjustment problems in school children and child guidance clinics. Though not as popular in evaluating adult personality, checklists of problems, such as the Mooney Problem Checklists, can help adults express any difficulties they are experiencing with respect to health, economic security, self-improvement, personality, home and family, courtship, sex, religion, or occupation. The results may facilitate self-exploration and serve as a source of data on what may be bothering the respondent and as an entrée to personal counseling.

Like the Mooney Problem Checklists, the adult version of the Problem Experiences Checklist helps pinpoint problems and identifies areas for further discussion. Those problems in a list of 200 that are bothering the respondent can be checked in 10 to 15 minutes. Problems are summarized in 10 categories: Marital-Relationship, Children-Parents, Financial-Legal, Bereavement, Personal Habits, Work Adjustment, Life Transition, Beliefs and Goals, Painful Memories, and Emotions. A similar procedure is used in completing the 208-item adult version of the Personal Problems Checklist. Problems are summarized in 13 categories: social, appearance, school, religion, legal, crises, health and habit, emotions, vocational, finances, sex, attitude, family and home.

RATING SCALES

Ratings and rankings are employed extensively in developmental assessments, psychodiagnosis, personnel selection and placement, performance evaluation, and determination of the effectiveness of treatments or interventions of various kinds. Ranking items, on which the rater simply ranks a set of n persons on a scale of 1 to n, are easy to construct but time-consuming and cumbersome for the rater. A related procedure consists of requiring the rater to compare every person to be evaluated with every other person in terms of the person's standing on a designated characteristic. However, this pair comparisons technique, which requires making $n(n - 1)/2$ comparisons, is also cumbersome.

Strategies for Constructing Rating Scales

As in designing a checklist or a personality inventory, various strategies may be adopted in constructing a rating scale. The designer may decide to stick close to a particular theory of personality, such as psychoanalytic theory, behavior theory, trait/factor theory, self-theory, or some other a priori conception of human nature. A related, *rational* or *deductive*, strategy consists of designing a rating scale according to what seems reasonable or logical to include in an instrument of this type. Such decisions are based on clinical and counseling experience, familiarity with the results of personality research, and logical reasoning.

The *inductive*, or *internal consistency*, construction strategy uses the results of correlational and factor-analytic research to decide which items to include on a rating scale. This strategy begins with the administration of many items, probably selected initially by means of theory and logical reasoning. Responses to the items are statistically analyzed, revealing a set of item clusters or factors constituting a few salient personality variables. An inductive strategy has been employed in the construction of many personality inventories, a good example being the 16 PF Questionnaire.

A third approach to rating scale construction is called the *empirical* or *criterion-groups strategy*. In this strategy, items are selected or retained according to their ability to distinguish between two or more diagnostic or other criterion groups of people. A variety of statistical indexes and significance tests may be used to determine which items and scales have this property. In any event, groups of items that, individually and collectively, differentiate between the criterion groups of interest are scored as a combined scale to identify or diagnose particular conditions and characteristics. For example, if you found that delinquent children tended to watch television significantly more often than nondelinquents, the following item might be included on a scale for measuring delinquency proneness: How many hours do you watch TV each week (0–4, 5–9, 10–14, 15–19, 20–24, or 25+)?

The three-scale construction strategies referred to previously are not mutually exclusive, and the design of many rating scales and checklists has employed two or more of them. Research findings have not made clear which strategy is best, but a combination would seem to be most appropriate. The first, or deductive, strategy was applied in the design of most rating scales now in use. However, scales constructed by this strategy alone tend to be more easily faked and have fairly low internal consistency reliabilities (Burisch, 1984a; Martin, 1988). Scales constructed by the inductive and empirical strategies also have their advantages and disadvantages.

Another condition that has traditionally been considered to yield low reliabilities is the inclusion of only a few items on a rating scale. Burisch (1984b) found that short scales are just as valid as long scales, simple scales are just as valid as sophisticated scales, and self-rating scales are just as valid as questionnaire scales. Consequently, he advised, and others have concurred that, in designing a rating scale or personality inventory one should "make it simple" (Wolfe, 1993).

Errors in Rating

Both checklists and rating scales are subject to response errors, in that the checker or rater is not completely objective in responding. Other factors than objective observation and knowledge of the ratee that come into play are the background and personality of the rater, and his or her perception and understanding of both the ratee and the rating task. To begin with, because of poor or ambiguous instructions concerning the rating task and unclear descriptions of the characteristics to be rated, the rater may not understand exactly what he or she is supposed to do or how to do it. Even when efforts have been made to construct a straightforward and unambiguous instrument and to explain the nature of the task as clearly as possible, various errors can bias ratings and reduce their value. The most common kinds of errors are constant errors, the halo effect, the contrast error, and the proximity error.

Constant Errors

Range restriction, or *constant errors*, occur when raters assign high, low, or average ratings more often than justified. Giving too many high ratings is known as the *leniency error*, giving too many low ratings is the *severity error*, and giving too many average (middle category) ratings is the *central tendency error*. Assuming that not all raters are subject to the same constant error, a rater's susceptibility to errors of this kind can be detected by comparing the ratings assigned by him or her with the mean of the ratings assigned by all other raters. Some statistical control over constant errors can also be exerted by transforming the ratings to standard scores. Ranking instead of rating people on the specified characteristics also controls for constant errors but provides only relative information. Although it by no means eliminates errors of this kind, training raters to be aware of these errors and how to avoid them is probably more effective than efforts to refine the rating questionnaire.

Halo Effect

Another common rating error is the *halo effect*—the tendency of raters to respond to the general impression made by a ratee or to overgeneralize by giving the ratee favorable ratings on all characteristics simply because he or she is superior on one or two of them. Perhaps less common than this *positive halo effect* is the *negative halo effect*, in which a single bad characteristic causes a person's ratings on all the other characteristics to be lower than they would otherwise be. Such a spread of effect also occurs in the *logical error* of giving similar ratings to characteristics that are deemed to be logically related.

Contrast Error

In interviewing, rating, or personality assessment in general, there is often a tendency to evaluate a person more positively if an immediately preceding person received a very negative evaluation, or to evaluate a person more negatively if an immediately preceding person received a very positive evaluation. This same sort of *contrast error* can occur when the rater compares or contrasts the ratee with himself (the rater) rather than with people in general. Because raters usually have some internalized standard of what constitutes high or low, good or bad, weak or strong, and so forth, the directions for making ratings should specify the reference group with which the ratee should be compared (e.g., "normal" people, members of one sex, ethnic group, or nationality, etc.).

Proximity and Most Recent Performance Errors

Not only the immediately preceding person but also previous items in a series can affect the rating assigned to a given item. A rater may be subject to the *proximity error* of assigning similar ratings to items or people that are closer together on the printed page. Another proximity factor is the *most recent performance error*, in which a ratee is judged on the basis of his or her most recent behavior rather than on a more representative sample of his or her behavior. Finally, errors in rating can occur because of inadequate information. Raters who do not possess sufficient information about the persons whom they are rating may be overly influenced by irrelevant or incorrect communications regarding the person and attach too much importance to insignificant details. They may also fall back on stereotypes about human nature, remember only information that confirms their beliefs about the ratee and people in general, and be swayed more by feelings than by knowledge of the ratee.

Types of Rating Scales

In its simplest form, a rating scale item consists of a word or phrase pertaining to the behavior or other characteristic to be rated and two or more *anchors*. The anchors may be a set of successive integers or letters designating different quantities or qualities of the rated person or thing (see Figure 4.3). Commonly employed are successive integers (1–5, etc.) of a *numerical scale*, where 1 represents the lowest and 5 the highest quantity or quality of whatever is being rated. Letters, such as the A, B, C, D, F series of the traditional academic grading (marking) system are also popular in rating performances and products. These numerals or letters are often arranged successively on a straight line, such as the following:

Not at all   Extremely
depressed   1   2   3   4   5   6   7 depressed

or

```
Not        0  1  2  3  4  5  6  7  8  9  10  As anxious as
anxious    └──┴──┴──┴──┴──┴──┴──┴──┴──┴──┘     I could be
```

Visual Analogue Scale

Determining the intensity of a patient's subjective experience (pain, anxiety, substance craving, etc.) poses a particular problem in clinical contexts. One technique that has been used to estimate the intensity of such experiences is a *visual analogue scale* (Wewers & Lowe, 1990). For example, the patient may be instructed to point to or mark the place on the line corresponding to the intensity of the felt experience of anxiety or pain. Or a young child may be asked to point to the picture of a face in a graded series of smiling and frowning faces that best

---

Directions: Answer each of the following items by entering a 1, 2, 3, 4, or 5 in the marginal dash:

1 = Not at all characteristic of you.
2 = Somewhat uncharacteristic of you.
3 = Neither characteristic nor uncharacteristic of you.
4 = Somewhat characteristic of you.
5 = Very characteristic of you.

_____ 1. I like to be with people.
_____ 2. I usually seem to be in a hurry.
_____ 3. I am easily frightened.
_____ 4. I frequently get distressed.
_____ 5. When displeased, I let people know it right away.
_____ 6. I am something of a loner.
_____ 7. I like to keep busy all the time.
_____ 8. I am known as hot-blooded and quick-tempered.
_____ 9. I often feel frustrated.
_____ 10. My life is fast paced.
_____ 11. Everyday events make me troubled and fretful.
_____ 12. I often feel insecure.
_____ 13. There are many things that annoy me.
_____ 14. When I get scared, I panic.
_____ 15. I prefer working with others rather than alone.
_____ 16. I get emotionally upset easily.
_____ 17. I often feel as if I'm bursting with energy.
_____ 18. It takes a lot to make me mad.
_____ 19. I have fewer fears than most people my age.
_____ 20. I find people more stimulating than anything else.

FIGURE 4.3 EAS Temperament Scale for Adults. (From *Temperament: Early Developing Personality Traits* by A. H. Buss & R. Plomin, 1984, Hillsdale, NJ: Erlbaum. Reprinted by permission.)

indicates how he or she feels. Though this procedure is perhaps more accurate than simply having patients tell how they feel in their own words, some patients have difficulty understanding it. The scales depicted in the last paragraph are examples of visual analogue scales with numerical anchors. An example of one with verbal anchors is the following:

Not	Mild	Moderate	Severe	As anxious as
anxious				I can be

Such scales can be periodically readministered to measure changes in feelings over time, but they have limitations. Many patients find it difficult to represent subjective experiences of pain, anxiety, and depression on visual analogue scales.

Semantic Differential

Rather than a straight line, a series of line segments may also be used on a numerical rating scale. An example is the *semantic differential scale*, on which a selected set of concepts (particular persons, objects, events, etc.) is rated on a series of 7-point bipolar adjectival scales. An illustration is the following:

Mother

bad _ _ _ _ _ _ _ good

weak _ _ _ _ _ _ _ strong

mean _ _ _ _ _ _ _ kind

The respondent checks the line segment that best indicates his or her feeling or impression of the ratee. Statistical analysis of the relationships among the rated connotative meanings of the set of persons or other concepts can provide insight into the personality and attitudes of the rater.

Graphic Rating Scale

In one of the most popular rating scale formats, the anchors are not numbers or letters but rather short descriptive phrases distributed at equidistant points along a continuous line. An example of such a *graphic rating scale* for rating "talkativeness" is the following:

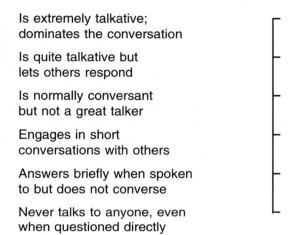

Is extremely talkative;
dominates the conversation

Is quite talkative but
lets others respond

Is normally conversant
but not a great talker

Engages in short
conversations with others

Answers briefly when spoken
to but does not converse

Never talks to anyone, even
when questioned directly

The anchors may be arranged either vertically, as they are in this example, or horizontally.

Standard Rating Scales

In rating performances or characteristics, the anchors need not be numbers, letters, or descriptions: they may be other people or things. This is the case in a *standard rating scale*, such as a *man-to-man* (or *person-to-person*) scale. For example, in rating a series of people on extroversion, the rater is asked to begin by thinking of the most extroversive person whom he or she knows, then the next most extroversive person, and so on down to the least extroversive person, building up a "scale" of five or so "standard" persons covering the entire range on a subjective scale of extroversion. Suppose John Jones is the most extroversive, Louise Smith the next most extroversive, Fred Brown the next, Paula Johnson the next, and George Green the least extroversive. The scale values assigned to these three standard persons (anchors) are 1 to 5, respectively. Then each new person to be rated is compared with the five "standard" persons and given a rating corresponding to the "standard" person whom he or she is most like in terms of extroversion.

Forced-Choice Scale

Several other types of rating scales have been devised to control for the subjectivity and potential biases in the rating process. Among these are the forced-choice scale and the behaviorally anchored scale. A *forced-choice rating scale* consists of set of phrases or statements that describe a particular behavior or characteristic but are equated in terms of their social desirability. When each item has two response choices, as on the Edwards Personal Preference Schedule, the rater is asked to indicate which description best applies to the person being rated. When the item consists of three or four response choices, the rater is asked which description is most applicable and which description is least applicable to the ratee. When there are four choices, two are equally socially desirable and two equally undesirable, but the rater presumably does not know which of the two desirable descriptions is the keyed one or which of the two undesirable descriptions is the keyed one. Consider the following forced-choice tetrad item for rating supervisory capacity:

Very rarely gets angry
Is able to control himself when angry
Gets angry fairly often
Has trouble controlling his anger

The first two descriptions are positive, and the last two are negative, but which of the positive statements and which of the negative statements is "keyed" for supervisory capacity?

Behaviorally Anchored Scales

Because the meanings of concepts such as "anxiety," "self-confidence," and "aggressiveness," as rated on traditional trait-oriented rating scales, vary from rater to rater, rating scales have often been viewed as subjective and biased. An attempt to make ratings more objective is represented by a *behaviorally anchored rating scale (BARS)*. To design the anchors for this kind of scale, a group of people who are experts in the behaviors to be rated is convened. By means of extensive, careful deliberation, they arrive at a consensus on behaviorally descriptive statements. The BARS technique, which has been applied primarily for designing job-rating scales, relies heavily on the method of *critical incidents*. A critical incident on a job, for example, is a behavior that significantly differentiates between good and poor workers (e.g., "secures machinery and tidies up work place when finished," "follows up customers' requests promptly"). Critical incidents for a released mental patient might be "Takes medication as prescribed," "Arrives at medical appointments promptly," and "Keeps self neat and clean."

Behavioral Expectation and Observation Scales

On a variation of the BARS technique known as the *behavioral expectation scale (BES)*, critical behaviors are rated in terms of what is expected rather than what actually occurs. On another variation of the BARS technique, the *behavioral observation scale (BOS)*, ratings are made in terms of the frequency ("never, seldom, sometimes, generally, always") with which critical behaviors are observed during a given period.

Both the emphasis on objective behaviors and group consensus would seem to make the BARS, the BES, and the BOS techniques psychometrically superior to other methods of rating. Unfortunately, this has not always been the case. In some studies, less bias in ratings has been found with BARS than other rating techniques. In most cases, however, BARS, BES, and BOS have not been shown to be demonstrably superior to traditional graphic scales (Champion, Green, & Sauser, 1988; Kinicki & Bannister, 1988).

Q-Sort

A final type of rating scale, which also has some similarity to a checklist, is the *Q-sort*. This technique requires respondents to sort a set of statements into a series of categories ranging from "most characteristic" to "least characteristic" of the respondent himself or another designated person. Respondents are also asked to sort the statements in such a way that a normal distribution of responses occurs across the several response categories. Special "homemade" Q-sorts have sometimes been constructed for a specific application, but a few Q-Sort decks are also commercially available. One example is the California Q-Sort Revised (Adult Set) (from Consulting Psychologists Press), consisting of 100 cards containing statements descriptive of personality. Another example is the Leadership Q-Sort Test, a test of leadership values designed for adults by R. N. Cassel and commercially available from Psychometric Affiliates.

Published Rating Scales for Clinical Assessment

Most rating scales were designed for a single research investigation to explore the relationships between certain personality variables and other aspects of behavior or to test hypotheses concerning such relationships. These scales are not commercially available, though they may have been published in a research paper or are available from the author(s). Most rating scales and checklists were developed from a trait/factor, psychodynamic, or psychophysiological orientation. Others were designed in the context of behavioral assessment or modification, and still others on a purely empirical basis.

Many published and unpublished rating scales for the assessment of personality and psychodiagnosis are available (Bech, 1994; Butcher,

1995; Goodwin & Jamison, 1990; Piacentini, 1993; Witt, Heffer, & Pfeiffer, 1990). A representative sample of commercially available instruments of this type is listed in Table 4.2.

Among the most popular of all rating scales are those designed to measure two common symptoms of mental disorders—anxiety and depression. Representative of rating instruments in these categories are the Hamilton Anxiety Scale and the Hamilton Depression Scale, the latter having become a standard for the identification of clinical depression. A Structured Interview Guide for the Hamilton Depression Scale, designed to standardize the administration of this instrument, is also

TABLE 4.2 Some Commercially Distributed Rating Scales for Personality and Behavioral Assessment of Adults

---

Brief Derogatis Psychiatric Rating Scale (L. R. Derogatis; NCS Assessments; adult and adolescent psychiatric and medical patients; for obtaining clinical observers' ratings on nine personality dimensions)

Clinical Rating Scale (D. H. Olson; Family Social Science; couples and families; to type marital and family systems and identify intervention targets; reviewed in MMYB 12:81)

Cognitive Behavior Rating Scales (CBRS) Research Edition (J. M. Williams; Psychological Assessment Resources; patients aged 30–89 with possible neurological impairment; allows a family member or other reliable observer to rate the presence and severity of cognitive impairments, behavioral deficits, and observable neurological signs in a patient; reviewed in MMYB 11:74; TC VII:119)

Dementia Rating Scale (S. Mattis; Psychological Assessment Resources; individuals aged 65–81 suffering from brain dysfunction; measures the cognitive status of individuals with known cortical impairment; reviewed in MMYB 11:107; TC X:199)

Derogatis Psychiatric Rating Scale (L. R. Derogatis; NCS Assessments; adults and adolescents; multidimensional psychiatric rating scale for use by clinicians to assist in validating patient-reported results)

Fels Parent Behavior Rating Scales (A. L. Baldwin, J. Kalhorn, F. H. Breese, & H. Champney; Fels Research Institute; parents; designed to measure certain aspects of parent-child relationships; reviewed in MMYB 4:43)

Global Assessment Scale (R. L. Spitzer, M. Gibbon, & J. Endicott; Dept. of Research Assessment & Training, N.Y. State Psychiatric Institute; psychiatric patients and possible psychiatric patients; ratings of Mental health–Illness on scale of 1–100; for evaluating the overall functioning of a person during a specified time period on a continuum ranging from psychological or psychiatric illness to health; reviewed in MMYB 11:147)

Revised Hamilton Rating Scale for Depression (W. L. Warren; Western Psychological Services; depressed adults; designed as a clinician-rated scale for evaluating individuals already diagnosed with depressive illness)

SCL-90 Analogue (L. R. Derogatis; NCS Assessments; adults and adolescents; a brief rating scale for collecting observer data on a patient's psychological symptomatic distress)

---

available. A Revised Hamilton Rating Scale was recently published by Western Psychological Services.

Goodwin and Jamison (1990) describe several other scales for rating the severity of depression and manic states. One of these scales—the Manic-State Rating Scale (Murphy, Beigel, Weingartner, & Bunney, 1974)—is somewhat unique in that the patient is rated (on a scale of 0–5) on both the frequency ("How much of the time?") and intensity ("How intense is it?") of 26 behavioral symptoms.

A broader-band instrument than any of the scales described thus far in this section is the Brief Psychiatric Rating Scale (BPRS) (Liberman, 1988; Overall & Gorham, 1962). The BPRS is scored on 18 scales (e.g., anxiety, emotional withdrawal, guilt feelings, hostility, somatic concern, suspiciousness, and unusual thought patterns). Ratings on these scales may be made during a patient interview and compared with ratings obtained on other psychodiagnostic groups.

Derogatis Series

This series comprises the most comprehensive group of commercially available checklists and rating scales designed for clinical applications. The five instruments in the series, designed to identify symptoms of psychopathology in adults, are the Symptom Checklist–90–Revised (SCL-90-R), the Brief Symptom Inventory (BSI), the Derogatis Psychiatric Rating Scale (DPRS), the Brief Derogatis Psychiatric Rating Scale (B-DPRS), and the SCL-90 Analogue. The SCL-90-R and the BSI are self-report instruments for screening patients with psychiatric disorders, recording their progress, and ascertaining the effectiveness of treatment. The DPRS, the B-DPRS, and the SCL-Analogue are observer-report instruments designed to measure the same variables as the first two instruments.

Patients respond to each of the 90 items on the SCL-90-R on a scale of 0 ("not at all") to 5 ("extremely"). It requires 12 to 15 minutes to complete and is scored on nine primary symptom dimensions: somatization, obsessive compulsive, interpersonal sensitivity, depression, anxiety, hostility, phobic anxiety, paranoid ideation, and psychoticism. Three measures indicate the current level or depth of a disorder, the intensity of the symptoms, and the number of patient-reported symptoms. Normative data on adult nonpatients, outpatients, and inpatients in psychiatric facilities are available. Numerous reliability, validity, and utility studies on the SCL-90-R have been conducted.

Like the items on the SCL-90-R, the 53 items on the BSI are written at a sixth-grade level and rated on a 5-point scale. The BSI was designed to reflect psychological symptom patterns in psychiatric and medical patients, and it measures the same nine primary symptoms dimensions as the SCL-90-R. Adult norms for psychiatric outpatients and inpatients, as well as for nonpatients, are available. Also like the SCL-90-R, the reliability and validity of the BSI appear to be satisfactory.

On both the DPRS and a shorter version—the B-DPRS, the observer-clinician rates the adult patient on the same nine dimensions as on the SCL-90-R and the BSI. Both scales can be filled out in less than 5 minutes. The DPRS is scored on 18 variables (9 primary dimensions, 8 additional dimensions, and a global index), the B-DPRS on 10 variables (9 primary dimensions and a global index).

Unlike the other instruments in the Derogatis series, the SCL-90 Analogue can be filled out by health professionals without the in-depth training or knowledge of psychopathology as a psychiatrist. The SCL-90 Analogue can be completed in 1 to 3 minutes by an observer of a patient for an initial evaluation and to monitor treatment progress. It is scored on the same nine primary dimensions and global psychopathology scale as the other instruments in the Derogatis series.

SUMMARY

Next to achievement tests, checklists and rating scales are the most popular of all psychometric instruments. They are administered in clinical, educational, industrial/organizational, and military contexts to assist in screening, performance evaluation, psychodiagnosis, and the evaluation of treatment effectiveness. Deductive, inductive, and criterion-group strategies have been applied to the construction of both checklists and rating scales. Most of these instruments have stemmed from a trait/factor orientation, but a combination of theoretical and empirical approaches to instrument design are common.

Checklists are designed for a variety of purposes, for example, to identify personal problems and symptoms of psychopathology, to evaluate physical and mental impairments and handicaps, to assist in taking a case history, and for research on personality and human development. Two of the most common types of checklists appropriate for "normal" personalities are adjective checklists and problem checklists. The Adjective Check List is a prominent example of instruments in the former category, and the Mooney Problem Check Lists are illustrative of instruments in the latter category.

Careful and thorough training of raters can contribute to the reliability and validity of ratings, but various types of errors still occur. These include constant errors (leniency, severity, central tendency), the halo effect, contrast error, and proximity error.

Numerical and graphic scales are the most popular of all rating scales, but standard and forced-choice scales also have their proponents. On a standard rating scale, such as the man-to-man scale, the rater compares the ratee with a set of "standard" people or other entities varying from very high to very low on some characteristic or very effective to very ineffective on some behavior.

To some extent, forced-choice scales can control for the social desirability response set, but raters typically find this format awkward and difficult. Semantic differential scales have proved helpful in understanding personality by analyzing the connotative meanings that selected concepts have for people. It might appear as if behaviorally anchored scales would yield more objective, and hence more reliable, ratings, but this assumption has not generally proved to be correct.

Numerous rating scales and checklists have been published in professional journals, and some have been distributed commercially. Examples of commercially available rating scales that have proved useful in clinical contexts are the Revised Hamilton Rating Scale for Depression, the Dementia Rating Scale, and the Cognitive Behavior Rating Scale. A series of five rating scales designed for psychodiagnostic and treatment evaluation purposes was prepared by L. R. Derogatis. Two of these—the SCL-90-R and the BSI—are self-report instruments, and three—the DPRS, the B-DPRS, and the SCL-Analogue—are observer-report instruments. Of the last three, only the SCL-90 Analogue can be administered by a health professional with limited training in psychiatry.

APPENDIX 4.1 Checklists for Evaluating Adult Personality and Behavior

---

Adjective Checklists

Adjective Check List (H. G. Gough & A. B. Heilbrun; Consulting Psychologists Press; high school students and older; designed to identify personal characteristics of individuals; reviewed in MMYB 9:52; TC I:34)

Depression Adjective Checklist (B. Lubin; Consulting Psychologists Press; grades 9–16 and adults; measures self-reported depressive mood; reviewed in MMYB 7:65; TC III:215)

Interpersonal Adjective Scales (J. S. Wiggins; Psychological Assessment Resources; measures dominance and nurturance dimensions of interpersonal behavior)

Multiple Affect Adjective Check List–Revised (M. Zuckerman & B. Lubin; Educational & Industrial Testing Service; ages 20–79; measures positive and negative affects as traits or states; reviewed in MMYB 10:205)

Personality Adjective Checklist (S. Strack; 21st Century; ages 16–adult; self-report measure of personality in normal adults; reviewed in MMYB 12:289)

Clinical Symptoms

Emotional Behavioral Checklist (J. G. Dial, C. Mezger, T. Masey, & L. T. McCarron; McCarron-Dial; ages 16 and over; assesses overt emotional behavior; reviewed in MMYB 11:130)

Hare Psychopathy Checklist-Revised (R. D. Hare; MultiHealth Systems; prison inmates; identifies psychopathic (antisocial) personality disorders in forensic populations; reviewed in MMYB 12:177)

S-D Proneness Checklist (W. T. Martin; Psychologists & Educators, Inc.; depressed or suicidal clients; a measure of depression and suicide-proneness; reviewed in MMYB 8:664; TC I:568)

Symptom Checklist-90-Revised (SCL-90-R) (L. R. Derogatis; NCS Assessments; adults and adolescents aged 13 and older; identifies psychological symptom patterns in psychiatric and medica; patients and nonpatients; reviewed in MMYB 9:1082; TC III:583)

The Time-Sample Behavioral Checklist (G. L. Paul, M. H. Licht, M. J. Mariotto, C. T. Power, & K. L. Engel; Research Press; adults in residential treatment settings; measures level and nature of functioning of adult residential patients and documents how and where residents and staff spend their time; reviewed in MMYB 12:401)

Cognitive/Mental Status

Cognitive Symptom Checklists (CSC) (C. O'Hara, M. Harrell, E. Bellingrath, & K. Lisicia; Psychological Assessment Resources; ages 16 and over; evaluates areas of impaired cognitive functioning)

Mental Status Checklist for Adults, 1988 Revision (J. A. Schinka; Psychological Assessment Resources; adults; surveys items that are commonly included in a comprehensive mental status examination; reviewed in MMYB 10:187)

Marital Evaluation

Marital Evaluation Checklist (L. Navran; Psychological Assessment Resources; married couples in counseling; surveys the fundamental characteristics and problem areas in a marital relationship; reviewed in MMYB 10:187)

Mental Retardation and Other Handicaps

Aberrant Behavior Checklist (M. G. Aman & N. N. Singh; Slosson; mentally retarded adolescents and adults; reviewed in MMYB 12:1; TC X:3)

Independent Living Behavior Checklist (R. T. Wells, T. Zane, & J. E. Thvedt; West Virginia Rehabilitation Research & Training Center; behaviorally impaired adults; reviewed in MMYB 9:503; TC VIII:301)

Personal History

Personal History Checklist for Adults (J. A. Schinka; Psychological Assessment Resources; adult clients of mental health services; used to obtain historical information during routine intake procedures; reviewed in MMYB 11:285)

Personal Problems

Mooney Problem Check Lists—Adult (R. L. Mooney & L. V. Gordon; The Psychological Corporation; adults; designed to help individuals express their personal problems; reviewed in MMYB 6:145; TC II:495)

Personal Problems Checklist—Adult (J. A. Schinka; Psychological Assessment Resources; adults; designed to facilitate the rapid assessment of an individual's problems as seen from that person's point of view; reviewed in MMYB 10:278)

Problem Experiences Checklist: Adult Version (L. Silverton; Western Psychological Services; adolescents and adults; used prior to the initial intake interview to identify potential problems for further discussion; reviewed in MMYB 12:309)

NOTE

1. *Directions for scoring.* Subtract your numerical answers to items 6, 16, and 19 from the value 6. Then score each of the five scales separately according to the following formulas:

$$
\begin{aligned}
\text{Ac (activity)} &= \text{item } 2 + \text{item } 7 + \text{item } 10 + \text{item } 17 \\
\text{An (anger)} &= \text{item } 5 + \text{item } 8 + \text{item } 13 + \text{item } 18 \\
\text{D (distress)} &= \text{item } 4 + \text{item } 9 + \text{item } 11 + \text{item } 16 \\
\text{F (fearfulness)} &= \text{item } 3 + \text{item } 12 + \text{item } 14 + \text{item } 19 \\
\text{S (sociability)} &= \text{item } 1 + \text{item } 6 + \text{item } 15 + \text{item } 20
\end{aligned}
$$

The mean scores of a sample of adult women are Ac = 13.4, An = 10.28, D = 10.08, F = 10.6, , and S = 15.24. The mean scores for a sample of adult men are D = 9.72, F = 8.95, An = 10.8, Ac = 12.8, and S = 14.6.

SUGGESTED READINGS

Aiken, L. R. (1996). *Rating scales and checklists.* New York: Wiley.

McReynolds, P., & Ludwig, K. (1987). On the history of rating scales. *Personality and Individual Differences, 8,* 281–283.

Pulakos, E. D. (1991). Rater training for performance appraisal. In J. W. Jones, B. D. Steffy, & D. W. Bray (Eds.), *Applying psychology in business: The handbook for managers and human resource professionals* (pp. 326–332). Lexington, MA: D. C. Heath.

Reckase, M. D. (1990). Scaling techniques. In G. Goldstein & M. Hersen (Eds.), *Handbook of psychological assessment* (2nd ed., pp. 41–56). New York: Pergamon.

Wolfe, R. N. (1993). A commonsense approach to personality measurement. In K. H. Craik, R. Hogan, & R. N. Wolfe (Eds.), *Fifty years of personality psychology* (pp. 269–290). New York: Plenum.

5

Personality Inventories

Paper-and-pencil measures of personality are referred to by a variety of names: test, checklist, rating scale, inventory, questionnaire, and scale. These terms, which are often used somewhat loosely and interchangeably, do not necessarily refer to different formats or designs. Despite the fact that "checklist," "rating scale," and "inventory" have similar connotations, their origins are different. Rating scales and checklists originated mostly in educational and employment contexts, where they were administered primarily for performance evaluation purposes. Personality inventories, conversely, were first used in clinical contexts, where they served as psychological screening and diagnostic devices. Furthermore, ratings are more often made by informants other than the person being rated, whereas most personality inventories are self-report instruments completed by the same person who is being assessed. Another difference between rating scales and personality inventories is that the latter are more likely to measure several variables. The score on each variable measured by a personality inventory is a composite of responses to many items, and the variable for which a particular item composite is scored is typically referred to as a "scale."

In the interest of providing a starting point for our discussion, we shall define a personality inventory as a self-report questionnaire consisting of items (words, phrases, and statements) concerned with personal characteristics and behaviors. The response format of the items may be dichotomous (true–false, yes–no, right–wrong, etc.), polychotomous (3–5 degrees of correctness, appropriateness, representativeness, or agreement), pair comparisons, ranking, or some other type of response. When there are multiple response possibilities and they are ordered in some way, each item is a kind of miniature rating scale. When the items are simply responded to as "true" or "false," as is the case on several of the most popular personality inventories, the instrument may be perceived as a multiple checklist.

Responding accurately to the items on a personality inventory requires that the respondent knows the truth about himself or herself and is willing to reveal it. However, the respondent may either not know the truth or be unwilling to reveal it even if it is known. Furthermore, it has been alleged that personality inventories tap only superficial aspects of personality—while the vast ocean of unconscious impulses, desires, and conflicts remains unexplored. It is debatable whether, by their very nature, personality inventories measure anything other than superficial aspects of behavior and personality. There is no denying, however, that people can dissimulate (fake) in responding to any self-report inventory. For example, they may try to place themselves in a more favorable light by answering in what they perceive as a socially desirable direction. Alternatively, they may even try to make themselves appear worse (i.e., more pathological) than they really are if appearing to be leads to a more desirable outcome.

Fairly early in the history of personality testing, it became clear that some method was needed to determine the extent to which respondents took the task of answering items on self-report inventories seriously and attempted to respond as truthfully as possible. Most people lie some of the time, and some people lie most of the time. It is impossible to detect every time that everyone lies, but the use of special scoring keys or scales on personality inventories may facilitate the task of deciding whether the responses are sufficiently valid to warrant further scoring and interpretation. Answering "true" to several items of the "I have never been late for an appointment" or "I am always completely happy" type is highly improbable when a person is answering truthfully. In addition, answering "yes" or "true" to every true/false item or answering "true" to items that connote more socially desirable responses suggest that the respondent's answers are of questionable validity. These and other special validation procedures and keys on modern inventories can reduce the frequency of efforts to score and interpret untruthful responses.

In addition to being concerned with dissimulation or faking, designers of self-report inventories have shown particular concern with the tendency on the part of some individuals to respond on the basis of form rather than the content of items. Two prominent examples of such *response sets* or *response styles* are *acquiescence*—the tendency to answer "true" an improbably large number of times—and *social desirability*—the tendency to make what is perceived as the socially desirable response more often than warranted. Although it is a good idea to be aware of such tendencies, attempting to control for the effects of these response styles by using special scoring keys or by other statistical procedures does not appear to improve the validity of the content scores on personality inventories to an appreciable degree.

EARLY PERSONALITY INVENTORIES

As was the case with the first intelligence tests, self-report inventories were initially constructed in response to the need for an efficient psychological screening device. As indicated in chapter 1, the first formal personality inventory was the Woodworth Personal Data Sheet. Some years earlier, Heymans and Wiersma (1906) had devised a list of psychopathological symptoms, a list that was later revised by Hoch and Amsden (1913) and Wells (1914). Based to some extent on these earlier lists, the Personal Data Sheet was a kind of paper-and-pencil psychiatric interview. Later known as the Woodworth Psychoneurotic Inventory, it consisted of 116 questions concerning psychopathological symptoms to be answered "yes" or "no" by respondents. This first personality inventory was designed as a brief screening instrument for the purpose of determining whether military recruits were likely to break down under the stress of combat. Although it did not become available in time to be used extensively in World War I, the Personal Data Sheet was the beginning of objective, standardized personality assessment and served as a model for the development of later personality inventories.

After the war, several other self-report inventories were devised for various applied and research purposes to be administered to relatively "normal" personalities. On one such inventory, the X–O Test (Pressey & Pressey, 1919), examinees crossed out each of a series of 600 words they viewed as unpleasant, activities they considered wrong (e.g., smoking, spitting in public, etc.), or things they worried about or that made them anxious (e.g., money, pain, etc.). Another early inventory was the A–S Reaction Study (Allport & Allport, 1928). This inventory was designed to measure the disposition to be ascendant (A) or submissive (S) in everyday social relationships, and it was used in several research investigations in social psychology. The A–S Reaction Study was a criterion-keyed inventory, in that items were included on this inventory only if they differentiated between groups of people whom their peers rated as ascendent or submissive.

The first personality inventories focused on a single variable, but during the 1930s several multiscore instruments were published and became popular in educational contexts. The first of these was the Bernreuter Personality Inventory. Consisting of 125 items answered "yes," "no," or "?," the Bernreuter could be completed in a half-hour or less by individuals aged 13 and older. It was scored on six variables: confidence, dominance-submission, introversion-extroversion, neurotic tendency, self-sufficiency, and sociability. A similar instrument published a bit later—the Bell Adjustment Inventory—was scored on six scales: home, health, submissiveness, emotionality, hostility, and masculinity. Like the Personal Data Sheet, the major purpose of the Bernreuter and Bell inventories was to identify personality problems or adjustment difficulties. Unlike the severe psychopathology orientation of the Woodworth inventory, the Bernreuter and Bell inventories focused on milder personal problems.

A list of representative, commercially available multiscore inventories of adult personality and behavior is given in Appendix 5.1. As suggested by this list, inventories designed for "normal personalities" outnumber those for "abnormal personalities" or personality disorders. Most inventories designed for normal personalities are appropriate in a wide range of situations, although a few are aimed exclusively at business and industrial contexts. The citation for a particular inventory listed in Appendix 5.1 provides the name(s) of the author(s) and publisher, the age range for which the inventory is appropriate, the number of variables on which it is scored, and the volume and number of reviews in the *Mental Measurements Yearbook* (MMYB) or *Test Critiques* (TC).

All of the inventories listed in Appendix 5.1 are currently in print, but the list is by no means exhaustive. Many other, less popular, inventories and others that are no longer available are not listed there. Among the many published inventories of personality are several that were published originally in the 1940s and are still available. An example is the Taylor–Johnson Temperament Analysis (T-JTA), which was designed expressly for premarital, marital, and family counseling and is available in five languages and in a special edition for the blind. The T-JTA can be taken in crisscross fashion, in which case each couple or family member describes both himself (herself) and the other person(s). It is scored on nine bipolar traits: nervous versus composed, depressed versus light-hearted, active-social versus quiet, expressive-responsive versus inhibited, sympathetic versus indifferent, subjective versus objective, dominant versus submissive, hostile versus tolerant, and self-disciplined versus impulsive; raw scores on these traits are converted to norms based on the 1992 standardization of the inventory.

RATIONAL-THEORETICAL INVENTORIES

The distinction between the deductive, inductive, and empirical construction strategies, which were discussed in chapter 4 for rating scales, is also applicable to personality inventories. The deductive strategy, also called the "rational-theoretical" strategy, consists of applying logical reasoning and theory pertaining to the structure and dynamics of personality to the design of personality assessment instruments. Many of the inventories constructed during the 1940s and 1950s, such as the California Test of Personality and the Omnibus Personality Inventory, were constructed by following the rational or content-validated approach. Items were included on these inventories because they were judged to tap important variables or constructs associated with personal and social adjustment. These constructs may have been derived from experience or research, logical reasoning, or some theory of personality. Like the Bernreuter and Bell inventories before them, most of the personality inventories devised by this strategy were multivariable instruments designed primarily for use in academic, work, and other organizational contexts.

Edwards Personal Preference Schedule

The construction of several self-report personality assessment instruments has been based to some extent on Henry Murray's need-press theory of personality. Included among these instruments are the Adjective Check List, the Personality Research Form, and the Edwards Personal Preference Schedule (EPPS). The EPPS, one of the most widely researched of all inventories, was designed to measure 15 of Murray's psychogenic needs: abasement, achievement, affiliation, aggression, autonomy, change, deference, dominance, endurance, exhibition, heterosexuality, intraception, nurturance, order, and succorance. Two additional scores—consistency and profile stability—can be computed as indicators of truthfulness or validity of responding on the EPPS.

The most unique feature of the EPPS is the procedure for controlling for the social desirability response set. The two statements comprising each of the 225 item pairs, each of which pits one of Murray's needs against another, were selected to be as nearly equal as possible in social desirability. Examinees are instructed to indicate which statement in each pair is personally more descriptive or characteristic of them.

The EPPS has been widely used in research on personality, but its forced-choice format is somewhat awkward for respondents. Furthermore, the ipsative nature of the scores produced by the forced-choice procedure are difficult to interpret and analyze statistically. This and other features of the EPPS have limited its practical applications, though it has been used extensively in research concerned with personality.

Personality Research Form

Another inventory based on Murray's theory of needs is the Personality Research Form (PRF). The PRF is scored on the same 15 needs as the EPPS, plus several other variables. Highly sophisticated psychometric procedures were applied to the construction and standardization of the five forms of the PRF, but it has been criticized for its impoverished theoretical conception of personality, inadequate reliabilities and norms, interpretive difficulties, and scant validity information. Consequently, like the EPPS, the PRF is recommended only for research purposes (Tinsley, 1985).

Myers–Briggs Type Indicator

Another theory-based inventory designed principally for research purposes but that, interestingly, has also proved to be popular in several practical contexts, is the Myers–Briggs Type Indicator (MBTI). Based on Carl Jung's theory of personality types, the two forms of the MBTI consist of a series of two-choice items concerned with preferences or inclinations in feelings and behaviors. Scores are in terms of four bipolar scales: extraversion–introversion, sensing–intuition, thinking–feeling, and judging–perceiving. The extraversion–introversion score indicates the degree to which the examinee relates to the outer world of people and things (extraversion) or to the inner world of ideas (introversion). The sensing–intuition score indicates the extent to which the examinee prefers to work with known facts (sensing) or to look for possibilities and relationships (intuition). The thinking–feeling score indicates the extent to which the examinee bases his or her judgments more on impersonal analysis and logic (thinking) or personal values (feeling). The judging–feeling score indicates the extent to which the examinee prefers a planned, decided, orderly way of life (judging) or a flexible, spontaneous way of life (perceiving). Combinations of scores on the four two-part categories yield 16 personality-type scores. A person whose highest scores are on extraversion, intuition, feeling, and perceiving is an ENFP type, whereas a person who scores highest on introversion, sensing, thinking, and judging is an ISTJ type. Although many psychologists have avoided the MBTI because of its "type" and Jungian orientations, Devito's (1985) review is positive. He concludes that the MBTI merits more serious considerations by psychologists, and he encourages its use with normal individuals in counseling and within organizations. A more recent review by Murray (1990) concludes that the reliability and validity indexes of the MBTI are acceptable and that the underlying constructs are supported by correlations with other measures. Conversely, a study by Lorr (1991) found poor agreement between the 16 categories of the MBTI and empirically derived clusters. The results of a study conducted in Australia led Boyle (1995b) to conclude that the MBTI has several psychometric limitations that raise concerns about its use. He recommended that it not be used routinely by practitioners and cautioned that it is likely to be misused in organizational and occupational settings.

Millon Index of Personality Styles

The four Jungian-type variables on which the Myers–Briggs Type Indicator is based are also assessed by the Cognitive Modes scales of the Millon Index of Personality Styles (MIPS) (Millon, 1994). This inventory consists of 180 true–false items and takes approximately 30 minutes to complete. The four pairs of Cognitive Modes scales on the MIPS, which were designed to assess the respondent's styles of processing information, are listed in Table 5.1. The table also lists the three pairs of Motivating Aims scales, for assessing the respondent's styles of obtaining reinforcement from the environment, and the five pairs of Interpersonal Behavior scales, for assessing the respondent's styles of relating to other people. In addition to scores on the 24 scales in Table 5.1, scores on three validating scales—Positive Impression, Negative Impression, and Consistency—may be obtained.

Raw scores on the MIPS scales are converted to Prevalence Scale (PS) values ranging from 0 to 100. The PS values on a particular scale are based on estimates of the percentage of males or females in the adult or college-student population falling into the corresponding trait category. Tables for converting raw scores to PS values, by gender and overall, in the adult and college-student samples are given in the manual. Persons having PS scores of 50 or above on a scale are assigned to the trait group defined by that scale, and their PS scores may then be converted to percentile ranks within that trait group.

The MIPS was standardized on two separate national samples: (1) 1,000 adults stratified by age (18–65 years), race/ethnicity, and geographical region; (2) 1,600 students considered representative of the U.S. college-student population. The average split-half reliabilities of the scales were .82 in the adult standardization sample and .80 in the college-student sample. The median test–retest reliability, based on a sample of 50 adults, was .85. Evidence for the construct validity of the MIPS scales is found in the pattern of intercorrelations among the scales and

TABLE 5.1 Scales on the Millon Index of Personality Styles

Motivating aims	Cognitive modes	Interpersonal behaviors
Enhancing Preserving	Extraversing Introversing	Retiring Outgoing
Modifying Accommodating	Sensing Intuiting	Hesitating Asserting
Individuating Nurturing	Thinking Feeling	Dissenting Conforming
	Systematizing Innovating	Yielding Controlling
		Complaining Agreeing

the correlations of the scales with scores on several other personality inventories. Empirical research on screening of military recruits for general adjustment, selection and training of law-enforcement officers, identification of management talent, and vocational guidance and career decision making are also described in the manual. Overall, the sophisticated theoretical foundation of this inventory, its good psychometric characteristics, and the availability of computer software for administration, scoring, and interpretation make it a real competitor among personality inventories designed for the assessment of normal personality.

FACTOR-ANALYZED INVENTORIES

The factor-analytic method of inventory construction, also known as the inductive or internal-consistency approach, has as its goal the discovery of groups of items that are highly intercorrelated but have low correlations with other groups of items. Factor analysis was first applied to the study of personality by Webb (1915), but the most concentrated and sophisticated efforts employing this approach were made by J. P. Guilford, R. B. Cattell, and H. Eysenck.

Guilford–Zimmerman Temperament Survey

J. P. Guilford was the first person to construct a standardized personality inventory by means of factor-analytic techniques. His earliest inventories—the Guilford–Martin Inventory of Factors, the Guilford–Martin Personnel Inventory, and the Inventory of Factors STDCR—were devised by correlating scores on many personality tests. Following Guilford's early work, Louis and Thelma Thurstone used factor-analytic methods to construct the Thurstone Temperament Schedule, which was scored on seven factors: active, dominant, impulsive, reflective, sociable, stable, and vigorous. Guilford subsequently published a 10-factor composite of his first three inventories—the Guilford–Zimmerman Temperament Survey (GZTS). Still in print, but with dated norms, the GZTS is scored on 10 personality traits (ascendance, emotional stability, friendliness, general activity, masculinity, objectivity, personal relations, restraint, sociability, and thoughtfulness), plus three verification scales.

The 16 Personality Factor Questionnaire

Perhaps the most widely administered of all personality inventories based on factor analysis is the 16 PF. An outgrowth of the R. B. Cattell's trait-factor theory of personality, the 16 PF measures the 16 source traits described in Table 5.2.

In addition to the 16 primary factors in Table 5.2, the fifth edition of the 16 PF is scored on five second-order factors (extraversion, anxiety, tough-mindedness, independence, and self-control); three response-style indices (impression management, infrequency, and acquiescence) are provided as a check on the validity of responses to the inventory.

As is the case with many other modern personality inventories, the 16 PF is scored by computer and several types of score reports can be generated. With a few exceptions (e.g., insufficient information in the form of an available technical manual), the 5th edition of the 16 PF has received positive reviews (McLellan, 1995; Rotto, 1995). Research with the 16 PF has centered on the role of personality factors in alcoholism, juvenile delinquency, various medical diseases (cancer, myocardial infarction, renal disease, somatic disorders, and stress) (see Butcher & Rouse, 1996 for references).

Adult Personality Inventory

Like the 16 PF, from which it stems, the Adult Personality Inventory (API) evolved from the personality research program of R. B. Cattell. This 324-item inventory was designed to measure personality differences among normal individuals, and it provides information on individual personality, interpersonal styles, and career factors. Responses are scored by computer on 21 trait scales divided into three groups, plus four validity scales. The seven Personal/Motivational scales are Extro-

TABLE 5.2 Descriptions of Factors on the 16 Personality Factor Questionnaire

A:	Warmth (reserved, impersonal, distant vs. warm, outgoing, attentive to others)
B:	Reasoning (concrete vs. abstract)
C:	Emotional stability (reactive, emotionally changeable vs. emotionally stable, adaptive, mature)
E:	Dominance (deferential, cooperative, avoids conflict vs. dominant, forceful, assertive)
F:	Liveliness (serious, restrained, careful vs. lively, animated, spontaneous)
G:	Rule consciousness (expedient vs. nonconforming)
H:	Social boldness (shy, threat sensitive, timid vs. socially old, venturesome, thick-skinned)
I:	Sensitivity (utilitarian, objective, unsentimental vs. sensitive, aesthetic, sentimental)
L:	Vigilance (trusting, unsuspecting, accepting vs. vigilant, suspicious, skeptical, wary)
M:	Abstractedness (grounded, practical, solution oriented vs. abstracted, imaginative, idea oriented)
N:	Privateness (forthright, genuine, artless vs. private, discreet, nondisclosing)
O:	Apprehension (self-assured, unworried, complacent vs. apprehensive, self-doubting, worried)
Q1:	Openness to change (traditional, attached to familiar vs. open to change, experimenting)
Q2:	Self-reliance (group oriented, affiliative vs. self-reliant, solitary, individualistic)
Q3:	Perfectionism (tolerates disorder, unexacting, flexible vs. perfectionistic, organized, self-disciplined)
Q4:	Tension (relaxed, placid, patient vs. tense, high energy, impatient, driven)

Adapted from the 16PF Fifth Edition Individual Record Form © 1993. Used by permission of the Institute for Personality and Ability Testing, Inc.

verted, Adjusted, Tough-Minded, Independent, Disciplined, Creative, and Enterprising. The eight Interpersonal Style scales are Caring, Adapting, Withdrawn, Submissive, Hostile, Rebellious, Sociable, and Assertive. The six Career/Life-Style scales are Practical, Scientific, Aesthetic, Social, Competitive, and Structured. The four Validity scales are Good Impression, Bad Impression, Infrequency, Uncertainty.

The API was standardized on 1,000 adults ranging in age from 16 to 70, in several locations throughout the United States. Initially there was no breakdown of the norms according to gender, age, race, or geographical region, although separate norms for men and women are now reported. However, the inventory has been criticized for the unrepresentativeness of its norms and for the limited reliability and construct validity information included in the manual (D'Amato, 1995). Despite these shortcomings, the API has found extensive use in a variety of counseling and personnel contexts. The computer-generated Narrative Report, in addition to the personal computer microcomputer software and the Career Profile software programs for scoring and preparing reports, make this inventory a highly attractive alternative for the assessment of adult personality.

Eysenck Personality Questionnaire

Holding something of a record for the smallest number of factors to be measured in a factor-analyzed inventory of personality are the questionnaires designed by H. J. Eysenck and his associates. These questionnaires have been used extensively in the research programs of Eysenck and others concerning the causes and correlates of introversion/extraversion, neuroticism, and other personality characteristics. The latest of these instruments, the Eysenck Personality Questionnaire–Revised, provides measures of Neuroticism or Emotionality (N), Extraversion (versus Introversion) (E), and Psychoticism or Tough-Mindedness (P), together with a Lie Scale (L). All of the instruments are fairly brief in length and completion time, but, for the most part, their reliability coefficients have been adequate.

Other Factor-Analyzed Inventories

Many other inventories have been designed or refined by using factor-analytic methodology. Two of the most popular are the Profile of Mood States (POMS) and the NEO Personality Inventory.

The POMS

Like the Multiple Affect Adjective Check List, the State-Trait Anxiety Inventory, and the Sickness Impact Profile, the POMS aspires to measure short-term or transitory conditions. It consists of a series of 65 adjectives that are descriptive of feelings and mood; the examinee marks one of the five response options (not at all, a little, moderately, quite a bit, or extremely) to describe how he or she has felt during the past week (including today). The POMS is fairly convenient and easy to use, yielding scores on six factors: tension–anxiety (T), depression–dejection (D), anger–hostility (A), vigor–activity (V), fatigue–inertia (F), and confusion–bewilderment (C). Peterson and Headen (1984) judged the POMS to be a relatively valid measure of momentary mood states, particularly in psychiatric outpatients and in research on the effects of medical or psychological interventions.

The NEO-PI-R and the NEO-FFI

The NEO Personality Inventory–Revised (NEO-PI-R) and an abbreviated version, the NEO Five-Factor Inventory (NEO-FFI), are based on a five-factor model of personality (Costa & McCrae, 1986). According to this model, five personality factors account for most of the variability in behavior across a wide range of situations. These factors are the following:

Neuroticism. Worry versus calm, insecure versus secure, self-pitying versus self-satisfied

Extraversion. Sociable versus retiring, fun-loving versus sober, affectionate versus reserved

Openness. Imaginative versus down to earth, preference for variety versus preference for routine, independent versus conforming

Agreeableness. Soft-hearted versus ruthless, trusting versus suspicious, helpful versus uncooperative

Conscientiousness. Well organized versus disorganized, careful versus careless, self-disciplined versus weak willed

Both the NEO-PI-R and the NEO-FFI are scored on these five factors or *domains*. Each domain is divided into six *facets*, providing a total of 30 facet scores, as indicated subsequently.

Neuroticism. Anxiety, hostility, depression, self-conscientiousness, impulsiveness, vulnerability

Extroversion. Warmth, gregariousness, assertiveness, activity, excitement seeking, positive emotions

Openness to Experience. Fantasy, aesthetics, feeling, actions, ideas, values

Agreeableness. Trust, modesty, compliance, altruism, straightforwardness, tender-mindedness

Consciousness. Competence, self-discipline, achievement striving, dutifulness, order, deliberation

Although the NEO Personality Inventory–Revised (NEO-PI-R) has received generally good reviews (Botwin, 1995; Juni, 1995; Piedmont & Weinstein, 1993), its usage in clinical contexts is limited. The absence of validity scales on the NEO-PI-R has been criticized by Ben-Porath and Waller (1992). Furthermore, Butcher and Rouse (1996) have questioned the utility of domain score analysis as a clinical diagnostic technique.

With respect to the five-factor model of personality, on which the NEO is based, a review by Ostendorf and Angleitner (1994), which focused on the structural validity of the model across several languages, is supportive. The reviewers maintain that the five-factor model provides a robust description of personality that proves to be highly replicable. However, as noted in chapter 2, the five-factor model was criticized by Block (1995) and by Butcher and Rouse (1996) as being an inadequate conceptualization of personality. In particular, Butcher and Rouse (1996, pp. 98–99) maintain that the model is inadequate for the following reasons:

1. Empirical research has not supported the hypothesized relationship between the five-factor approach and the disorders on Axis II of the DSM-IV.
2. Many of the concepts that are important in the assessment of personality pathology were systematically underrepresented in the development of the five-factor approach.
3. The method by which the five-factor approach was developed could represent an analysis of common linguistic structure, not one of personality or behavior.

Other critics of the five-factor model recognize that the factors are related to psychopathology but not sufficiently to provide a valid differentiation between diagnostic categories. One alternative that has been proposed to represent disorders on Axis II is the Personality Psychopathology Five (Harkness & McNulty, 1994), which Butcher and Rouse (1996) suggest as perhaps more appropriate than the five-factor approach as a model from which the assessment of abnormal behavior can proceed.

MMPI AND OTHER CRITERION-KEYED INVENTORIES

Before the 1940s, most psychologists plied their trade in lecture halls, libraries, and laboratories. Some psychologists worked in consulting rooms and other clinical settings, but they were in the minority. After 1940, psychology retained its emphasis on the scientific study of human behavior, but it became much more clinical in orientation as increasing numbers of psychologists were needed by the Veterans Administration and other organizations. In addition, the private practice of psychology grew as the former emphasis of mental health professionals on severer mental disorders gave way to a concern with diagnosing and treating less serious disorders outside the confines of mental hospitals. Initially, psychologists in mental health settings were members of a team of professionals headed by a psychiatrist. An important function of the psychologist member of such a team was to administer various kinds of psychological tests, from which diagnostic and prognostic conclusions were drawn and summarized in the form of a report.

MMPI

By 1940, several personality inventories had become available for use with children, adolescents, and "normal" adults, but there were no standardized inventories designed expressly for differentiating between and diagnosing various mental disorders. This vacuum was filled by publication of the MMPI (Hathaway & McKinley, 1940, 1943). Based to some extent on earlier inventories, such as the Humm-Wadsworth Temperament Scale (1935), the MMPI was designed as an instrument that could be used for diagnostic and research purposes in clinics and mental hospitals. Substantially more research has been conducted during the past 5 years on the MMPI and its successor, the MMPI-2, than on other personality inventories used in clinical assessment.

The MMPI consisted of 550 statements concerned with attitudes, emotions, motor disturbances, psychosomatic symptoms, and other feelings and behaviors indicative of psychiatric problems. Respondents were instructed to read each statement and answer "true," "false," or "cannot say." In constructing the scoring keys, the statement items were administered to groups of psychiatric patients who had previously been diagnosed as hypochondriacal, depressed, hysterical, psychopathic, paranoid, psychasthenic, schizophrenic, or hypomanic and to groups of nonpatient "normals." Items that significantly differentiated between patients in a particular diagnostic category and the "normals" were then keyed for that diagnosis. These keys were subsequently cross-validated on new groups of patients and normals, yielding nine clinical "scales": 1 or Hs (hypochondriasis), 2 or D (depression), 3 or Hy (conversion hysteria), 4 or Pd (psychopathic deviate), 5 or Mf (masculinity–femininity), 6 or Pa (paranoia), 7 or Pt (Psychasthenia), 8 or Sc (Schizophrenia), and 9 or Ma (Hypomania).

The 504 items constituting the MMPI clinical scales were subsequently expanded to a pool of 566 items by inclusion of a Masculinity–Femininity (Mf) scale, which presumably could be used to identify homosexuality but actually only distinguished between males and females. Another "content scale," the Social Introversion (0 or Si) scale, was constructed from 70 items that differentiated between college women who were highly involved in extracurricular activities and those who were less involved (e.g., "I have the time of my life at parties") (Drake, 1946).

The nine clinical scales, together with the Si scale and four validity scales—Cannot Say (?), Lie (L), Frequency or Infrequency (F), and Correction (K)—brought the total number of scales on which the MMPI could be scored to 14. A person's score on the ? scale consisted of the number of items he or she left unanswered. The L scale consisted of 15 items of overly good self-report, such as "I smile at everyone I meet" (answered "true"). The F scale consisted of 64 items answered in the scored direction by 10% or less of normals, such as "There is an international plot against me" (true). The K scale consisted of 30 items reflecting defensiveness in admitting to problems, such as "I feel bad when others criticize me" (false).

The interpretation of responses to the MMPI begins with an inspection of the scores on the four validity scales. A high score on the ? scale is considered indicative of defensiveness in responding, a high L ("fake good") score suggests that the examinee is attempting to place himself or herself in a more favorable light, and a high F ("fake bad") score indicates that the examinee is attempting to place himself or herself in an unfavorable light. Faking bad might occur, for example, when the respondent was attempting to avoid going to prison, serving in the military, or engaging in other "unpleasant" activities. High scorers on the K scale (a measure of overcriticalness or overgenerosity in evaluating oneself) tend to deny personal inadequacies and deficiencies in self-control, whereas low K scorers are willing to make socially desirable statements about themselves. A fraction of the K score is applied as a correction factor to the raw score on scales 1, 4, 7, 8, and 9.

MMPI-2

By the 1980s the MMPI was more than 40 years old, so the norms and the wording of some of the statements were dated. To provide up-to-date norms, broaden the item pool, and revise the language of some of the items, a revision of the inventory was undertaken. Two forms of the revised version of the MMPI—the MMPI-2 for adults and the MMPI-A for adolescents—were constructed. Items on the MMPI were retained in both revised versions, but they were edited for dated, awkward, or sexist language. The 567 true–false items on the MMPI-2 also include 154 new experimental items for assessing eating disorders, type A personality, drug abuse, and other areas of psychopathology.

In scoring the MMPI-2, the first 370 items are scored for the four validity scales and the 10 basic clinical scales; the remaining items are scored for the supplementary content and research scales (see Table 5.3). In addition to the four traditional validity scales, there are three supplementary validation scales:

Back F (F_B). For detecting possible deviant responding to items located toward the end of the item pool

Variable Response Inconsistency (VRIN) scale. For detecting tendency
of examinee to answer items in an indiscriminate manner

True Response Inconsistency (TRIN) scale. For detecting the tendency
to answer "True" ("acquiescence") or "False" ("nonacquiescence") indiscriminately

Raw scores on the content scales of the MMPI-2 are converted to
uniform T scores like those in Table 5.3. Because of differences in raw
score distributions of the various scales, traditional T scores on the
MMPI were not strictly comparable from scale to scale. Converting the
T scores computed on the distribution of scores for each scale to
averages based on eight of the basic clinical scales and the Content
Scales retained the general shape of the raw score distributions on
these scales and made the scores comparable (Hathaway & McKinley,
1989). Scores on clinical scales 5 and 0 and the supplementary scales,
however, are linear rather than uniform T scores.

The MMPI-2 was standardized on a fairly representative sample of
U.S. adults, but the test–retest reliabilities of several of the basic scales
are rather low. Consequently, differences between scores on the various
scales should be interpreted cautiously.

The MMPI-2 can be scored and coded for interpretive purposes by
hand, but computer-based scoring and interpretation have become
more common (Butcher, 1993). Several computer programs based on
rules for analyzing the pattern or configuration of MMPI-2 scores are
available. The interpretative portion of one such report is given in
Report 5.1. This interpretation is based on item responses, the T scores
listed in Table 5.3, and various special indices, including the Welsh
Codes (based on MMPI-2 and MMPI norms), F–K Dissimulation Index,
Percentage True and False, Average Profile Elevation, Psychopathology
F Scale, Megargee Classification, Pain Classification, Henrichs Rules,
Goldberg Index, and Cooke's Disturbance Index. For the case in Report
5.1, the percentage true = 37, the percentage false = 63, the Profile
Elevation is 54.00, and the Pain Classification is 0. The Welsh Code
(new) for the profile of the 13 clinical and validity scales is 02'+458–67/
1:<u>93</u>#F'+–L/K. In this code, the numerical designations of the nine clinical
scales and the Social Introversion scale (scale 0), are arranged from
left to right in descending order of their T scores. A prime (') is placed
after the number of the last scale having a T score of 70 or greater, and
a dash (–) is placed after the number of the last scale having a T score
of 60 or greater. The numerical designations of scales having T score

TABLE 5.3 MMPI-2 Scales and T Scores for Case in Report 5.1

Basic validity and clinical scales			T score
Validity			
L	Lie		52
F	Infrequency		70
K	Defensiveness		41
?	Cannot Say (reported as raw score)		0
Clinical			
(1)	*Hs*	Hypochondriasis	45
(2)	*D*	Depression	76
(3)	*Hy*	Conversion Hysteria	38
(4)	*Pd*	Psychopathic Deviate	64
(5)	*Mf*	Masculinity-Femininity	62
(6)	*Pa*	Paranoia	57
(7)	*Pt*	Psychasthenia	51
(8)	*Sc*	Schizophrenia	62
(9)	*Ma*	Hypomania	39
(0)	*Si*	Social Introversion	79

Content Scales

ANX	Anxiety	62
FRS	Fears	74
OBS	Obsessiveness	50
DEP	Depression	66
HEA	Health Concerns	53
BIZ	Bizarre Mentation	51
ANG	Anger	48
CYN	Cynicism	65
ASP	Antisocial Practices	51
TPA	Type A	38
LSE	Low Self-Esteem	72
SOD	Social Discomfort	76
FAM	Family Problems	77
WRK	Work Interference	59
TRT	Negative Treatment Indicators	59

Content Component Scales

Fears Subscales		
FRS1	Generalized Fearfulness	89
FRS2	Multiple Fears	61
Depression Subscales		
DEP1	Lack of Drive	62
DEP2	Dysphoria	68
DEP3	Self-Depreciation	69
DEP4	Suicidal Ideation	45
Health Concerns Subscales		
HEA1	Gastrointestinal Symptoms	57
HEA2	Neurological Symptoms	40

(Continued)

TABLE 5.3 (Continued)

HEA3	General Health Concerns	64
Bizarre Mentation Subscales		
BIZ1	Psychotic Symptomatology	44
BIZ2	Schizotypal Characteristics	47
Anger Subscales		
ANG1	Explosive Behavior	52
ANG2	Irritability	46
Cynicism Subscales		
CYN1	Misanthropic Beliefs	68
CYN2	Interpersonal Suspiciousness	53
Antisocial Practices Subscales		
ASP1	Antisocial Attitudes	57
ASP2	Antisocial Behavior	38
Type A Subscales		
TPA1	Impatience	34
TPA2	Competitive Drive	40
Low Self-Esteem Subscales		
LSE1	Self-Doubt	75
LSE2	Submissiveness	69
Social Discomfort		
SOD1	Introversion	68
SOD2	Shyness	74
Family Problems		
FAM1	Family Discord	60
FAM2	Familial Alienation	76
Negative Treatment Indicators		
TRT1	Low Motivation	54
TRT2	Inability to Disclose	60

Supplementary Scales

TRIN	True Response Inconsistency	50
VRIN	Variable Response Inconsistency	38
F(B)	Back F	55
S	Experimental Scale	45
A	Anxiety	56
R	Repression	65
Es	Ego Strength	40
MAC-R	MacAndrew Alcoholism—Revised	44
O-H	Overcontrolled Hostility	52
Do	Dominance	31
Re	Social Responsibility	55
Mt	College Maladjustment	
GM	Gender Role–Masculine	
GF	Gender Role–Feminine	
PK	Post-Traumatic Stress Disorder–Keane	68
PS	Post-Traumatic Stress Disorder–Schlenger	
MDS	Marital Distress Scale	

(Continued)

TABLE 5.3 *(Continued)*

Basic validity and clinical scales		T score
APS	Addiction Potential Scale	49
AAS	Addiction Admission Scale	41
Social Introversion Subscales		
Si_1	Shyness/Self-Consciousness	77
Si_2	Social Avoidance	67
Si_3	Alienation—Self and Others	56
Harris-Lingoes Subscales		
D_1	Subjective Depression	69
D_2	Psychomotor Retardation	70
D_3	Physical Malfunctioning	75
D_4	Mental Dullness	58
D_5	Brooding	68
Hy_1	Denial of Social Anxiety	34
Hy_2	Need for Affection	32
Hy_3	Lassitude–Malaise	66
Hy_4	Somatic Complaints	43
Hy_5	Inhibition of Aggression	48
Pd_1	Familial Discord	78
Pd_2	Authority Problems	48
Pd_3	Social Imperturbability	40
Pd_4	Social Alienation	67
Pd_5	Self-Alienation	63
Pa_1	Persecutory Ideas	70
Pa_2	Poignancy	55
Pa_3	Naivete	41
Sc_1	Social Alienation	80
Sc_2	Emotional Alienation	59
Sc_3	Lack of Ego Mastery, Cognitive	48
Sc_4	Lack of Ego Mastery, Conative	49
Sc_5	Lack of Ego Mastery, Defective Inhibition	61
Sc_6	Bizarre Sensory Experiences	51
Ma_1	Amorality	42
Ma_2	Psychomotor Acceleration	44
Ma_3	Imperturbability	35
Ma_4	Ego Inflation	37

values within 1 point of each other are underlined, and scores on the L, F, and K scales are placed after the profile code.

The computer-based interpretation of MMPI-2 responses and scores can provide many interesting hypotheses concerning the examinee, but the report is based on a prototype and is not tailor-made. A particular examinee may not match the prototype on which the interpretation is

REPORT 5.1 MMPI-2 Sample Report Based on T Scores in Table 5.3, Item Responses, and Other Indices

ID Number 10101010
Male   Age 40   Divorced   11 Years of Education
Correctional Setting   Chronic Pain Program
April 13, 1994

Profile Validity

This is a valid MMPI-2 clinical profile. The client has cooperated in the evaluation, admitting a number of psychological problems in a frank and open manner. Individuals with this profile tend to be blunt and may openly complain to others about their psychological problems. The client tends to be quite self-critical and may appear to have inadequate psychological defense mechanisms. He may be seeking psychological help at this time because he feels that things are out of control and unmanageable.

Symptomatic Patterns

The clinical scale configuration that includes Scale D was used as the prototype for this report. This configuration shows very high profile definition, that is, the clinical scale pattern is greater than 10 points above the adjacent scale. This clear pattern increases confidence that the following narrative report is a good indication of the client's current symptomatic behavior. The client's MMPI-2 clinical profile suggests that he is presently experiencing many psychological problems. Individuals with this profile tend to exhibit a pattern of chronic psychological maladjustment. He is presently quite depressed and anxious, extremely pessimistic, and uninterested in life. He blames and belittles himself to the point that he cannot function in routine daily activities. He may experience vague physical problems and feel as if he cannot "get going." His depression may be partly situational and may diminish over time, with treatment, or as stress dissipates. Nevertheless, his profile also indicates a stable pattern of behavior or a personality-trait pattern reflecting social withdrawal. His many passive traits, including dependency, low self-esteem, and social isolation, are likely to persist even after the symptom pattern of depression and anxiety subsides.

In addition, the following description is suggested by the content of the client's item responses. He has endorsed a number of items suggesting that he is experiencing low morale and a depressed mood. He reports a preoccupation with feeling guilty and unworthy. He feels that he deserves to be punished for wrongs he has committed. He feels regretful and unhappy about life, and he seems plagued by anxiety and worry about the future. He feels hopeless at times and feels that he is a condemned person. He endorsed response content that reflects low self-esteem and long-standing beliefs about his inadequacy. He has difficulty managing routine affairs, and the items he endorsed suggest a poor memory, concentration problems, and an inability to make decisions. He appears to be immobilized and withdrawn and has no energy for life. He views his physical health as failing and reports numerous somatic concerns. He feels that life is no longer worthwhile and that he is losing control of his thought processes.

According to his response content, there is a strong possibility that he has seriously contemplated suicide. The client's response content suggests that

REPORT 5.1 *(Continued)*

he feels intensely fearful about a large number of objects and activities. This hypersensitivity and fearfulness appear to be generalized at this point and may be debilitating to him in social and work situations.

Profile Frequency

Profile interpretation can be greatly facilitated by examining the relative frequency of clinical scale patterns in various settings. The client's high-point clinical scale score (D) occurs in 7.2% of the MMPI-2 normative sample of men. However, only 2.4% of the sample have D as the peak score at or above a T score of 65, and only 1.1% have well-defined D spikes.

His MMPI-2 profile peak score on the D scale occurs as a high point in 17% of men in chronic pain samples.

Profile Stability

The relative elevation of the highest scales in his clinical profile shows very high profile definition. His peak scores on this testing are likely to be very prominent in his profile pattern if he is retested at a later date. His high-point score on D is likely to remain stable over time. Short-term test–retest studies have shown a correlation of .75 for this high-point score.

Interpersonal Relations

He is socially withdrawn, is fearful of others, does not make friends easily, and lacks expressiveness and spontaneity in social situations. He tends to allow others to dominate him and fails to defend himself even when he has been wronged. He may become involved in relationships in which he is mistreated or taken advantage of because he feels he doesn't deserve better.

The content of this client's MMPI-2 responses suggests the following additional information concerning his interpersonal relations. He appears to be an individual who has rather cynical views about life. Any efforts to initiate new behaviors may be colored by his negativism. He may view relationships with others as threatening and harmful. He views his home situation as unpleasant and lacking in love and understanding. He feels like leaving home to escape a quarrelsome, critical situation and to be free of family domination. His social relationships are likely to be viewed by others as problematic. He may be visibly uneasy around others, sits alone in group situations, and dislikes engaging in group activities.

Diagnostic Considerations

A Dysthymic Disorder is the most likely clinical diagnosis. He would probably also be considered to have a Dependent Personality Disorder.

Treatment Considerations

Medical or pain patients with this MMPI-2 clinical profile are usually experiencing a great deal of emotional distress along with their physical symptoms. Some individuals with this profile require antidepressant medication to elevate their mood. This patient is probably feeling quite tense and may be motivated to receive help for his depressive symptoms.

Individual psychotherapy, although possibly considered appropriate in his case, may not be very easy to conduct. Individuals with this MMPI-2 pattern are very inhibited, have very few social skills, and have difficulty relating well to others. They are likely to have problems establishing a therapeutic relationship.

Directive psychological treatment that requires limited initial activity on the part of the patient might have more chance of succeeding than insight-oriented psychotherapy. He might also benefit from some social-skills training.

Examination of item content reveals a considerable number of problems with his home life. He feels extremely unhappy and alienated form his family. He reports that his home life is unpleasant and that he does not expect to improve. Any psychological intervention will need to focus on his negative family feelings if progress is to be made.

He has expressed a number of specific fears with which he is concerned at this time. Behavioral therapy to alleviate these fears might be considered.

based, so the descriptions, inferences, and recommendations contained in the report need to be checked against other sources of information. In addition, the report should be kept confidential and used by only a trained, qualified interpreter.

California Psychological Inventory (CPI)

Like its parent instrument—the MMPI—the CPI is a criterion-keyed inventory. Approximately one-third of the 480 true–false items on the first edition of the CPI were taken from the MMPI, and the remaining half were written expressly for this inventory. These items were concerned principally with more positive, normal aspects of personality rather than problems of adjustment or signs of mental disorders. The CPI was scored on 18 content scales, three of which (Well-Being, Good Impression, and Communality) were validity scales designed to detect whether the examinee was faking bad (Well-Being), faking good (Good Impression), or selecting highly popular responses (Communality). As on other personality inventories, scores on the validity scales were examined before proceeding to an analysis of scores on the content scales.

The psychometric characteristics (standardization, reliability, validity) of the CPI were acceptable. It fulfilled its role as the "sane person's MMPI" quite well and became one of the most popular of all personality inventories. As with the MMPI, by the 1980s it was clear that the CPI needed revising. The Revised CPI, published in 1986, consists of 462 items retained or reworded from the original CPI.

The most recent edition of this California Psychological Inventory— the revised CPI™, Third Edition—contains 434 items and is scored on 20 Folk Scales, three Vector Scales, and 13 Special Purpose Scales. The Folk Scales, which are listed in Table 5.4, consist of the 18 scales on

TABLE 5.4 Folk Scales on the Revised CPI™ (3rd ed.)

Interpersonal Style and Manner of Dealing with Others

*Dominance	*Self-acceptance
*Capacity for Status	Independence
*Sociability	Empathy
*Social Presence	

Internalization and Endorsement of Normative Conventions

*Responsibility	*Communality
*Socialization	*Tolerance
*Self-Control	*Well-being
*Good Impression	

Cognitive and Intellectual Functioning

*Achievement via Conformance	*Achievement via Independence
*Intellectual Efficiency	

Thinking and Behavior

*Psychological-Mindedness	*Femininity–Masculinity
*Flexibility	

*Scales on original version of California Psychological Inventory.
Modified and reproduced by special permission of the publisher, Consulting Psychologists Press, Inc., Palo Alto, CA 94303 from *California Psychological Inventory* by Harrison G. Gough, PhD. Copyright 1987 by Consulting Psychologists Press, Inc. All rights reserved. Further reproduction is prohibited without the publisher's written consent.

the original edition plus the Empathy and Independence Scales. The 13 Special Purpose Scales include Creative Temperament, Managerial Potential, Work Orientation, Leadership Potential, Amicability, Tough-Mindedness, Law Enforcement Orientation, Anxiety, and five others.

The three Vector Scales on the CPI™, Third Edition, define a theoretical model of personality structure. Scores on these three scales are independent of each other, although they are significantly related to scores on the Folk Scales. Scale v.1 measures the role or interpersonal orientation theme (from externality to internality). Scores on v.1 reflect how examinees express their self-interest in interpersonal situations. Scale v.2 measures the normative perspective or character theme (from norm questioning to norm favoring). Scale v.3 measures the competence or realization theme (from level 1 to level 7).

Combinations of scores on the three Vector Scales yield four personality types: alphas, betas, gammas, and deltas. *Alphas* are externally oriented and norm-favoring, *betas* are internally oriented and norm-favoring, *gammas* are externally oriented and norm questioning, and *deltas* are internally oriented and norm-questioning. Each of these four personality types has seven levels, varying from level 1—dispirited or poorly integrated with little or no realization of the positive potential of the type—through level 7—self-fulfilled or highly integrated with realization of the positive potential of the type. Level 1 alphas are described as "authoritarian," level 4 alphas as "strong willed," and level 7 alphas as "steadfast." Level 1 betas are described as "self-blaming," level 4 betas as "conventional," and level 7 betas as "humane." Level 1 gammas are described as "wayward," level 4 gammas as "impulsive," and level 7 gammas as "creative." Level 1 deltas are described as "alien-ated," level 4 deltas as "conflicted," and level 7 deltas as "visionary."

Reviews of the CPI have been mostly positive (e.g., Bolton, 1992; Engelhard, 1992). The inventory has good reliability, although the norms on the first two editions were not completely adequate and some important technical information was omitted from the manuals. Be that as it may, the three editions of the CPI have received positive evaluations as research and instructional instruments, and they can provide useful information for counseling purposes in the hands of an expert clinician. Their business uses include finding and developing successful employees, developing leaders, creating efficient and productive organizations, and promoting teamwork.

Millon Clinical Multiaxial Inventory-III (MCMI-III)

Of all the personality inventories listed in Appendix 5.1, it would probably have been predicted that the Millon Clinical Multiaxial Inventory (MCMI) would be the most competitive with the MMPI. Like the MMPI-2, the 3rd edition of the MCMI (MCMI-III) (Millon, Millon, & Davis, 1994) was designed primarily to assess personality disorders and clinical syndromes. Coordinated with Theodore Millon's theory of personality and with the 4th edition of the *Diagnostic and Statistical Manual (DSM-IV)* (American Psychiatric Association, 1994), the MCMI-III consists of 175 items and is scored on 27 diagnostic scales. As shown in Figure 5.1, three of these scales are Modifying Indices, 11 are Clinical Personality Pattern scales based on Axis II of DSM-IV, three are Severe Personality Pathology scales, seven are Clinical Syndrome scales based on Axis I of DSM-IV, and three are Severe Syndrome scales.

The MCMI-III can be scored by hand with a set of templates or by using the NCS Assessments' MICROTEST Q System computer software. Scores are weighted and converted to *base rate scores* that consider the incidence of particular characteristics or disorders in the general population. Use of these base-rate scores maximizes the ratio of correct classifications (valid positives) to the number of incorrect classifications (false positives).

MILLON CLINICAL MULTIAXIAL INVENTORY - III

CONFIDENTIAL INFORMATION FOR PROFESSIONAL USE ONLY

ID NUMBER: 12566
PERSONALITY CODE: 8A 3 2B 2A ** - * 8B 6A 1 + 6B 5 " 4 7 '' // C ** - * //
SYNDROME CODE: A ** T H D R * // CC ** - * //
DEMOGRAPHIC: 12566/ON/F/44/W/D/10/MD/AL/——/05/——/

Valid Profile

CATEGORY		SCORE		PROFILE OF BR SCORES	DIAGNOSTIC SCALES
		RAW	BR	0 60 75 85 115	
MODIFYING INDICES	X	163	93		DISCLOSURE
	Y	4	20		DESIRABILITY
	Z	28	91		DEBASEMENT
CLINICAL PERSONALITY PATTERNS	1	13	64		SCHIZOID
	2A	20	86		AVOIDANT
	2B	20	87		DEPRESSIVE
	3	22	88		DEPENDENT
	4	7	16		HISTRIONIC
	5	12	46		NARCISSISTIC
	6A	14	66		ANTISOCIAL
	6B	14	56		AGGRESSIVE (SADISTIC)

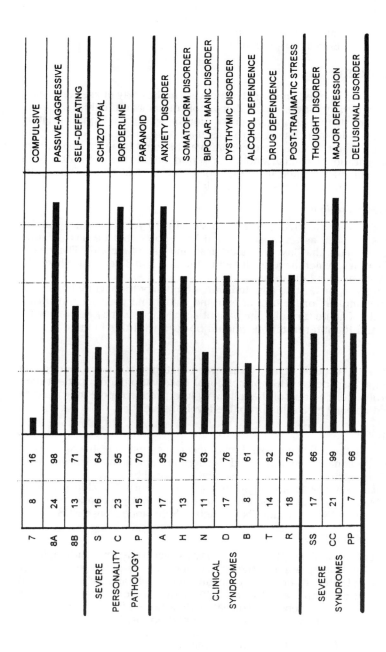

		COMPULSIVE	7	8	16
		PASSIVE-AGGRESSIVE	8A	24	98
		SELF-DEFEATING	8B	13	71
SEVERE		SCHIZOTYPAL	S	16	64
PERSONALITY		BORDERLINE	C	23	95
PATHOLOGY		PARANOID	P	15	70
		ANXIETY DISORDER	A	17	95
		SOMATOFORM DISORDER	H	13	76
		BIPOLAR: MANIC DISORDER	N	11	63
		DYSTHYMIC DISORDER	D	17	76
		ALCOHOL DEPENDENCE	B	8	61
CLINICAL		DRUG DEPENDENCE	T	14	82
SYNDROMES		POST-TRAUMATIC STRESS	R	18	76
SEVERE		THOUGHT DISORDER	SS	17	66
SYNDROMES		MAJOR DEPRESSION	CC	21	99
		DELUSIONAL DISORDER	PP	7	66

FIGURE 5.1 Sample MCMI–III Profile. (Copyright by DICANDRIEN, INC. Reproduced by permission of NCS Assessments.)

REPORT 5.2 Summary of MCMI-III Interpretative Report for Scores in Figure 5.1

ID Number 12566   Male   Age 37   White
Divorced   10 Years Education   Inpatient

CAPSULE SUMMARY

MCMI-III reports are normed on patients who were in the early phases of assessment or psychotherapy for emotional discomfort or social difficulties. Respondents who do not fit this normative population or who have inappropriately taken the MCMI-III for nonclinical purposes may have distorted reports. The MCMI-III report cannot be considered definitive. It should be evaluated in conjunction with additional clinical data. The report should be evaluated by a mental health clinician trained in the use of psychological tests. The report should not be shown to patients or their relatives.

Interpretive Considerations

The client is a 37-year-old divorced white male with 10 years of education. He is currently being seen as an inpatient, and he reports that he has recently experienced problems that involve moodiness and use of alcohol. These self-reported difficulties, which have occurred in the last 1 to 3 years, are likely to take the form of an Axis I disorder.

This patient's response style may indicate a tendency to magnify illness, an inclination to complain, or feelings of extreme vulnerability associated with a current episode of acute turmoil. The patient's scale scores may be somewhat exaggerated, and the interpretations should be read with this in mind.

Profile Severity

On the basis of the test data, it may be assumed that the patient is experiencing a severe mental disorder; further professional observation and inpatient care may be appropriate. The text of the following interpretive report may need to be modulated upward given this probable level of severity.

Possible Diagnoses

He appears to fit the following Axis II classifications best: Passive-Aggressive (negativistic) Personality Disorder, and Borderline Personality Disorder, with Dependent Personality Traits, and Depressive Personality Traits.

Axis I clinical syndromes are suggested by the client's MCMI-III profile in the areas of Major Depression (recurrent, severe, without psychotic features). Generalized Anxiety Disorder, and Psychoactive Substance Abuse NOS.

Therapeutic Considerations

Inconsistent and pessimistic, this patient may expect to be mishandled, if not harmed, even by well-intentioned therapists. Sensitive to messages of disapproval and lack of interest, he may complain excessively and be irritable and erratic in his relations with therapists. Straightforward and consistent communication may moderate his dependent/negativistic attitude. focused, brief treatment approaches are likely to overcome his initial oppositional outlook.

In addition to a scoring service, NCS Assessments provides an interpretive report and a profile report that graphically represents the base-rate scores on all scales. The interpretative report gives an integrated interpretation of scores on all scales, a description of the examinee's personality characteristics, an assessment of clinical syndromes related to those characteristics, and a list of possible DSM-IV diagnoses. A capsule summary of an interpretative report associated with the profile in Figure 5.1 is given in Report 5.2.

Reviews of the MCMI-II, the predecessor of the MCMI-III, have been mixed: Both Haladyna (1992) and Reynolds (1992) were impressed with the conceptual foundations of the MCMI-II, but Reynolds (1992) described it as "psychometrically somewhere between a nightmare and an enigma" (p. 534).

The MCMI-III was fairly well standardized, and the reliability coefficients of the scales are good for a personality inventory. Because samples of normal people were not used in standardizing the MCMI-III, but rather base-rate scores were used to differentiate between different samples of psychologically disordered people, Butcher & Rouse (1996) warn that using the MCMI-III with nonpatients is likely to result in many false-positive errors in diagnosis. Some of the criticisms of the MCMI-II would appear to be muted in MCMI-III, although it is still good advice to restrict the use of this inventory to clinical populations.

Basic Personality Inventory

Using a combination of construction strategies and sophisticated psychometric procedures, D. N. Jackson has produced several personality inventories. One of these, the Personality Research Form, was described earlier in the chapter. Another instrument designed for "normal" personalities is the Jackson Personality Inventory. The latest inventory by Jackson and his coworkers—the Basic Personality Inventory (BPI)—has a different orientation from the first two.

Like the Personality Assessment Inventory (Morey, 1991), the BPI is intended as a shorter and psychometrically purer alternative to the MMPI for use with both clinical and normal populations. It focuses on identifying sources of maladjustment and personality strength in juveniles and adults. Scores are provided on the following 12 basic scales: Alienation, Anxiety, Denial, Depression, Hypochondriasis, Impulse Expression, Interpersonal Problems, Persecutory Ideas, Self Depreciation, Social Introversion, Thinking Disorder, and Deviation (Critical Item Scale).

Because of its maladjustment orientation, the BPI is more appropriate than its predecessors for mental health and correctional contexts. Profiles for psychiatric patients (anorexics, suicidal patients, hallucinatory patients, etc) are provided in the manual (Jackson et al., 1989). Although the norms would appear to be somewhat limited, the test–retest reliabilities of the BPI scales are moderate to high. In addition to inadequate norms, data on the validity of the BPI are not as extensive as one might wish.

Reviews of the BPI (Urbina, 1995; Yelland, 1995) assign high marks to its psychometrically sophisticated construction methodology. However, reviewers point to the need for a more representative set of adult norms based on different ethnic groups and clinical populations. A comparison of the clinical effectiveness of the BPI and the MMPI-2 found that both inventories significantly discriminated among psychopathological symptoms, and had comparable hit rates (Grigoriadis, Fekken, & Nussbaum, 1994).

ASSESSMENT OF SPECIFIC CLINICAL SYMPTOMS AND SYNDROMES

All of the adult-oriented inventories discussed in the previous sections of this chapter are multiscore or multiphasic instruments, in that they provide measures of many different variables having relatively low correlations with each other. As shown in Appendix 5.2, however, several personality inventories focus on a single clinical construct, such as alcoholism, anger, anxiety, depression, neuroticism, stress, and suicide ideation. Among the most popular of these are Spielberger's anxiety and anger inventories and Beck's anxiety, depression, hopelessness, and suicide ideation inventories.

State-Trait Anxiety and Anger Scales

The State-Trait Anxiety Inventory (STAI) was designed to differentiate between the temporary condition of "state anxiety" and the more general and long-standing quality of "trait anxiety" in adults. The 20 4-point items on the State Anxiety scale measure feelings of apprehension, tension, nervousness, and worry, which increase with physical danger and psychological stress. The 20 4-point items on the Trait Anxiety scale measure the relatively stable tendency to be anxious in a wide range of stressful situations. The STAI has been used for screening students and military recruits, and for assessing the immediate and long-term outcomes of counseling, psychotherapy, and other intervention programs.

The State-Trait Anger Expression Inventory (STAXI)–Research Edition measures the intensity of anger as an emotional state (State Anger) and the disposition to experience angry feelings as a personality trait (Trait Anger). Subscales on the Trait Anger scale differentiate between "angry temperament" and "angry reaction." Like the STAI, the STAXI has been used extensively in research on the effects of psychotherapy, behavioral medicine, and related stress management programs. Both the STAI and the STAXI have received good reviews for construction, psychometric characteristics, and research applications (Biskin, 1992; Dreger, 1978; Katkin, 1978; Retzlaff, 1992).

Beck Scales

All four of the inventories authored by Aaron Beck—the Beck Depression Inventory, the Beck Hopelessness Scale, the Beck Anxiety Inventory, and the Beck Scale for Suicide Ideation—can be administered in 5 to 10 minutes to adults aged 17 to 89 years in clinical situations. Of the four inventories, the Beck Depression Inventory (BDI), which was designed to detect and determine the intensity of depression in both normal and psychiatric populations, has been the most widely used. It consists of 21 item sets, each composed of four statements reflecting increasing levels of depression. The response to each item is weighted on a scale ranging from 0 ("no complaint") to 3 ("severe complaint"). Total scores as well as subscores on cognitive-affective and somatic-performance scales may be determined. Total scores of 0 to 9 are "normal," scores of 10 to 18 indicate "mild to moderate depression," scores of 19 to 29 indicate "moderate to severe depression," and scores of 30 or higher indicate "extremely severe depression."

The Beck Hopelessness Scale (BHS) was designed to measure negative beliefs concerning the future. It consists of 20 true-false items in which the examinee either endorses a pessimistic statement or denies an optimistic statement. Scores on the BHS are moderately correlated with scores on the BDI, but the latter instrument is a better predictor of suicidal intention and behavior. The Beck Anxiety Inventory (BAI) was designed to measure the severity of anxiety in adolescents and adults. It also consists of 21 items, each item being descriptive of a symptom of anxiety and rated on a sale of 0 to 3. The Beck Scale for Suicide Ideation was designed to evaluate suicidal thinking and attitudes, and thereby to identify individuals at risk for suicide. It contains 21 items, including five screening items for reducing the length of the question-naire and its intrusiveness to nonsuicidal respondents.

The reliability and standardization of all four Beck inventories are adequate. Research on the validity of the inventories is reported in the respective manuals. Among the reported findings are that BDI scores are highly correlated with clinical ratings of depression, and that BAI scores significantly discriminate between anxious and nonanxious diagnostic groups. In a review of the BDI, Sundberg (1992) concluded that it "has made an important contribution to clinical and research work on depression" (p. 80). Although Owen's (1992) review of the BHS was less positive, Dowd (1992) concluded that it is "a well-constructed and validated instrument, with adequate reliability" (p. 82).

SUMMARY

Personality inventories are among the most numerous of all objective measures of personality designed for applied and research purposes. Deductive (rational/theoretical), inductive (internal consistence/factor analytic), and empirical (criterion-keyed) strategies have all been employed in constructing such inventories. No single construction strategy has been found to be generally superior to any of the others, and a combination of approaches is considered best.

Personality inventories made their debut with the Woodworth Personal Data Sheet during World War I. These devices became popular during the ensuing decades, finding uses in selection, diagnosis, and research in educational, clinical, and industrial/organizational contexts. Problems of faking and response sets in answering items on personality inventories have been controlled to some extent by specially constructed validity scales, but the scores on these instruments can still be affected by dissimulation.

Personality inventories tend to have somewhat lower reliabilities than tests of achievement and ability, and they typically do not contribute as much to the prediction of performance in academic or employment situations. Scores on clinically based inventories, such as the MMPI-2, the MCMI-III, and the Basic Personality Inventory, however, often make significant contributions to the diagnosis and prognosis of disorders of personality and behavior and to the prediction of the behavioral outcomes of clinical interventions. Inventories designed for more "normal" personalities, such as the CPI and the 16 PF, can also assist in the identification of adjustment problems and in forecasting behavioral changes produced by training or counseling programs.

In addition to multivariable, or multiphasic, inventories that assess many different personality variables for various applied and research purposes, several inventories focus on a specific psychological or behavioral state (anger, anxiety, depression, etc.) or condition (alcoholism, eating disorders, severe stress, neuroticism, type A behavior, suicide, etc.). Prominent among instruments of this type are Spielberger's state-trait inventories of anger and anxiety and Beck's inventories of anxiety, depression, hopelessness, and suicide ideation. These instruments, as well as the more comprehensive multiphasic inventories, are typically not used alone, but rather they form a part of a battery of psychodiagnostic instruments and procedures designed to achieve particular clinical, educational, or employment goals.

APPENDIX 5.1 Representative Multiscore Inventories of Adult Personality and Behavior

Normal Personality

Adult Personality Inventory (S. E. Krug; MetriTech; ages 16–adult; 25 scores; designed as a tool for analyzing and reporting individual differences in personality, interpersonal styles, and career-style preferences; reviewed in MMYB 9:54 & 12:20; TC VI:21)

The APT Inventory (Training House, Inc.; adults; 10 traits; designed to measure an individual's relative strength on 10 personality traits)

Association Adjustment Inventory (M. M. Bruce; normal and institutionalized adults; 13 scores; designed for use as a screening instrument for maladjustment and immaturity; reviewed in MMYB 6:201; TC I:70)

California Psychological Inventory (rev. ed.) (H. G. Gough, Consulting Psychologists Press; ages 13 and older; designed to assess personality characteristics and to predict what people will say or do in specified contexts; reviewed in MMYB 11:54; TC VII:66)

California Test of Personality (E. W. Tiegs, W. W. Clark, & L. P. Thorpe; CTB/McGraw-Hill; children and adults; 15 scores; designed to identify and reveal the status of certain factors in personality and social adjustment; reviewed in MMYB 9:183)

Comprehensive Personality Profile (Wonderlic Personnel Test & L. L. Craft; adults; 17 scores; designed to identify individuals with personality traits that are compatible with occupational and organizational demands)

Edwards Personal Preference Schedule (A. L. Edwards; The Psychological Corporation; college and adults; 16 scores; developed to measure a number of relatively independent *normal* personality variables; reviewed in MMYB 7:72; TC I:252)

Eysenck Personality Inventory (H. J. Eysenck & S. B. G. Eysenck; Educational & Industrial Testing Service; adults; 3 scores; measures to independent dimensions of personality: extraversion–introversion and neuroticism–stability; reviewed in MMYB 9-I:405; TC II:258)

Eysenck Personality Questionnaire (rev.) (H. J. Eysenck & S. B. G. Eysenck; Educational & Industrial Testing Service; college and general adults including those with lower education levels, ages 7–15, 16 and older; 4 scores; designed to measure four dimensions of personality in adults; earlier edition reviewed in MMYB 8:553 and TC I:27)

The Guilford–Zimmerman Temperament Survey (J. P. Guilford & W. S. Zimmerman; Consulting Psychologists Press; ages 16 through adult; 10 scores; designed to measure multiple facets of personality; reviewed in MMYB 9:460; TC VIII:251)

Hogan Personality Inventory (rev.) (R. Hogan & J. Hogan; Hogan Assessment Systems; college students and adults; 14 scores; measures of normal personality designed for use in personnel selection, individualized assessment, and career-related decision making; earlier edition reviewed in MMYB 10:140; TC VI:216)

Jackson Personality Inventory—Revised (D. N. Jackson; Sigma Assessment Systems; grades 9–16 and adults; 16 scores; provides a set of measures of personality reflecting a variety of interpersonal, cognitive, and value orientations; earlier edition reviewed in MMYB 8:593; TC II:369)

Maudsley Personality Inventory (H. J. Eysenck & R. R. Knapp; Hodder & Stoughton; college and adults; 2 scores; designed to measure two dimensions of personality: extraversion–introversion and neuroticism–stability; reviewed in MMYB 6:138; TC IV:387)

Millon Index of Personality Styles (T. Millon; The Psychological Corporation; ages 18–65; 26 scores; measure of personality for use in employee development, career guidance, and job screening)

Myers–Briggs Type Indicator (I. B. Myers, K. C. Briggs; Consulting Psychologists Press; grades 9–16 and adults; 4 scores; designed to identify the basic preferences of people in regard to perception and judgment; reviewed in MMYB 9:739; MMYB 10:206; TC I:482)

NEO Five-Factor Inventory (P. T. Costa, Jr., & R. McCrae; Sigma Assessment Systems; ages 17 and older; shortened measure of the five domains of personality; designed to provide measures of the five domains of adult personality)

NEO Personality Inventory—Revised (P. T. Costa, Jr. & R. R. McCrae; Psychological Assessment Resources; ages 17 and older; analyzes personality using the "Five Factor" model; 35 scores; reviewed in MMYB 12:330)

Personal Relationship Inventory (R. L. Mann; Behaviordyne; ages 15 and older; assesses the capacity to love and engage in intimate interpersonal relationships; 13 scores; reviewed in MMYB 12:288)

Personal Styles Inventory (J. T. Kunce, C. S. Cope, & R. M. Newton; Educational & Psychological Consultants, Inc.; provides a comprehensive assessment of normal personality characteristics; 24 scores)

Personality Research Form (3rd ed.) (D. N. Jackson; Sigma Assessment Systems; grade 6–college, adults; designed to yield scores for personality traits relevant to the functioning of individuals in a wide variety of situations; 22 scales; earlier edition reviewed in MMYB 10:282; TC III:429)

Profile of Mood States (D. M. McNair, M. Lorr, & L. F. Droppleman; Educational & Industrial Testing Service; college and psychiatric outpatients; 6 scores; designed to measure mood or affective states; reviewed in MMYB 8:651; TC I:522)

Psychological Screening Inventory (R. I. Lanyon; Sigma Assessment Systems; adolescents through adults; brief true–false mental health screening inventory designed to identify people who might benefit from more intensive examination and professional attention; 5 scores)

Sixteen Personality Factor Questionnaire (5th ed.) (R. B. Cattell et al.; Institute for Personality & Ability Testing; ages 16 and over; 24 scores; designed as a comprehensive measure of personality traits; reviewed in MMYB 12:354)

Taylor–Johnson Temperament Analysis (1992 ed.) [R. H. Johnson (original edition); revised by R. M. Taylor et al.; Psychological Publications; adolescents and adults–individuals and couples; measures personality traits that influence personal, interpersonal, scholastic, and vocational functioning and adjustment; a "standard" test for marital/family evaluation and counseling; 9 traits; reviewed in MMYB 10:357]

Temperament and Values Inventory (C. B. Johansson & P. L. Webber; NCS Assessments; ages 15 and over; 14 scores; designed to measure individual differences that may affect contentment in work situations; reviewed in MMYB 11:423; TC I:660)

Temperament Inventory (R. J. Cruise, W. P. Blitchington, & W. G. A. Futcher; Andrews University Press; college and adults; 4 scores; designed to measure a set of four genetically determined temperaments; reviewed in MMYB 9:1235)

Business and Industry

Inwald Personality Inventory—Revised (R. Inwald; Hilson Research; public safety, security, and law enforcement applications [police, correction, fire, security];

26 scores; developed to aid public safety/law enforcement and security agencies in selecting new officers; reviewed in MMYB 11:183; 12:194)

Occupational Personality Questionnaire (Saville & Holdsworth Ltd.; business or industry; self-report measure of personality and motivational characteristics particularly relevant to the world of work; 31 scores; reviewed in MMYB 11:267)

Sales Personality Questionnaire (Saville & Holdsworth Ltd.; sales applicants; to assess personality characteristics necessary for sales success; 12 scores; reviewed in MMYB 12:337)

Personality Disorders

Basic Personality Inventory (D. N. Jackson; Sigma Assessment Systems; ages 12 and over; multiphasic measure of psychopathology; 12 scores; reviewed in MMYB 12:42; TC VIII:38)

Carlson Psychological Survey (K. A. Carlson; Sigma Assessment Systems; adolescent and adult criminal offenders; 5 scores; psychometric instrument intended primarily for individuals accused or convicted of crimes; reviewed in MMYB 9:203; TC IV:144)

Clinical Analysis Questionnaire (S. E. Krug; Institute for Personality & Ability Testing; ages 16 and over; 21 normal personality traits and 16 clinical factors; designed to assess both deviant behavior and normal coping skills; reviewed in MMYB 9:232; TC I:202)

Millon Clinical Multiaxial Inventory—II & III (T. Millon; NCS Assessments; adults 18 years and older; provides a profile of the scale scores and a detailed analysis of personality and symptom management; MCMI-II reviewed in MMYB 11:239; TC VIII:457)

Minnesota Multiphasic Personality Inventory-2 (S. R. Hathaway, J. C. McKinley, & J. N. Butcher; published by University of Minnesota, distributed by NCS Assessments; ages 18 and older; designed to assess a number of the major patterns of personality and emotional disorders; reviewed in MMYB 11:244; TC VIII:485; TC X:424)

Personality Assessment Inventory (L. C. Morey; Psychological Assessment Resources; ages 18–adult; 54 scores; designed to provide information relevant to clinical diagnosis, treatment planning, and screening for psychopathology; reviewed in MMYB 12:290)

Schedule for Nonadaptive or Adaptive Personality (L. A. Clark, 1994; University of Minnesota Press; ages 18 and older; 34 scores; designed to assess trait dimensions in the domain of personality disorders)

Wisconsin Personality Disorder Inventory (M. H. Klein, L. S. Benjamin, R. Rosenfeld, C. Treece, & J. H. Greist, 1993; adults; self-report questionnaire derived from an interperson perspective on DSM-III-R personality disorders)

APPENDIX 5.2 Inventories for Assessing Specific Clinical Symptoms or Syndromes in Adults

---

Anger

State-Trait Anger Expression Inventory (research ed.) (C. D. Spielberger; Psychological Assessment Resources; ages 13 and over; to measure the experience and expression of anger; reviewed in MMYB 11:379; TC IX:510)

Anxiety

Beck Anxiety Inventory (1993 ed.) (A. T. Beck & R. A. Steer; The Psychological Corporation; adolescents and adults; measures the severity of anxiety in adults and adolescents)

Endler Multidimensional Anxiety Scales (N. S. Endler, J. M. Edwards, & R. Viteli; Western Psychological Services; ages 16 and over; to assess state and trait anxiety and the perception of threat in the immediate situation; reviewed in MMYB 12:138)

IPAT Anxiety Scale (R. B. Cattell, S. E. Krug, & I. H. Scheier; Institute for Personality & Ability Testing; ages 14 and over; a measure of clinical information regarding anxiety; reviewed in MMYB 8:582; TC II:357)

State-Trait Anxiety Inventory (C. D. Spielberger; Psychological Assessment Resources; adults; designed to differentiate between state and trait anxiety; reviewed in MMYB 8-I:683; TC I:626)

Depression and Hopelessness

Beck Depression Inventory (1993 rev.) (A. T. Beck & R. A. Steer; The Psychological Corporation; ages 13–80; designed to assess the severity of depression in adolescents and adults; previous edition reviewed in MMYB 11:31)

Beck Hopelessness Scale (rev.) (A. T. Beck & R. A. Steer; The Psychological Corporation; ages 13–80; measures the extent of negative attitudes about the future (pessimism) as perceived by adolescents and adults; reviewed in MMYB 11:32; TC X:82)

The Grief Experience Inventory (C. M. Sanders, P. A. Mauger, & P. N. Strong; Consulting Psychologists Press; bereaved adults; multidimensional measure of grief; reviewed in MMYB 12:168)

IPAT Depression Scale (S. E. Krug & J. E. Laughlin; Institute for Personality & Ability Testing; adults; designed to estimate depression level; reviewed in MMYB 8:583; TC I:377)

Multiscore Depression Inventory (D. J. Berndt; Western Psychological Services; ages 13 through adult; to provide an objective measure of the severity of self-reported depression; reviewed in MMYB 11:251)

Neuroticism

The Neuroticism Scale Questionnaire (I. H. Scheier & R. B. Cattell; Institute for Personality & Ability Testing; ages 13 and over; brief measure of neurotic trends in the normal or abnormal adult and adolescent; reviewed in MMYB 6:148; TC V:283)

NPF (Second Edition) (R. B. Cattell, J. E. King, & A. K. Schuettler; MetriTech; adults; to assess stress tolerance and overall adjustment; reviewed in MMYB 12:261)

Stress and Coping

Coping Inventory for Stressful Situations (N. Endler & J. Parker; Psychological Publications; adults; measures three major coping styles—Task Oriented Coping, Emotion Oriented Coping, and Avoidance Coping)

Coping Resources Inventory (A. L. Mammer & M. S. Marting; Consulting Psychologists Press; high school and over; to assess a person's resources for coping with stress; reviewed in MMYB 12:95; TC VIII:111)

Coping With Stress (Training House, Inc.; adults; to identify sources of stress and responses to stress; reviewed in MMYB 12:96)

Daily Stress Inventory (P. J. Brantley & G. N. Jones; Sigma Assessment Systems; age 17 and older; to measure the number and relative impact of minor stresses in a person's life; reviewed in MMYB 11:101)

Hassles and Uplifts Scales (R. S. Lazarus & S. Folkman; Consulting Psychologists Press; to identify sources of stress and aspects of daily living that help counteract the damaging effects of stress; reviewed in MMYB 11:155)

Millon Behavioral Health Inventory (T. Millon; C. J. Green, & R. B. Meagher; NCS Assessments; 18 years and older; brief self-report personality inventory designed to assess psychological coping factors related to the physical health care of adult medical patients)

Occupational Stress Inventory (research version) (S. J. Osipow & A. R. Spokane; Sigma Assessment Systems; adults; measures 3 dimensions of occupational adjustment: occupational stress, psychological strain, and coping resources; reviewed in MMYB 11:269 and TC X:498)

Understanding and Managing Stress (J. D. Adams; Pfeiffer & Co. International Publishers; adults; assesses stress level and health-related behaviors)

Suicidal Ideation

Adult Suicidal Ideation Questionnaire (W. M. Reynolds; Psychological Assessment Resources: ages 18 and over; designed to evaluate the presence and frequency of suicidal thoughts)

Beck Scale for Suicide Ideation (A. T. Beck & R. A. Steer; The Psychological Corporation; adults and adolescents; designed to detect and measure the severity of suicidal ideation in adults and adolescents)

Substance Abuse

Alcohol Use Inventory (J. L. Horn, K. W. Wanberg, & F. M. Foster; NCS Assessment; adults suspected of problem drinking; to assess a person's pattern of alcohol and problems associated with it, reviewed in MMYB 12:25)

Personal Experience Inventory for Adults (K. C. Winters; Western Psychological Services; adults; provides comprehensive information concerning substance abuse patterns in adults; used to identify alcohol and drug problems, make referrals, and plan treatment)

Substance Abuse Subtle Screening Inventory (G. A. Miller; The Sassi Institute; ages 12–18 and adults; for identifying alcohol-and drug-dependent individuals and to differentiate them from social users and general psychiatric patients; reviewed in MMYB 12:381)

SUGGESTED READINGS

Burisch, M. (1986). Methods of personality inventory development: A comparative analysis. In A. Angleitner & J. S. Wiggins (Eds.), *Personality assessment via questionnaires* (pp. 109–123). New York: Springer-Verlag.

Butcher, J. N. (1995). Interpretation of the MMPI-2. In L. E. Beutler & M. R. Berren (Eds.), *Integrative assessment of adult personality* (pp. 206–239). New York: Guilford Press.

Finn, S. E., & Butcher, J. N. (1991). Clinical objective personality assessment. In M. Hersen, A. E. Kasdin, & A. S. Bellack (Eds.), *The clinical psychology handbook* (2nd ed., pp. 362–373). New York: Pergamon.

Gough, H. G. (1990). The California Psychological Inventory. In C. E. Watkins (Ed.), *Testing in counseling practice. Vocational psychology* (pp. 37–62). Hillsdale, NJ: Erlbaum.

Hogan, R., & Nicholson, R. A. (1988). The meaning of personality test scores. *American Psychologist, 43,* 621–626.

Keller, L. S., Butcher, J. N., & Slutske, W. S. (1990). Objective personality assessment. In G. Goldstein & M. Hersen (Eds.), *Handbook of psychological assessment* (2nd ed., pp. 345–386). New York: Pergamon Press.

McAdams, D. P. (1992). The five-factor model of personality: A critical appraisal. *Journal of Personality, 60,* 329–361.

Millon, T., & Davis, R. D. (1996). The Millon Clinical Multiaxial Inventory–III. In C. S. Newmark (Ed.), *Major psychological assessment instruments* (2nd ed., pp. 108–147). Needham Heights, MA: Allyn & Bacon.

6

Projective Techniques

As the song goes in one of the James Bond thrillers, "You only live twice, or so it seems; one life for yourself and one for your dreams." Certainly, most people spend at least some time dreaming, fantasizing about what might be—typically but not invariably pleasant fantasies. Often those flights of imagination are triggered by a sight or sound that is reminiscent of something and initiates the mental association process. In this imaginary excursion, desires are satisfied, problems are solved, and you become admired and loved. Like sleeping dreams, these waking fantasies often reveal more clearly the kind of person you are, or at least what you would like to be or to possess, than the persona that is donned to get you through the situation or the day with a modicum of disagreement and dissatisfaction.

BACKGROUND AND VARIETIES

Projective techniques often serve as the stimuli of fantasy, a fact that Alfred Binet and other pioneers in personality assessment undoubtedly realized. The concept of "projective test" actually has a psychoanalytic origin. In psychoanalytic theory, *projection* is an ego defense mechanism in which the ego "projects" feelings onto some other person or thing in the interest of protecting itself from conflict and anxiety. For example, an individual who has strong aggressive feelings toward another person but is unable to admit those feelings may decide that the person actually harbors hostile impulses toward him.

Except for the most automatic reflexes or simple habits, all behavior is projective: It is shaped to some extent by the desires, conflicts, and other idiosyncrasies of individual personality. This is as true of responses to an interviewer's questions and the form and content of personal documents (autobiographies, diaries, etc.) as it is of responses to inkblots and ambiguous pictures. However, the term *projective technique* has generally been reserved for a collection of formal assessment procedures that attempt to break down the examinee's resistance to self-revelation and get at the underlying, often unconscious, forces and factors that are reflected in behavior and personality.

History and Current Status

As originally coined by Lawrence K. Frank, the term *projective technique* refers to a procedure or device that makes use of the projection mechanism by evoking from a person "what is in various ways expressed in his private world and personality processes" (Frank, 1948, p. 42). More formally, Frank (1948) defined a projective technique as "a method of studying the personality by confronting the subject with a situation to which he will respond according to what the situation means to him and how he feels when so responding" (p. 46). Frank saw projective techniques as revealing a person's conscious and unconscious conflicts, desires, fears, needs, and ways of perceiving and responding to the world. This is especially true when the stimulus material is ambiguous and the response format relatively unstructured.

Francis Galton (1879) rather than Lawrence Frank is usually credited with having introduced the projective technique into psychological assessment. At the turn of the century, Galton's *word association* procedure of having people produce verbal associations to a series of stimulus words was adapted as a diagnostic and therapeutic tool by Emil Kraepelin and Carl Jung. During that same period, the seeds of two other projective techniques—sentence completions and verbal responses to pictures—were sown by Hermann Ebbinghaus and Alfred Binet, respectively.

Interest in the development and use of projective techniques proceeded rapidly from the 1920s to the 1950s, a period during which psychoanalysis had an increasing influence on psychiatry and clinical psychology. The Rorschach Inkblot Test, the Thematic Apperception Test, sentence completion tests, and many other projectives were widely administered in clinical and research contexts during and immediately following World War II. In the 1950s, however, interest in projectives began to decline. Among the events leading to this decline were psychoactive drug therapies, the community mental health movement, the increasing growth of biological psychiatry, in addition to economic problems and the availability of competing assessment techniques (Bellak, 1992; Elias, 1989). According to Bellak (1992), however, in the past few years there has been a resurgence of interest in projective techniques, and especially apperceptive techniques, such as the Thematic Apperception Test. A recent report by Watkins, Campbell, Nieberding, and Hallmark (1995) concludes that "although much ado has been made about the decline of and academics' negative opinions about projective techniques, from the standpoint of practice, all that truly appears to be much ado about nothing" (p. 54). Conversely, certain psychologists maintain that most projective techniques should no longer be used in clinical situations (Dawes, 1994).

Types of Projective Techniques

Descriptions of the most popular projective techniques for assessing personality are given in Appendix 6.1. As suggested by this list, apperception tests and sentence completions are the most numerous of all projectives. However, inkblot techniques, such as the Rorschach and the Holtzman, are also popular. Although not exhaustive, Appendix 6.1 is a fairly complete list of the projective techniques in print. In addition to identifying information and a brief description, documentation is provided concerning reviews of the instruments in the *Mental Measurements Yearbook* and *Test Critiques*.

The headings given in Appendix 6.1 may not be the best way of classifying projective techniques. Lindzey (1959), for example, grouped projective techniques into five categories according to the type of response required: association, construction, completions, arrangement, and expression. *Association techniques* consist of word associations, early memories, and the Rorschach Inkblot Test. *Construction techniques* include such instruments as the Thematic Apperception Test (TAT), the House–Tree–Person Technique (HTP), and the Make-a-Picture Story. Illustrative of *completion techniques* are sentence completion tests and the Rosenzweig Picture Frustration Study. With respect to *arrangement or selection techniques*, many older instruments, including the Szondi Test, the Tomkins-Horn Picture Arrangement Test, and the Kahn Test of Symbol Arrangement, are no longer commercially available. Examples of *expression techniques* include the Machover Draw-a-Person Test, handwriting analysis, finger painting, play activities of various sorts, and psychodrama. Many instruments and procedures in this last category are more appropriate for children than adults; the last three, for example, have also been used extensively in child therapy. In any event, we shall begin our review of projective techniques with two association, two construction, and two completion techniques, and proceed from there to a discussion of the two most popular types of projectives— inkblots and apperception techniques.

SIMPLER ASSOCIATION AND CONSTRUCTION TESTS

Word Associations

It has been said that language is the mirror of the soul. Whether or not it reflects our spiritual side, the way in which we express ourselves in words can certainly reveal a great deal about our culture, education, cognitive abilities, and personality. We can hide the real "us" by means of verbal window dressing, but how we think and what our sources of concern and contentment may be are often inadvertently revealed in how and what we speak and write.

As noted previously, the word association technique was pioneered by Francis Bacon and first employed clinically by Carl Jung as a method of detecting mental complexes and neurotic conflicts. A list of words, at least some of which were presumed to be related to the patient's particular situation and problems, was read aloud to the patient. After each word was read, the patient was supposed to respond as quickly as possible with the first word that came to mind. In theory, those words of significance to the patient's conflicts and problems should stimulate unconscious material, which might be expressed in the form of abnormal associations. Delayed responding and blocking (inability to produce associative response) were also considered to be indicative of an emotional reaction.

Although a special list of words may be devised for a particular patient, standard lists, such as the Kent–Rosanoff Free Association Test and the Revised Word List (Rapaport, Gill, & Schafer, 1946), have also been prepared. Variations on the word association technique, including delayed responding (Siipola, Walker, & Kolb, 1955) and Sutherland and Gill's (1970) combination of the word association and sentence completion techniques, have been devised. In addition, word associations have sometimes been used in conjunction with the polygraph ("lie detector test") to determine whether or not a person possesses information about a crime that he or she has not revealed to the authorities. Despite its continued use in research (Pons, 1989), psychodiagnostic applications of the word association technique have diminished considerably during the past few decades.

Early Recollections

Like the word association technique, clinical applications of the projective method of early recollections originated in psychodynamic therapy. This technique, proposed initially by Alfred Adler (Munroe, 1955), begins by instructing the examinee to relate the earliest, specific, concrete memories that he or she has. Respondents occasionally report experiences dating back to their early preschool years, but it is questionable whether adults can truly recall experiences they had before the age of 5 years. The events they do recall frequently involve emotional experiences, such as the following:

> I remember being on a train seated between my parents and I was bored and restless. I was looking through the window and all I saw was telephone poles and I wanted to get away but I was hemmed in and so I began to inch my way down without my parents knowing and I finally got to the floor and began to look around and I noticed the legs of people and I remember the smell of the floor and the dust there. And I began to move forward being careful not to let anyone know I was there. And I came upon an oil can; it was brass and shiny. And I picked it up and began to squirt oil on the shoes of a man. Suddenly the man cried out and he reached down and pulled me out. And the conductor came and picked me up while I was screaming and I was brought to my father who began to spank me. (Corsini & Marsella, 1983, p. 605)

The process of interpreting early memories is rather subjective and impressionistic, but it can be made more objective by determining the broad themes underlying the memories and the frame of reference reflected by them. A scoring scheme devised by Manaster and Perryman (1973) categorizes the content of early recollections into seven categories: characteristics, themes, concern with detail, setting, activity level, source of control, and emotion. Application of this scheme to the memory quoted previously yielded the following interpretation:

> You are a wanderer, and you move not only from place to place but also from person to person, a kind of Don Juan. You are easily bored and always restless, and on the go, and you want excitement and will do things in a mischievous manner to get excitement. However, you know you won't succeed in getting away with your mischief and you expect to be caught and to be punished. (Corsini & Marsella, 1983, p. 605)

Recently, several personality tests based on early memories have become commercially available. One such test is the Early Memories Procedure (by A. R. Bruhn; Western Psychological Services; Bruhn, 1995). Examinees, who may be 10 years old are older, are told to write down both their general and specific memories in a 32-page booklet or to record them electronically. Next, the examinee rates those memories according to a specified set of criteria, and then the examiner interprets the responses according to Bruhn's (1992) cognitive-perceptual model.

Public and professional interest in early memories that have supposedly been "hidden" for many years has recently been stimulated by reports of adults suddenly recalling emotionally disturbing and abusive acts that presumably occurred when they were children. An adult may remember being raped or beaten by a relative, seeing a friend abused or even murdered, or having some other traumatic childhood experience that has not been thought about or even recalled during the intervening years. However, a continuing question pertaining to these "recovered memories" is whether they represent events that actually occurred or are simply fantasies prompted by the persuasion and suggestions of psychotherapists or drugs ("Dubious Memories," 1994).

Construction Tests

Projective techniques of the construction type involve an analysis of the way in which a person orders, arranges, or in other ways puts something together. The construction may consist of drawings, the arrangement of figures, or any other manipulation task. One of the earliest examples of a figure construction test, which also has elements of a completion test, was provided by the famous artist Leonardo da Vinci. Leonardo presented ambiguous figures to prospective students and evaluated a student's imagination by the quality of the artistic form produced.

Although drawings of a human figure, arranging dolls, and similar types of activities have been employed more often as diagnostic and therapeutic devices with children, such procedures have also been used on occasion with adults. For example, while undergoing basic training in the U.S. Marine Corps in 1954, I took the Machover Draw-a-Person Test. This test, which entailed drawing a human figure on one side of a sheet of paper and a person of the opposite sex on the other side, was being used as a screening device to detect homosexuality or other "psychological problems" in recruits. The figure-drawing task had been a respected, supposedly culture-fair test of general mental ability for years, but it did not fare well in the assessment of personality.

Several variations on the draw-a-person theme have been published as assessment instruments. Two of these are the Kinetic Family Drawings (Burns & Kaufman, 1970, 1972) and the Draw a Person: Screening Procedure for Emotional Disturbance (DAP:SPED) (J. A. Naglieri, T. J. McNeish, & A. N. Bardos; CPPC). On the former test, the examinee is asked to draw a picture of his or her family doing something. The examinee is then asked to identify each family member in the drawing, indicate what the person is doing in the picture and why, and discuss the relationships of the family members with each other. On the DAP:SPED, which is designed for children, the examinee is required to draw a man, a woman, and the self. Two other construction tests with a somewhat better reputation than the Machover are the House–Tree–Person Technique (HTP) and the Bender Visual-Motor Gestalt Test (see Report 6.1).

House–Tree–Person Technique

The HTP, administered to either children or adults, was ranked by Craig and Horowitz (1990) as among the top 10 tests used by clinical and counseling psychologists. The task is fairly simple: to draw freehand pictures of a house, a tree, and a person on sheets of white paper. The house drawing is made with the sheet in landscape orientation; the tree and person pictures are drawn in the portrait orientation on opposite sides of the same sheet. After completing the drawings in pencil, the examinee is asked to draw a house, a tree, and a person with crayons. Lastly, the examinee is asked 20 descriptive and interpretive questions about each drawing. Although the drawings may be scored quantitatively on several variables (drive level and control, primary needs and assets, psychosexual satisfaction and conflicts, and interpersonal relationships and interenvironmental matters), they are usually interpreted impressionistically. Several books and manuals to facilitate this process are available from Western Psychological Services.

Because the house drawing is presumed to represent the examinee's home, it should arouse associations or perceptions about his or her home life and family relationships. In theory, the tree drawing reflects deeper, more unconscious feelings about the self. The condition of the tree is considered to be related to the examinee's vivacity or attitude toward life: A dead tree indicates emotional emptiness, a full-blown tree represents liveliness, a weeping willow tree suggests weakness, and a spiky tree connotes aggressiveness. The drawing of a person is said to represent the self and reflects a more conscious view of the examinee's self and his or her relationships with the environment. In a variation on the HTP technique, Burns (1987) has the respondent draw the house, the tree, and the person on the same page. In this procedure, designated the Kinetic House–Tree–Person Drawings (KHTP), the three drawings are often seen as being in dynamic interaction. Many of the analysis methods used by Burns and Kaufman (1970) in the Kinetic-Family-Drawing are applied to the analysis of the KHTP drawings.

REPORT 6.1 Diagnosis from a Drawing

During the Vietnam War, a Veterans Administration psychologist tested a young soldier who had accidentally shot himself in the leg with a .45 caliber pistol while practicing quick draw in the jungle. Surgeons found it necessary to amputate the soldier's leg from the knee down. He was quite depressed, and everyone assumed that he suffered from grief and guilt over his great personal tragedy. He was virtually mute and nearly untestable. He was persuaded to complete a series of figure drawings, however. In one drawing he depicted himself as a helicopter gunner, spraying bullets indiscriminately into the jungle below. When questioned about this drawing, he became quite animated and confessed that he relished combat. Guided by the possible implications of the morbid drawing, the psychologist sought to learn more about the veteran's attitudes toward combat. In the course of several interviews, the veteran revealed that he particularly enjoyed firing upon moving objects—animals, soldiers, civilians—it made no difference to him. Gradually, it became clear that the young veteran was an incipient war criminal who was depressed because his injury would prevent him from returning to the front lines. Needless to say, this information had quite an impact on the tenor of the psychological report.

From Gregory, R. J. *Psychological testing* (2nd ed.). Copyright 1996 by Allyn and Bacon. Reprinted by permission.

Despite its extensive use in clinical practice and research, representative norms are not available on the HTP. The reliability coefficients for the instrument are modest, and evidence for its validity is rather skimpy.

Hutt Adaptation of the Bender-Gestalt Test

This brief test, which was originally introduced as a measure of visual-motor coordination, requires the examinee to copy nine geometric designs presented individually on 4×6 inch white cards. The test is now used primarily to detect central nervous system impairment in children and adults, but the drawings can also be evaluated as projective responses. For example, exact reproductions are said to indicate obsessive-compulsive tendencies (Tolor & Schulberg, 1963) and figure reversals suggest negativism (Hutt, 1977).

In the Hutt Adaptation of the Bender-Gestalt Test, responses to nine designs similar to but more uniform in size than those on the original test, are evaluated by an objective approach, a projective approach, or a configurational analysis approach. The *objective approach* yields scores on a Psychopathology Scale and a Scale for Perceptual Adience-Abience. Scores on the Psychopathology Scale have been found to differentiate between normal and psychotic people but not between brain-damaged and chronic schizophrenic patients. A person's scores on the Perceptual Adience-Abience Scale reveals his or her perceptual orientation or style—openness (approach) versus closedness (avoidance).

In evaluating responses to the Hutt Adaptation by the *projective approach*, the drawings are examined for signs of the examinee's adaptation style, cognition, affect, areas of conflict, defensive methods, and maturational characteristics. The required data are obtained by having the examinee copy the designs, redraw them to make them more pleasing, and then saying what the originally copied and redrawn designs look like or suggest. In the last approach to analyzing the drawings from the Hutt Adaptation—*configurational analysis*, the drawings are examined for specific signs characteristic of brain damage, depression, mental retardation, psychoneuroses, and schizophrenia. Unfortunately, neither the projective approach nor the configurational analysis approach yields sufficiently valid data for making good diagnostic decisions. The objective approach has earned higher marks than the other two approaches, but the norms for all three approaches are based on relatively small samples of normal and mentally disordered groups. In a review of the Hutt Adaptation of the Bender-Gestalt Test, Sattler (1985) counseled extreme caution is using it as a projective technique.

COMPLETION TESTS

Sentence Completion Tests

One of the most popular and, according to Goldberg (1965), one of the most valid of all projective techniques for the purposes of psychodiagnosis and research is a sentence completion test. A typical sentence completion test consists of a set of 20 to 100 sentence fragments or stems; examinees are directed to complete each stem to make a complete, sensible sentence. Examples of stems designed to elicit attitudes, emotions, and conflicts are the following:

My greatest fear is _____.
I only wish my mother had _____.
The thing that bothers me most is _____.

Like word association tests, sentence completion tests can be devised for a particular patient, purpose, or situation.

Ebbinghaus introduced the sentence completion technique in 1897 as an intelligence test, but Payne (1928) and Tendler (1930) are credited with initiating its use in personality assessment. During World War II, sentence completion tests were designed for the psychological evaluation and selection of pilots, army officers and OSS candidates. They have also been applied extensively in personnel selection and clinical contexts.

Clinicians who use sentence completions for diagnostic purposes generally interpret the responses impressionistically and in combination with other data obtained on the respondent. The accuracy of these interpretations depends on the interpreter's experience and skill, and his or her understanding of the limits of the technique. An effective clinician possesses high interpersonal sensitivity and clinical judgment and is able to consider observational data, interview findings, and other psychometric information when formulating conclusions from the results of a sentence completion test.

Rabin and Zlotogorski (1981) describe the effective interpreter of sentence completions as attending to the affective tone (negative or positive) of the responses, the role of the examinee (active or passive), the form of the response (specific or qualified, imperative or declarative), temporal orientation (past, present, future), degree of commitment (wholehearted vs. hedging), degree of definiteness from one response to another (definite vs. vague), and variation in verbalization from one response to another. In addition to content aspects of the responses, noncontent features, such as the length of the completions, the use of personal pronouns, response times, verb/adjective ratio, range of words used, grammatical errors, and first word used, may be scored (Benton, Windle, & Erdice, 1957).

Numerous sentence completion tests are commercially available, 12 of which are described in Appendix 6.1. Of these, the Forer Structured Sentence Completion Test and the Rotter Incomplete Sentences Blank have been the most popular, although the Sentence Completion Tests and the Sentence Completion Series are the most versatile.

Rotter Incomplete Sentences Blank

The most carefully constructed and standardized of all sentence completion tests is the Rotter Incomplete Sentences Blank (2nd ed.) (RISB). Each of the three forms of the RISB—high school, college, and adult—contains 40 sentence fragments and takes approximately 30 minutes to complete. In the semiobjective scoring system, based on college norm groups, responses are rated on a 7-point scale for conflict (C) or unhealthy response (e.g., "I hate . . . almost everyone"); positive response (P) (e.g., "The best . . . is yet to come"); and neutral responses (N) (e.g., "Most girls . . . are females"). Failure to respond or a response that is too short to be meaningful counts as an omission. Overall scores range from 80 to 205 on a 0 to 240 scale. The case examples in the 1992 manual facilitate the scoring process, but, like other sentence completion tests, the RISB does not lend itself well to computer-based scoring.

The internal consistency reliabilities of scores on the RISB are high enough to justify its use, but the low to moderate test–retest coefficients indicate that the scores are not always reliable. Because it correctly classifies most examinees into adjusted and maladjusted categories, the RISB can serve as a useful screening device in clinical contexts. In general, it is viewed as a quick, efficient way of uncovering major conflicts, but, as Boyle (1995a) indicates in his review, the low reliabilities and certain deficiencies in the manual are causes for concern.

Rosenzweig Picture Frustration Study

Another widely respected projective instrument of the completion type, but one with limited clinical use, is the Rosenzweig Picture Frustration Study (P-F). Like the Children and Adolescent forms, the Adult form of this instrument consists of 24 comic-strip pictures in an eight-page booklet. Each picture shows two people, the one on the left saying something that is presumably frustrating to the one on the right or that describes the frustrating situation. The examinee is instructed to write in the space ("balloon") above the head of the person on the right the first verbal response that this person might make. After the examinee has responded to all items, a posttest interrogation or inquiry is conducted to facilitate classification and interpretation of responses. Responses are interpreted, following a psychodynamic framework, according to Direction and Type of Aggression expressed. *Extraggression* (E-A, outwardly or toward the environment), *intraggression* (I-A, inwardly or toward oneself), and *imagggression* (M-A, avoidance or nonexpression of aggression) are the three Direction of Aggression categories. *Obstacle-dominance* (O-D, the frustrating object stands out), *etho-defense* (E-D, the examinee's ego predominates to defend itself), and *need-persistence* (N-P, the goal is pursued despite the frustration) are the three Type of Aggression categories. The scores on these six variables are combined to yield nine factors and a total of 15 scores. A Group Conformity Rating, indicating correspondence between the examinee's responses and those given most frequently by the norm group, and a Trends score reflecting changes in responses from the first to the second half of the test may also be determined. Responses may also be interpreted impressionistically.

The percentage agreement in scoring the nine factors on the P-F test is reported as approximately 85, but the split-half and test–retest reliabilities of these factors are mostly in the .50s and .60s. Recognized as the premier test for research on frustration, the P-F test has been used for nearly a half-century throughout the world. P-F scores are related to age trends, cultural differences, hypnotizability, scores on other personality tests, psychiatric reports, sex differences, and various physiological measures. Be that as it may, the norms for adults are dated, and there are problems with the way the scores are interpreted (Wagner, 1985).

RORSCHACH AND OTHER INKBLOT TESTS

Ambiguous figures and other visual stimuli have been used informally as projective devices since time immemorial. For example, two of the characters in Shakespeare's play *Hamlet* have a conversation concerning what they see in clouds:

> *Hamlet*: Do you see yonder cloud, that's almost in shape of a camel?
>
> *Polonius*: By the mass, and 't is like a camel, indeed.
>
> *Hamlet*: Methinks, it is like a weasel.
>
> *Polonius*: It is backed like a weasel.
>
> *Hamlet*: Or, like a whale?
>
> *Polonius*: Very like a whale.
>
> —*Hamlet*, Act III, Scene II

Pictures of clouds were actually employed in one early projective, test, the Cloud Picture Test of Wilhelm Stern.

The Rorschach Psychodiagnostic Technique, published initially by Hermann Rorschach in 1921, consists of a set of ten inkblots, each on a 5 1/2- × 9 1/2-inch white card. Most of the blots are symmetrical, with those on cards I, IV, V, VI, and VII being achromatic and those on cards II, III, VIII, IX, and X multicolored. The assumption on which the test is based is that responses to the ambiguous shapes formed by the blots are affected by the needs and conflicts of the respondents and their own idiosyncratic manner of perceiving and organizing the environment.

Administering the Rorschach

Administering the Rorschach consists of presenting one card at a time to the examinee, who views it at approximately arm's length and can turn it any way that he or she likes. The first part of the testing procedure is the *association* phase, in which the examinee is asked to tell what he or she sees in each blot or what it represents. The examiner records the examinee's oral responses, the response time, and the way in which the card is held. After the association phase has been completed, an *inquiry* phase, in which the examiner attempts to discover what features of the blot determined each response, is conducted. From the examinee's responses to direct questions and suggestions, the examiner decides whether form, color, shading, animal or inanimate movement, or some other *determinant* influenced the perception. A third, final phase known as *testing the limits* may also be conducted to determine whether certain aspects of the blot could possibility have influenced a percept.

Scoring and Interpreting Rorschach Responses

Several *systems* for scoring and interpreting Rorschach responses have been proposed over the years. The Beck and Klopfer systems were the most popular in the United States until the past two decades. In recent years, John Exner's *comprehensive system* for Rorschach scoring and interpretation has replaced most of the older systems (Exner, 1993). This system represents an integration of the other Rorschach systems. *Structural* components of Rorschach responses are emphasized, although *content* components also play a role in the interpretation. The two main structural categories are location and determinant. *Location* is where on the blot the percept is seen: in the blot as a whole, as a common or uncommon detail, or in the white space. Use of the blot as a whole is coded as *W*; a large, well-defined, common detail is coded as *D*, and an uncommon detail is coded as *Dd*. Use of the white space in the percept is coded as *WS, DS,* or *DdS*, depending on whether the white space involved the blot as a whole, a common detail, or an uncommon detail, respectively. For example, responses such as "a butterfly" to card I, "a monster" to card IV, or a "a bat" to card V are coded as *W*.

Exner's coding system for the various *determinants*—what aspects of the blot determined the response—is described in Table 6.1, and his list of content codes is given in Table 6.2. The content of a response is also coded as popular (*P*) or original (*O*). Popular responses include such percepts as bat or butterfly on cards I and V, the head of an animal on cards II, human figures on cards III and IV, an animal skin or hide on card VI, a human head or face on card VII, a whole animal figure on card VIII, human or human-like figures on card IX, and a spider or crab on card X. Depending on the particular card, these responses may involve the whole blot or a specific detail.

A final coding of Rorschach responses is according to whether they are "popular" or "original." Popular responses (P) are indicative of conventional thinking or good contact with reality. A list of popular responses to the ten Rorschach cards is given in Table 6.3.

TABLE 6.1 Rorschach Determinant Coding

Form (F). To be used separately for responses based exclusively on form features of the blot, or in combination with other determinant symbols (*except M* and *m*) when the form features have contributed to the formulation of the answer.

Human movement (M). To be used for responses involving the kinesthetic activity of a human, or of an animal or fictional character in human-like activity.

Animal movement (FM). To be used for responses involving a kinesthetic activity of an animal. The movement perceived must be congruent to the species identified in the content. Animals reported in movement not common to their species should be coded as *M*.

Inanimate movement (m). To be used for responses involving the movement of inanimate, inorganic, or insensate objects.

Pure color (C). To be used for answers based exclusively on the chromatic color features of the blot. *No* form is involved.

Color-form (CF). To be used for answers that are formulated primarily because of the chromatic color features of the blot. Form features are used, but are of secondary importance.

Color naming (Cn). To be used when the colors of the blot or blot areas are identified by *name*, with the intention of giving a response.

Pure achromatic color (C'). To be used when the response is based exclusively on the gray, black, or white features of the blot, when they are clearly used as color. *No* form is involved.

Achromatic color-form (C'F). To be used for responses that are formulated *mainly* because of the black, white, or gray features, clearly used as color. Form features *are* used, but are of secondary importance.

Form-achromatic color (FC'). To be used for answers that are based *mainly* on the form features. The achromatic features, clearly used as color, are also included, but are of secondary importance.

Pure texture (T). To be used for answers in which the shading components of the blot are translated to represent a tactual phenomenon, with no consideration to the form features.

Texture-form (TF). To be used for responses in which the shading features of the blot are interpreted as tactual, and form is used secondarily, for purposes of elaboration or clarification.

Form-texture (FT). To be used for responses that are based *mainly* on the form features. Shading features of the blot are translated as tactual but are of secondary importance.

Pure vista (V). To be used for answers in which the shading features are interpreted as depth or dimensionality. No form is involved.

Vista-form (VF). To be used for responses in which the shading features are interpreted as depth or dimensionality. Form features are included, but are of secondary importance.

Form-vista (FV). To be used for answers that are based *mainly* on the form features of the blot. Shading features are also interpreted to note depth or dimensionality, but are of secondary importance to the formulation of the answer.

Pure shading (Y). To be used for responses that are based exclusively on the light-dark features of the blot that are completely formless and do not involve reference to either texture or dimension.

Shading-form (YF). To be used for responses based primarily on the light-dark features of the blot. Form features are included but are of secondary importance.

(Continued)

TABLE 6.1 *(Continued)*

Form-shading (FY). To be used for responses that are based *mainly* on the form features of the blot. The light-dark features of the blot are included as elaboration or clarification and are secondary to the use of form.

Form based dimension (FD). To be used for answers in which the impression of depth, distance, or dimensionality is created by using the elements of size or shape of contours. No use of shading is involved in creating this impression.

Pair ([2]). To be used for answers in which two identical objects are reported, based on the symmetry of the blot. The objects must be equivalent in all respects, but must *not* be identified as being reflected or as mirror images.

Reflection-form (rF). To be used for answers in which the blot or blot area is reported as a reflection or mirror image, because of the symmetry of the blot. The object or content reported has no specific form requirements, as in clouds, landscape, shadows, etc.

Form-reflection (Fr). To be used for answer in which the blot or blot area is identified as reflected or a mirror image, based on the symmetry of the blot. The substance of the response is based on form features, and the object report has a specific form demand.

Source: Exner (1993, pp. 104–105). Adapted by permission.

TABLE 6.2 Rorschach Content Coding

Whole human (H). Whole human form. If the percept involves real historical figures, such as Napoleon, Joan of Arc, etc., the content coded *Ay* should be added as a secondary code.

Whole human (fictional or mythological) ([H]). Whole human form that is fictional or mythological, such as clowns, fairies, giants, witches, fairy tale characters, ghosts, dwarfs, devils, angels, science fictional creatures that are humanoid, human-like monsters.

Human detail (Hd). Incomplete human form, such as an arm, leg, fingers, feet, the lower part of a person, and a person without a head.

Human detail (fictional or mythological) ([Hd]). Incomplete human form that is fictional or mythological, such as the head of the devil, the arm of a witch, the eyes of an angel, parts of science fiction creatures that are humanoid, and all masks.

Human experience (Hx). Human emotion or sensory experience, such as love, hate, depression, happiness, sound, smell, fear, etc. Most answers in which *Hx* is coded will also include the use of *AB* as a special score.

Whole animal (A). Whole animal form.

Whole animal (fictional or mythological ([A]). A whole animal that is fictional or mythological, such as a unicorn, dragon, magic frog, flying horse, Black Beauty, and Jonathan Livingston Seagull.

Animal detail (Ad). An incomplete animal form, such as the hoof of a horse, claw of a lobster, head of a dog, and animal skin.

Animal detail (fictional or mythological) ([Ad]). An incomplete animal form that is fictional or mythological, such as the wing of Pegasus, the head of Peter Rabbit, and the leg of Pooh Bear.

Anatomy (An). Skeletal, muscular, or internal anatomy, such as bone structure, rib cage, heart, lungs, stomach, liver, muscle fiber, vertebrae, and brain. If the response involves a tissue slide, the code *Art* should be added as secondary.

(Continued)

TABLE 6.2 *(Continued)*

Art (Art). Paintings, drawings, or illustrations, either abstract or definitive, art objects, such as statues, jewelry, chandelier, candelabra, crests, badges, seals, and decorations.

Anthropology (Ay). Objects with a specific cultural or historical connotation, such as a totem, Roman helmet, Magna Carta, Santa Maria, Napoleon's hat, Cleopatra's crown, arrowhead, and prehistoric axe.

Blood (Bl). Blood, either human or animal.

Botany (Bt). Any plant life, such as bushes, flowers, seaweed, trees, or parts of plant life such as leaves, petals, tree trunk, roots.

Clothing (Cg). Any article of clothing, such as hat, boots, belt, necktie, jacket, trousers, and scarf.

Clouds (Cl). Used specifically for the content cloud. Variations of this category, such as fog or mist are coded *Na*.

Explosion (Ex). A blast or explosion, including fireworks.

Fire (Fi). Fire or smoke.

Food (Fd). Any edible, such as fried chicken, ice cream, fried shrimp, vegetables, cotton candy, chewing gum, steak, a filet of fish.

Geography (Ge). A map, specified or unspecified.

Household (Hh). Household items, such as bed, chair, lamp, silverware, plate, cup, glass, cooking utensil, carving knife, lawn chair, garden hose, and rug (excluding animal skin rug, which is coded *Ad*).

Landscape (Ls). Landscape, such as mountain, mountain range, hill, island, cave, rocks, desert, swamp, or seascapes, such as coral reef or underwater scene.

Nature (Na). Used for a broad variety of contents from the natural environment, that are not coded as *Bt* or *Ls*, such as sun, moon, planet, sky, water, ocean, river, ice, snow, rain, fog, mist, rainbow, storm, tornado, night, and raindrop.

Science (Sc). Percepts that are associated with, or are the products of science or science fiction, such as microscope, telescope, weapons, rocket ships, motors, space ships, ray guns, airplane, ship, train, car, motorcycle, light bulb, television aerial, and radar station.

Sex (Sx). Sex organs or activity of a sexual nature, such as penis, vagina, buttocks, breast (except if used to delineate a female figure), testes, menstruation, abortion, intercourse. *Sx* is usually scored as a secondary content. Primary contents are typically *H*, *Hd*, or *An*.

X-ray (Xy). Used specifically for the content of X-ray and may include either skeletal or organs. When *Xy* is coded, *An* is not included as a secondary code.

Source: Exner (1993, pp. 158–159). Adapted by permission.

After all responses have been coded, a *structural summary* of location features, determinants, form quality, contents, organizational activity, populars, pairs and reflections, and special scoring indices is prepared.[1] The various ratios, percentages, and derivations incorporated in the structural summary are grouped into several sections: core, ideation, affect, mediation, processing, interpersonal, and self-perception (see Exner, 1993, pp. 183–188). The completion of a structural summary is the first step in the process of interpreting a Rorschach protocol. The interpretation process typically focuses on the maturity and complexity

TABLE 6.3 Rorschach Popular Responses

Card I.	Bat or butterfly; always involves the whole blot.
Card II.	Animal forms, usually heads of dogs, bears, elephants, or lambs.
Card III.	Two human figures, or representations thereof, such as dolls and caricatures.
Card IV.	Human or human-like figure, such as a giant, monster, science fiction creature, etc.
Card V.	Butterfly or bat, including the whole blot; the apex of the card upright or inverted.
Card VI.	Animal skin, hide, rug, or pelt.
Card VII.	Human head or face, specifically identified as female, child, Indian, or with gender not identified.
Card VIII.	Whole animal figure. The content varies considerably, such as a bear, dog, rodent, fox, wolf, and coyote.
Card IX.	Human or human-like figures, such as witches, giants, science fiction creatures, monsters, etc.
Card X.	Spider or crab with all appendages restricted to a specified area (D1). Other variations of multilegged animals are not coded as P (popular responses).

Source: Exner (1993, p. 162). Adapted by permission.

of the respondent's thought processes, contact with reality, affect or mood, coping styles and defense mechanisms, and effectiveness of interpersonal functioning. Predominant emotions (anxiety, depression, mania, etc.), sources of conflict, self-orientation, psychopathic behavior, and schizophrenic ideation are also important to note. Finally, a (tentative) diagnosis and a prognosis may also be formulated if desired.

Among the simpler indexes in a Rorschach protocol is the total number of responses, the number of good whole (W) responses, the number of color responses ($C + CF + Cn + C' + C'F + FC'$), the number of movement responses ($M + FM + m$), the number of shading responses (T + TF + FT + V + VF + FV + Y + YF + FY), the number of popular responses (P), and the number of white-space responses (S). The total number of responses to the 10 inkblots is one of the most reliable scores and a rough index of cognitive ability; several good whole responses also point to integrated or organized thinking. Original responses with good form are consistent with high cognitive ability, but many original responses with poor form, especially when combined with other signs of confused thinking, suggest a psychotic process. Color responses suggest emotionality and impulsivity, movement responses reveal imagination, and shading responses are indicative of self-control. Many color responses may be indicative of mania, and few color and movement responses are consistent with a diagnosis of depression. White-space responses are considered indicative of oppositional tendencies.

Of particular importance in the structural summary is *experience balance* (EB), computed as the ratio of all human movement responses to the weighted sum of the chromatic color responses. The EB ratio is said to be related to the degree to which the respondent is thought-minded rather than action oriented. A preponderance of human movement responses is more characteristic of an introversive personality, whereas many color responses is indicative of an extroversive personality. Another index included in the structural summary is the *form-color ratio*, which is interpreted as an indicator of the extent to which the respondent is controlled by cognition rather than emotion. Among the other ratios or indexes included in a structural summary are the active:passive ratio, the intellectualization index, the affective ratio, the complexity index, the economy index, the aspirational ratio, the egocentricity index, the schizophrenic index, the depression index, the coping deficit index, the suicide constellation, the hypervigilance index, and the obsessive style index (see Exner, 1993, pp. 183–188).

Also important in the structural interpretation of the Rorschach are the speed and accuracy of the responses. Delays in responding suggest anxiety, and degree of accuracy—how well the responses fit the respective parts of the blots (good, poor, indeterminate)—can be helpful in diagnosing psychopathology. An analysis of the sequence of responses, comments made during the test, and other observed behaviors may also contribute to an understanding of the personality and problems of the respondent (Hurt, Reznikoff, & Clarkin, 1995).

Some clinicians eschew structural interpretation of the Rorschach and concentrate exclusively on content, using the Rorschach test as a kind of semistructured interviewed. Content interpretation, which is admittedly a rather subjective process and of questionable reliability, is typically guided by a psychodynamic perspective. Unreal characters, such as ghosts and clowns, are considered to be indicative of an inability to identify with real people. Masks are interpreted as role playing to avoid exposure, food is interpreted as dependency needs or emotional hunger, death as loneliness and depression, and eyes as sensitivity to criticism. The content of responses to the 10 Rorschach cards may be varied. For example, the person on whom Report 6.2 was generated gave two "fire" responses and one response each of "man, women, girls, monster, penis, face, genitals, beetle, bird, monster-animal, skin-animal, intestines, blood, leaf, stump, shoes, cap, boots, hat, cracker, rock."

Computer-Based Interpretation of the Rorschach

Several computer-based test interpretation programs for the Rorschach have been constructed. One interpretive service, Version 3 of the Rorschach Interpretation Assistance Program, was devised by J. E. Exner and K. S. C. Tuttle and is available through Psychological Assessment Resources and The Psychological Corporation. In addition to responses to the Rorschach cards, this service accepts behavioral, cognitive, and interpersonal data, as well as information on the client's physical symptoms and complaints in order to personalize the interpretive hypotheses generated by the program. The interpretive report begins with a series of tables consisting of "Subject Information," "Sequence of Scores," "Summary of Approach," "Structural Summary," "Constellations Table," and "Summary of Response Contents." Then the scores and the corresponding narrative descriptions are presented in seven clusters: Ideation, Cognitive Mediation, Information Processing, Capacity for Control and Tolerance for Stress, Affect, Self Perception, and Interpersonal Perception and Relations. The report is completed with a general interpretive summary (see Report 6.2).

Evaluation of the Rorschach

When judged by conventional psychometric criteria—reliability, validity, standardization, etc., the Rorschach does not fare very well. Research studies have found it to be susceptible to the faking of psychosis (Albert, Fox, & Kahn, 1980; Netter & Viglione, 1994), and the findings of reliability and validity studies have frequently been discouraging. To be fair, the results of some reliability studies have been promising (Thomas, Alinsky, & Exner, 1982; Haller & Exner, 1985), especially when they are based on Exner's comprehensive system (Exner & Andronikof-Sanglade, 1992; Ornberg & Zalewski, 1994). Though far from uniformly positive, the results of certain investigations of the validity of the Rorschach have also been encouraging (Reznikoff, Aronow, & Rauchway, 1982; Zubin, Eron, & Schumer, 1965). But as Peterson (1978) pointed out many years ago, "the general lack of predictive validity for the Rorschach raises serious question about its continued use in clinical practice" (p. 662).

Despite its psychometric deficiencies, the Rorschach continues to be the most popular of all projective techniques. Most practicing clinical psychologists and psychiatrists, who tend to prefer a more impressionistic, idiographic method of analyzing human behavior, still consider the Rorschach to be the centerpiece of a comprehensive clinical evaluation. Although many psychologists have noted that projective testing is not as important as it once was, most doctoral-level training programs in clinical psychology still include formal instruction in the Rorschach. It remains one of the most frequently used personality assessment methods in clinical situations and second only to the MMPI in terms of

REPORT 6.2 Synopsis of a Rorschach Interpretation Assistance Program Report

---

Client: John Jones   *Gender:* Male   *Date of Birth:* 11/12/58
Age: 35   *Education:* 16   *Marital Status:* Married   *Test Date:* 8/8/94

Ideation

His protocol contains many features similar to those found among schizophrenics. It appears likely that his thinking is seriously disturbed. He lacks a marked stylistic approach to decision making or problem solving. Apparently, he does not react very much to subtle ideational stimuli, that is, those not in the focus of attention, as is common in people. He tends to react hastily to demands created by such stimuli.

Cognitive Mediation

He has some chronic and pervasive problems that promote perceptual inaccuracy and/or mediational distortion. His peculiarities in thinking often lead to considerable perceptual inaccuracy, which, in turn, creates an impairment in reality testing.

Information Processing

He is hypervigilant, investing considerable energy to maintain a state of hyperalertness. His processing activity includes an overincorporative style. Some of his processing is not very thorough and seems to reflect a conservative motivation. The quality of his processing generally appears to be similar to that of most others. However, the quality of his processing activity falters significantly at times to an unsophisticated, less mature level. His processing habits tend to be regular and predictable.

Capacity for Control and Tolerance for Stress

This person has a sturdier tolerance for stress and is far less likely to experience problems in control than the average person.

Affect

His emotions are not consistent in the way in which they influence his thinking, problem solving, and decision making behaviors. He has a marked tendency to avoid emotional stimuli. He is very lax about modulating or controlling his emotions. When lapses occur in the modulation of his emotional displays, the resulting behaviors are likely to be inappropriate and potentially maladaptive. His level of psychological complexity is not unlike that of others of this age who have a similar approach to decision making.

Self Perception

His estimate of his personal worth tends to be more negative than should be the case. He appears to engage in self inspection more often than most people. His self image and/or self value tend to be based largely on imaginary rather than real experience.

Interpersonal Perception and Relations

He has a hypervigilant style, which is a core element of his psychological structure. It is likely that he will manifest many more dependency behaviors than usually is expected. His interest in, and expectations concerning needs for closeness are dissimilar to those of most people. He appears to be as interested in others as much as most people. He is apparently quite insecure about his personal integrity and tends to be overly authoritarian or argumentative when interpersonal situations appear to pose challenges to the self. It is likely that much of his interpersonal behavior will be marked by forcefulness and/or aggressiveness that is usually obvious to the frequent observer.

General Summary

He has serious problems in thinking and perceptual accuracy. This composite is markedly similar to that found among schizophrenics. The likelihood that a schizophrenic picture has been produced by some alternative condition is remote, but could occur if he is currently suffering from toxicity or is actively psychotic due to some other condition. In that he is also hypervigilant, the schizophrenic, toxic, or psychotic state will be marked by noticeable paranoid features.

   He is very lax about controlling his emotional displays. He is not very consistent in his problem solving or decision making behaviors. This lack of consistency makes him less efficient in his everyday life and more prone to make judgmental errors. He tends to regard himself less favorably when he compares himself to others. His conception of himself is not well developed and is probably rather distorted. A hypervigilant style forms a core element of his personality. He uses considerable energy to maintain a state of preparedness. This hyperalert state has its origins in a very negative or mistrusting attitude toward people. He is cautious about interpersonal relations and does not usually anticipate being close to others. He seems to be reasonably interested in people. He probably is more aggressive or forceful than most people in his relations with others.

Excerpted from pages 74–81 of RIAP 3™ Plus Rorschach Interpretation Assistance Program™ by John E. Exner, Jr., Ph.D. Copyright © 1976, 1985, 1990, 1994, 1995 by Psychological Assessment Resources, Inc. Reprinted by permission.

research citations (Butcher & Rouse, 1996). Exner's Comprehensive System has provided a more objective and reliable basis for interpreting Rorschach responses, but better information on the accuracy of the diagnoses proposed by users of the test is needed. Without such data one is forced to rely on expert opinion and belief.

Holtzman Inkblot Test

The Rorschach has undergone many modifications in administration procedure, scoring, and interpretation. There is the consensus Rorschach for couples and family therapy (Klopfer, 1984), the Rorschach Prognostic Rating Scale for evaluating the outcomes of psychotherapy (Garwood, 1977; Shields, 1978), and other approaches (Blatt & Berman, 1984). In addition, entirely new inkblot tests have been designed to be more objective and more psychometrically sound than the Rorschach. Such is the Holtzman Inkblot Test (HIT). The 45 inkblots on each of the two forms (A and B) of the HIT were selected on the basis of their high split-half reliabilities and their ability to differentiate between normal and pathological responses. Examinees are limited to one response per blot, a restriction that increases the discrimination among comparisons of the content, determinants, and other structural features in interpreting responses to the blots. The HIT blots are more varied in color, form, and shading than those on the Rorschach: Some are symmetrical, and some have colors and different visual textures.

The HIT is usually administered to one individual at a time, but group-administration by means of a projector is possible. After each response, the examinees are asked to indicate where the percept was seen and what about the blot suggested that percept. Responses are scored on the following variables:

Reaction Time (Form A only)	Integration
Rejection	Content (human, animal, anatomy,
Location	sex, abstract)
Space	Anxiety
Form Definiteness	Hostility
Form Appropriateness	Barrier
Color	Penetration
Shading	Balance (Form A only)
Movement	Popular
Pathognomic Verbalization	

Scores on these variables are converted to percentile norms based on over 1,400 people ranging in age from 5 years to adulthood, consisting of normal, schizophrenic, depressive, and mentally retarded individuals. Because the construction and standardization procedure for this test were more like those for a personality inventory than a typical projective test, the reliability of HIT scores are higher than those of the Rorschach. Split-half reliabilities are in the .70s and .80s and interscorer agreement indexes in the .90s. The scores are related to developmental level in children and have found use in the differential diagnosis of psychopathology.

Despite the fact that it is psychometrically superior to the Rorschach, the HIT has not been widely adopted by clinicians. This instrument represents a noteworthy effort to construct an inkblot test with respectable psychometric properties, but it has not and undoubtedly will not replace the Rorschach. A new version, the HIT 25, requires two responses to each of 25 cards selected from Form A. This variant of the HIT shows promise in schizophrenic diagnoses (Holtzman, 1988).

TAT AND OTHER APPERCEPTION TESTS

A generally accepted psychological principle is that personality affects perception: Our needs and characteristic ways of thinking and acting organize and give meaning to our sense impressions. Depending on the similarities between our genetic structure and experiences and those of other people, the meanings that we attribute to what we see, hear, smell, taste, and feel are somewhat different from those of others. Psychoanalysts have emphasized the importance of defense mechanisms, such as projection and identification in determining how we perceive our world in a psychosocial sense. The operation of identification is particularly apparent in how we interpret and appreciate plays, films, novels, and other stories involving people whose lives and problems can be imagined as our own.

An example of a now discredited projective test that presumably appealed to the mechanism of identification is the Szondi Test. It consisted of six sets of photographs, eight pictures per set, of psychiatric patients who had been diagnosed as hysterics, catatonics, paranoids, depressed, manic, and so on. People who took the Szondi were told to select from each set the two pictures that they liked most and the two they liked least. The assumption was that the needs and personality of people who take this test are related to those of the patients depicted in the photographs, and that people prefer the photographs of patients who are most like them and reject those who are least like them.

The identification mechanism also has an influence on stories told about ambiguous pictures. The use of pictures and stories in the assessment of personality, in particular with children, goes back to the beginning of the century. Most of these *apperception tests* consist of pictures of people or animals, but one is composed of pictures of hands (Hand Test) and another of auditory stimuli (Auditory Apperception Test). One of the first published picture story tests was Van Lennep's Four Picture Test, but the Thematic Apperception Test (TAT) became the second most popular projective test among clinical practitioners and personality researchers in the United States.

The TAT, published initially by Morgan and Murray in 1935 and later by Murray (1938, 1943), consists of 30 white cards containing black-and-white pictures and one blank card (see Table 6.4). Each picture is a drawing of one or more persons in an ambiguous situation. From the entire set, 20 pictures can be selected that are appropriate for adult males (M), adult females (F), boys (B), girls (G), or a combination. Typically, however, only 10 picture cards are administered to a particular person.

TABLE 6.4 Descriptions of TAT Pictures

Picture 1. A young boy is contemplating a violin that rests on a table in front of him.

Picture 2. Country scene: In the foreground is a young woman with books in her hand; in the background a man is working in the fields and an older woman is looking on.

Picture 3BM. On the floor against a couch is the huddled form of a boy with his head bowed on his right arm. Beside him on the floor is a revolver.

Picture 3GF. A young woman is standing with downcast head, her face covered with her right hand. Her left arm is stretched forward against a wooden door.

Picture 4. A woman is clutching the shoulders of a man whose face and body are averted as if he were trying to pull away from her.

Picture 5. A middle-aged women is standing on the threshold of a half-opened door looking into a room.

Picture 6BM. A short elderly women stands with her back turned to a tall young man. The latter is looking downward with a perplexed expression.

Picture 6GF. A young women sitting on the edge of a sofa looks back over her shoulder at an older man with a pipe in his mouth who seems to be addressing her.

Picture 7. A gray-haired man is looking at a younger man who is sullenly staring into space.

Picture 7GF. An older woman is sitting on a sofa close beside a girl, speaking or reading to her. The girl, who holds a doll in her lap, is looking away.

Picture 8BM. An adolescent boy looks straight out of the picture. The barrel of a rifle is visible at one side, and in the background is the dim scene of a surgical operation, like a reverie image.

Picture 8GF. A woman sits with her chin in her hand looking off into space.

Picture 9BM. Four men in overalls are lying on the grass taking it easy.

Picture 9GF. A young woman with a magazine and a purse in her hand looks from behind a tree at another young woman in a party dress running along a beach.

Picture 10. A young woman's head against a man's shoulder.

Picture 11. A road skirting a deep chasm between high cliffs. On the road in the distance are obscure figures. Protruding from the rocky wall on one side are the long head and neck of a dragon.

Picture 12M. A young man is lying on a couch with his eyes closed. Leaning over him is the gaunt form of an elderly man, his hand stretched out above the face of the reclining figure.

Picture 12F. The portrait of a young woman. A weird old woman with a shawl over her head is grimacing in the background.

Picture 12BG. A rowboat is drawn up on the bank of a woodland stream. There are no human figures in the picture.

Picture 13MF. A young man is standing with downcast head buried in his arm. Behind him is the figure of a woman lying in bed.

Picture 13B. A little boy is sitting on the doorstep of a log cabin.

Picture 13G. A little girl is climbing a winding flight of stairs.

Picture 14. The silhouette of a man (or woman) against a bright window. The result of the picture is totally black.

Picture 15. A gaunt man with clenched hands is standing among gravestones.

Picture 16. Blank.

(Continued)

TABLE 6.4 (Continued)

Picture 17BM. A naked man is clinging to a rope. He is in the act of climbing up or down.

Picture 17GF. A bridge over water. A female figure leans over the railing. In the background are tall buildings and small figures of men.

Picture 18BM. A man is clutched from behind by three hands. The figures of his antagonists are invisible.

Picture 18GF. A woman has her hands squeezed around the throat of another woman whom she appears to be pushing backward across the banister of a stairway.

Picture 19. A weird picture of cloud formations overhanging a snow-covered cabin in the country.

Picture 20. The dimly illuminated figure of a man (or women) in the dead of night leaning against a lamppost.

From Bellak, Leopold. *The T.A.T., C.A.T., and S.A.T. in clinical use.* Copyright © 1993 by Allyn and Bacon. Adapted by permission.

Administering the TAT

The directions for administering the TAT are simple: The examinee is told to make up a story, telling what's going on now, what happened before, and how it will turn out. According to Karon (1981), the following directions are satisfactory:

> I'm going to show you a set of ten pictures, one at a time. I want you to tell me what is going on, what the characters might be feeling and thinking, what led up to it, and what the outcome might be. In other words, tell me a good story.

The examiner then presents each card and writes down the story told in response to it. For example, the following story was told by a your woman in response to picture 12F. This picture shows a young woman in the foreground and a weird old woman with a shawl over her head grimacing in the background.

> This is a woman who has been quite troubled by memories of a mother she was resentful toward. She has feelings of sorrow for the way she treated her mother; her memories of her mother plague her. These feelings seem to be increasing as she grows older and sees her own children treating her the same way as she treated her mother. She tries to convey the feeling to her children, but does not succeed in changing their attitudes. She is living the past in her present, because this feeling of sorrow and guilt is reinforced by the way her children are treating her.

Such "family" stories are typical of responses to the pictures on the TAT, which has been considered useful in analyzing family relationships.

After all cards have been presented, a follow-up inquiry may be conducted to determine if the examinee has followed the instructions properly and if the stories include the three As—action, antecedents, and aftermath—as well as the thoughts and feelings of the characters. Although not the standard procedure, the TAT cards can be self-administered or administered to a group of people simultaneously by having them write down their stories.

Scoring and Interpreting TAT Stories

As with other projective tests, it is assumed in analyzing TAT stories that the examinee has projected his or her own needs, desires, and conflicts into the story and its characters. A number of formal scoring systems have been devised, the oldest being Henry Murray's (1943). This scoring system consists of identifying the *needs*, trends, and feelings of the characters (especially the "hero" of the story), the inimical or benign environmental forces (*press*) impinging upon them, the happy or unhappy *outcomes* of the stories and whether they were the results of actions by the hero or environmental forces, the predominant *themas* in the stories, and the *interests* and *sentiments* expressed in them (see Table 6.5). The interpretation process begins with the identification of the character(s) (the "heroes") in which the storyteller is most interested. Next to be determined are the personalities of the heroes, including what they feel, what their motives are, what unusual or unique characteristics they possess, what their needs are, and how those needs are satisfied. The third step in Murray's analysis consists of an assessment of the physical and interpersonal environment of the hero, and the fourth step involves an analysis of the relative strengths of the hero and the press. The fifth step entails the consideration of simple and complex themas, and the sixth and last step is an evaluation of interests and sentiments (Aiken, 1995, pp. 360–362).

Though systems for formal scoring of TAT stories abound and continue to be developed (Hibbard et al., 1994; Ronan, Colavito, & Hammontree, 1993; Ronan, Date, & Weisbrod, 1995), most clinicians who administer the test do not employ a formal scoring system. Rather, they interpret the stories impressionistically and in light of other information about the examinee. The interpretation focuses on the dominant needs, emotions, sentiments, complexes, and conflicts of the storyteller and the pressures to which he or she is subjected. Especially significant in this regard is an analysis of the needs and personality of the main character—the hero or heroine who presumably represents the examinee—and the pressures impinging on him or her. It should be cautioned, however, that the interpersonal situations described in TAT stories do

TABLE 6.5 Typical Themes Elicited by TAT Pictures

Picture 1. Relationship toward parental figures; achievement; symbolic sexual responses; aggression, anxiety, body image or self-image; obsessive preoccupations; sexual activity.

Picture 2. Family relationships; autonomy versus compliance; heterosexual and homosexual attitudes; pregnancy; compulsive tendencies; role of the sexes.

Picture 3BM. Latent homosexuality; aggression.

Picture 3GF. Depressive feelings.

Picture 4. Male-female relationships; triangular jealousy.

Picture 5. Mother who may be watching; masturbation; voyeurism; primal scene; fear of attack; rescue fantasies.

Picture 6BM. Mother-son relationships.

Picture 6GF. Relationship of females to father; father-son relationships.

Picture 7GF. Relationship between mother and child in females; attitude toward expectancy of children.

Picture 8BM. Aggression, ambition; Oedipal relationship.

Picture 8GF. Contemporary man-to-man relationships; homosexual drives and fears; social prejudices.

Picture 9GF. Depression and suicidal tendencies; paranoia.

Picture 10. Relationship of men to women; latent homosexuality.

Picture 11. Infantile or primitive fears; fears of attack; oral aggression, anxiety.

Picture 12M. Relationship of a younger man to an older man; passive homosexual fears.

Picture 12F. Conceptions of mother figures.

Picture 12BG. Suicidal tendencies; depression.

Picture 13MF. Sexual conflicts in both men and women; economic deprivation; oral tendencies; obsessive-compulsive trends.

Picture 13B. Stories of childhood.

Picture 13G. Not a very useful picture.

Picture 14. Sexual identification; fears in relation to darkness; suicidal tendencies; aesthetic interests.

Picture 15. Death in the immediate family; fears of death; depressive tendencies.

Picture 16. May be extremely valuable with verbally gifted subjects.

Picture 17BM. Oedipal fears; homosexual feelings; body image.

Picture 17GF. Suicidal tendencies in women.

Picture 18BM. Anxiety in males.

Picture 18GF. How aggression is handled by women; mother–daughter conflicts.

Picture 19. Sometimes useful with children, but otherwise not notable.

Picture 20. Fear of dark (females).

From Bellak, Leopold. *The T.A.T., C.A.T., and S.A.T. in clinical use.* Copyright © 1993 by Allyn and Bacon. Adapted by permission.

not necessarily reflect the actual experiences or relationships of the examinee. The analysis of TAT stories is an analysis of fantasy, and the interpreter must consider the stories against a background of findings from other sources: psychiatric interview, mental status examination, observational and historical data, and psychological test information. It is particularly important in analyzing the stories to search for recurring themes and to determine how they are expressed in other psychological data concerning the examinee.

Personalized impressionistic interpretations of TAT stories may also consider the frequency, intensity, and duration of the story as well as certain "signs." For example, signs of depression include slowness or delays in responding, signs of homosexuality include stories by men involving negative comments about women, and signs of obsessive-compulsive disorder include overcautiousness and preoccupation with details. These "signs," however, should not be treated as definitive but rather as hypotheses to be substantiated by data from other sources. Furthermore, some clinicians are better than others at impressionistic interpretation. Although training does not guarantee expertise, an extensive background of clinical experience can help. For this reason, it has been recommended that interpreters of TAT stories should have received considerable practice in analyzing TAT stories in contexts where they can be checked against objective facts.

Reliability and Validity of the TAT

As with other projective techniques, the relatively unstructured nature of the TAT and the lack of objective scoring, combined with situational factors, transient internal need states, and intentional faking, contribute to the fairly low reliability coefficients that have been reported for this instrument (Kraiger, Hakel, & Cornelius, 1984; Winter & Stewart, 1977; Singh, 1986). It would seem that picture stories would be more reliable and valid than responses to inkblots, but the particular environmental context in which the TAT is administered has a pronounced effect on the content of the stories and hence the test's reliability.

When responses are scored on specific variables, such as achievement motivation, higher reliability coefficients are obtained with the TAT (Exner, 1976; Murstein, 1963). Furthermore, newer, more objective methods of scoring the TAT (Cramer & Blatt, 1990; McGrew & Teglasi, 1990; Ronan, Colavito, & Hammontree, 1993) have tended to yield higher reliability coefficients. Scores determined by one of the more systematic procedures have greater reliability and can be interpreted in terms of norms based on standardization studies (Bellak, 1993).

Because the TAT was designed to analyze fantasy, which may or may not be indicative of actual behavior, assessment of the validity of TAT responses has proved extremely difficult. When conventional methods of determining validity are employed, a wide range of results has been produced. Studies have found significant differences among normals, neurotics, and psychotics on certain TAT variables but not on others

(Dana, 1955, 1959; Eron, 1950; Ritter & Effron, 1952; Sharkey & Ritzler, 1985). Significant correlations between TAT responses and other variables have also been obtained (Barends, Westen, Leigh, Silbert, & Byers, 1990).

Not only the instrument itself but also the skills of the test administrator and interpreter affect the validity of the TAT. In fact, Worchel and Dupree (1990) concluded that the information obtained from administering the TAT is more a function of the test administrator/interpreter than of the test itself. Several years ago, the lack of information on the reliability and validity of the TAT at that time led Swartz (1978) to conclude that "if the TAT were published today with the same amount of information on its reliability, validity, and standardization, it is very doubtful that it would ever attain anywhere near its present popularity" (p. 1127). This conclusion would appear to be as sound today as then.

TAT-Like Tests for Minorities and the Elderly

In addition to problems concerning its reliability and validity, the use of the TAT in evaluating nonwhite ethnic groups and older adults has been criticized. Several modifications, such as the Thompson Modification of the TAT (Thompson, 1949) (T-TAT), Tell-Me-a-Story (TEMAS) (Costantino, Malgady, & Rogler, 1988; also see Lang, 1992), and the Senior Apperception Test (Bellak & Bellak, 1973), were devised to be more appropriate for nonwhites and the elderly. Unfortunately, the reliability coefficients of the T-TAT and TEMAS are no higher than those of the TAT; therefore, these instruments should probably be used for only research purposes.

The Senior Apperception Technique (SAT) consists of 16 pictures depicting older people in a wide range of human situations. Some situations reflect the themes of helplessness, illness, loneliness, family difficulties, dependence, and lowered self-esteem, whereas others are happier, more positive situations. The SAT has been criticized for inadequate norms, stereotyping older adults, and as possessing no advantage over the TAT in testing older age groups (Schaie, 1978). Klopfer and Taulbee (1976) maintained that the way in which the SAT portrays older adults discourages active responding and reveals only superficial aspects of personality.

Picture Projective Test

Another shortcoming of the TAT is the probability that the negative, sad tone of many of the pictures induces pessimistic, depressive responses that are not necessarily characteristic of the respondent (Eron,

Terry, & Callahan, 1950; Goldfried & Zax, 1965). For this reason, the Picture Projective Test (PPT) was heralded as a much-needed improvement when it was first published (Ritzler, Sharkey, & Chudy, 1980; Sharkey & Ritzler, 1985). A more rigorous construction methodology and a wider range of picture materials than the TAT were employed in designing the PPT. The 30 pictures, which stress interpersonal involvement and a balance between positive and negative stimulus cues, were selected from the *Family of Man* photographic collection of the Museum of Modern Art (1955). Consequently, the PPT produces more upbeat stories with an emphasis on adaptive, "healthier" responses than the TAT.

In a comparison of the responses of small samples of normals, nonhospitalized depressives, hospitalized depressives, hospitalized psychotics with good premorbid histories, and hospitalized psychotics with poor histories, the TAT and PPT proved approximately equal in their ability to differentiate between normal and depressed subjects. The PPT was better at distinguishing between psychotics and normals or depressives: The depressives told gloomier stories, and the stories told by the psychotics contained more perceptual distortions and thematic-interpretive deviations. All things considered, it may be concluded that the PPT is a "very promising instrument" but that further research is needed to determine whether it is psychometrically superior to the TAT.

SUMMARY

Most proponents of projective techniques have a psychodynamic orientation, maintaining that human behavior and thought processes are governed to a great extent by unconscious motives and conflicts. They believe that projective tests are more effective than self-report inventories in revealing deeper, less superficial layers of personality and are more difficult to fake. The assumption that projectives get at unconscious mental forces may or may not be true; even the most unstructured technique for assessing personality possesses some structure, and that structure, combined with culturally common experiences, affect a person's responses to the stimulus material. Furthermore, verbal report is not necessarily identical to perception: A person may see or think one thing, but, from a desire to please, to be socially accepted, to appear brighter or more bizarre, or to stimulate a reaction in the listener, may report having seen or thought about something else than was actually the case. Certainly projectives do not provide an X-ray of the mind or an undeviating path to the truth. Like personality inventories, rating scales, and other measures of behavior and personality, projectives can be faked in either a "good" or a "bad" direction.

Responses to projectives can be influenced by the way in which the directions and questions are phrased, the examiner's personality, and the degree of encouragement and approval given to the examinee (Klopfer & Taulbee, 1976). Furthermore, the way in which these responses are scored depends on the theoretical orientation, skill, and personal characteristics of the examiner. With respect to their psychometric characteristics, on the whole projectives have low to moderate reliabilities, are usually poorly validated, and are either not standardized at all or standardized on unrepresentative samples.

Despite all of the shortcomings of projective techniques and some decline in their use during the past quarter century, psychological practitioners and researchers continue to use these instruments (Bellak, 1992; Butcher & Rouse, 1996). For example, Butcher and Rouse (1996) conclude that

> Whether viewed from the perspective of research attention or practical usage, the Rorschach Inkblot technique remains among the most popular personality assessment methods, and predictions about the technique's demise appear both unwarranted and unrealistic. (p. 91)

Regarding the Thematic Apperception Tests, Butcher and Rouse (1996) state that

> The TAT continues to be used as a clinical assessment tool and research instrument to study motivation and fantasy. Although much research on the TAT centers around nonclinical studies, . . . clinical samples are still emphasized. (p. 92)

Thus, reports of the death of projectives seem premature or at least exaggerated. Despite the negative attitudes toward projectives shown by some psychology faculty, graduate programs in clinical psychology continue to require at least some course work in projective techniques (Piotrowski & Zalewski, 1993). As seen by the many apperception and sentence completion tests in particular, many of which are of recent origin, projective techniques continue to be constructed, administered, and studied as measures of personality.

APPENDIX 6.1 Projective Techniques Appropriate for Adults

Apperception Tests

The Facial Interpersonal Perception Inventory (J. J. Luciani & R. E. Carney; Timao
 Foundation for Research and Development; for ages 5 and older; designed
 to evaluate real versus ideal perceptions of self and others by soliciting
 responses to simplified line drawings of faces displaying different emotional
 expressions; 15 scores; reviewed in MMYB 9:407)

Family Apperception Test (A. Julian III, W. M. Sotile, S. Henry, & M. O. Sotile;
 Western Psychological Services; for ages 6 and over; 35–40 scores; designed
 to assess family system variables; reviewed in TC X:251)

Four Picture Test (3rd rev. ed.) (D. J. Van Lennep; Swets Test Services; ages 10
 and over; a projective test of the TAT-type, requiring written rather than
 verbal responses; earlier edition reviewed in MMYB 6:213; TC III:288)

The Group Personality Projective Test (R. N. Cassel & T. C. Kahn; Psychological
 Test Specialists; for ages 12 and over; test of personality concerned with
 assessing personal, social, and emotional need projections; 7 scores; reviewed
 in MMYB 7:167)

The Hand Test, Revised 1983 (E. E. Wagner; Western Psychological Services; for
 ages 5 and over; a diagnostic technique that uses pictures of hands as a
 projective medium; the examinee "projects" by telling what the hand is doing;
 41 scores; reviewed in MMYB 10:134; TC I:317)

Pain Apperception Test (D. V. Petrovich; Western Psychological Services; for
 adults functioning at an elementary school level; to assess and evaluate
 psychological variables involved in the experience of pain; 3 area scores and
 total; reviewed in MMYB 8:639 and TC VII:404)

Projective Assessment of Aging Method (B. D. Starr, M. B. Weiner, & M. Rabetz;
 Springer Publishing Co.; for older adults; designed as a projective method
 for exploring thoughts and feelings about significant themes and problems
 of aging; reviewed in MMYB 9:1008; TC III:539)

The Rosenzweig Picture-Frustration Study (S. Rosenzweig; Psychological Assessment Resources; for ages 4–13, 12–18, 18 and over; designed to measure the
 pattern of responding to everyday stress; 15 scores; reviewed in MMYB 9:1060;
 TC V:388)

The Senior Apperception Technique (1985 revision) (L. Bellak; C.P.S., Inc.; ages
 65 and over; a projective instrument to gather information on forms of depression, loneliness, or rage in the elderly; no scores; reviewed in MMYB 8:676
 and TC III:604)

Thematic Apperception Test (H. A. Murray; Harvard University Press; for ages 4
 and over; a method of revealing to the trained interpreter some of the dominant drives, emotions, sentiments, complexes, and conflicts of personality;
 total score only; reviewed in MMYB 8:697; TC II:799)

Construction Tests

House–Tree–Person Projective Technique (J. N. Buck & W. L. Warren; Western
 Psychological Services; for ages 3 and over; total score only; designed to
 provide diagnostically and prognostically significant data concerning a person's total personality; review of earlier edition in MMYB 6:215; TC II:436;
 TC IX:358)

Inkblot Tests

Holtzman Inkblot Technique (W. H. Holtzman, J. S. Thorpe, J. D. Swartz, & E. W. Herron; The Psychological Corporation; for ages 5 and over; 20–22 scores; inkblot test of personality; reviewed in MMYB 9:480; TC I:328)

Rorschach (H. Rorschach; Grune & Stratton; for ages 5 and over; projective inkblot technique for clinical assessment and diagnosis; reviewed in MMYB 8:661; TC IV:523)

Somatic Inkblot Series (W. A. Cassell; Aurora Publishing Co.; for ages 3 and over; 4 scores; projective test for personality, diagnostic, and clinical assessment; reviewed in TC V:444)

Memory Techniques

Early Memories Procedure (A. R. Bruhn, Arnold R. Bruhn and Associates; for ages 10 and over with at least a fourth-grade reading level; method of exploring personality organization, especially life currents, based on the examinee's memory of the past; no scores; see Bruhn, 1992)

Sentence-Completion Tests

Activity Completion Technique (J. M. Sachs; Psychological Assessment Resources; high school and over; 60 sentence stems covering the areas of Family, Interpersonal, Affect, and Self-Concept; reviewed in MMYB 10:8)

Bloom Sentence Completion Survey (W. Bloom; Stoelting; for students aged 6–21 and adults; designed to reveal subject's attitudes [positive, neutral, or negative] toward important factors in everyday living; reviewed in MMYB 9:153)

Curtis Completion Form (J. W. Curtis; Western Psychological Services; for grades 11–15 and adults; sentence completion test designed to evaluate emotional maturity and adjusted; reviewed in MMYB 6:208)

EPS Sentence Completion Technique (D. C. Strohmer & H. T. Prout; Psychological Assessment Resources; for mildly mentally handicapped ages 14 and over; 4 levels of scores; semi-projective instrument designed specifically for use with individuals in the mildly retarded and borderline intelligence ranges)

The Forer Structured Sentence Completion Test (B. R. Forer; Western Psychological Services; for ages 16–18 and adults; designed to measure personality variables and attitudes that may be of some value in treatment planning; reviewed in MMYB 5:134; TC IV:300)

Geriatric Sentence Completion Form (P. LeBray; Psychological Assessment Resources; adults aged 60 and over; 30 items; scored for 4 content domains— physical, psychological, social, and temporal orientation; reviewed in MMYB 9:436)

Miner Sentence Completion Scale (J. B. Miner; Organizational Measurement Systems; for workers and prospective workers in management, professional, and entrepreneurial or task-oriented occupations; reviewed in MMYB 11:241)

Politte Sentence Completion Test (A. J. Politte; Psychologists & Educators, Inc.; for grades 1–8, 7–12, and adults; designed to elicit information from individuals concerning their immediate environment, especially the people in the environment)

Rotter Incomplete Sentences Blank (2nd ed.) (J. B. Rotter, M. T. Lah, & J. E. Rafferty; The Psychological Corporation; for high-school and college students, adults; used primarily as a screening instrument of overall adjustment; reviewed in MMYB 12:335)

Sentence Completion Series (L. H. Brown & M. A. Unger; Psychological Assessment Resources; for adolescents and adults; consists of 8 self-report forms, each with 50 content-valid sentence stems pertaining to a specific area of concern: adult, adolescent, family, marriage, parenting, work, illness, aging)

Sentence Completion Test (F. S. Irvin; Psychologists and Educators; high school and college students; designed to assess feelings, urges, beliefs, attitudes, and desires; 35 item scores in six areas)

Sentence Completion Tests (A. Roe; Diagnostic Specialists; 10 sentence-completion tests, eight of which [General Incomplete Sentence Test, Short Incomplete Sentences, Full Incomplete Sentences Test, Full I Am Test, Marriage Incomplete Sentences Test, Relationship Incomplete Sentences Test, Full Length Alcohol Sentence Completion, and Drug Inquiry Sentence Completion] are appropriate for adults)

NOTE

1. Calculation of the structural summary, ratios, percentages, and constellations can be facilitated by a computer software package, Exner's Rorschach Scoring Program (J. E. Exner & K. S. C. Tuttle; The Psychological Corporation).

SUGGESTED READINGS

Bellak, L. (1992). Projective techniques in the computer age. *Journal of Personality Assessment, 58*, 445–453.

Bruhn, A. R. (1995). Early memories in personality assessment. In J. N. Butcher (Ed.), *Clinical personality assessment: Practical approaches* (pp. 278–301). New York: Oxford University Press.

Dana, R. H. (1996). The Thematic Apperception Test (TAT). In C. S. Newmark (Ed.), *Major psychological assessment instruments* (2nd ed., pp. 166–206). Needham Heights, MA: Allyn & Bacon.

Erdberg, P. (1996). The Rorschach. In C. S. Newmark (Ed.), *Major psychological assessment instruments* (2nd ed., pp. 148–165). Needham Heights, MA: Allyn & Bacon.

Handler, L. (1996). The clinical use of drawings. In C. S. Newmark (Ed.), *Major psychological assessment instruments* (2nd ed, pp. 206–293). Needham Heights, MA: Allyn & Bacon.

Hertz, M. R. (1992). Projective techniques in crisis. In E. I. Megargee & C. D. Spielberger (Eds.), *Personality assessment in America: A retrospective on the occasion of the fiftieth anniversary of the Society for Personality Assessment* (pp. 99–112). Hillsdale, NJ: Erlbaum.

Klopfer, W. G. (1992). The metamorphosis of projective methods. In E. I. Megargee & C. D. Spielberger (Eds.), *Personality assessment in America: A retrospective on the occasion of the fiftieth anniversary of the Society for Personality Assessment* (pp. 96–98). Hillsdale, NJ: Erlbaum.

Kutash, S. B. (1992). The impact of projective techniques on basic psychological science. In E. I. Megargee & C. D. Spielberger (Eds.), *Personality assessment in America: A retrospective on the occasion of the fiftieth anniversary of the Society for Personality Assessment* (pp. 34–46). Hillsdale, NJ: Erlbaum.

Lerner, P. M. (1995). Assessing adaptive capacities by means of the Rorschach. In J. N. Butcher (Ed.), *Clinical personality assessment: Practical approaches* (pp. 317–325). New York: Oxford University Press.

7

Other Personality Variables and Measures

The concept of *personality* is not limited to emotions, motives, temperament, or even the affective domain in general. Any habit, stylistic behavior, preference, orientation, or ability that is expressed often enough to become characteristic of a person can be construed as a component of personality. Such characteristics are shaped by the interaction of a person's biological makeup and encounters with the environment, manifested fairly early in the life cycle. Barring serious brain damage or psychological trauma, these characteristics remain a part of personality from childhood to senescence. Experience and learning can alter personality, but only partially. Much of what a person is—how he or she copes with other people, things, and events—persists and becomes typical of the individual.

In a sense, this is a cleanup chapter, and something of a mixed-up chapter as well. It is not so much that the topics—interests, values, personal orientations, cognitions, and biological factors—have been overlooked in previous chapters. The variables considered in this chapter are certainly associated with those assessed by observations, interviews, rating scales, inventories, and projective techniques, but they have not been explicitly discussed before now. Although a *holistic* definition of personality encompasses interests, values, attitudes, personal orientations, cognitive abilities, and styles, in the research literature these variables are often referred to as *correlates* rather than components of personality. This distinction emphasizes the notion that, although related to personality and shaped by many of the same factors, the variables considered in the present chapter do not actually consti-tute a part of what is generally referred to as personality. However, we shall follow Cattell (1965), who conceptualized personality as being made up of dynamic traits, ability traits, and temperament traits, a conception that encompasses both affective and cognitive variables. Certainly measures of interests, values, personal orientations, and cog-nitive abilities predict the same behaviors as more traditional measures of personality, and typically no less reliably or accurately.

INTERESTS AND PERSONALITY

Interests are defined as feelings of concern, involvement, or curiosity about something or someone. Interests can be assessed in a variety of ways—by observing the activities in which a person engages, by lis-tening to what he or she says, and by means of self-report inventories. Because interests are aspects of motivation, they affect how much effort one exerts in playing certain games, studying certain subjects, and pursuing certain jobs or careers.

Interest inventories have been designed for a variety of purposes, but primarily for use in academic and vocational guidance. Academic and vocational counselors use the results of interest inventories, along with measures of ability, achievement, and experience, in advising ado-lescents and adults about courses, programs, and careers in which they are most likely to find success and satisfaction.

The most prominent and time-honored of all interest inventories is the Strong Interest Inventory (SII), a 317-item instrument concerned with responses to various occupations, school subjects, activities, leisure activities, types of people, preferences between two activities, personal characteristics, and choices in the world of work (Harmon et al., 1994). Because the item weights and scoring procedure for the SII are a trade secret, the completed inventory must be sent to the publisher and scored by computer. Scores are obtained on five groups of measures: Administrative Indexes, General Occupational Themes, Basic Interest Scales, Occupational Scales, and Personal Style Scales. Before beginning the process of interpreting a person's scores on the last four groups of measures, scores on the three Administrative Indexes are checked. The first of these, the Total Responses Index, should not be below 300; the second—the Like, Indifferent, and Dislike Percent Indexes—should be between 14 and 60; the last, the Infrequent Response Index, should not be less than zero. Next, T scores on the six General Occupational Themes (Realistic, Investigative, Artistic, Social, Enterprising, and Con-ventional), which are the six categories in John Holland's (1985) theory of vocational personalities, are examined. Then the high and low T scores on the 25 Basic Interest Scales falling under the General Occupational Themes are examined. Next, the 109 Occupational Scales are arranged into highs and lows according to T scores. T scores on the four Personal Style Scales (Work Style, Learning Environment, Leadership Style, Risk Taking/Adventure) can also be helpful in vocational counseling and career exploration.

Because interest measurement occurs most often for vocational or academic counseling purposes, and personality characteristics are measured most often for purposes of clinical or personality counseling, interests are usually viewed as different from personality variables. However, it has long been recognized that the decision to engage in a particular occupation or to prepare for a certain career is guided to some extent by personality characteristics. For example, it may be that the decision to become a meat cutter or a surgeon is affected by aggressive impulses and that becoming an actor or other performer reflects exhibitionistic needs. In fact, psychoanalytic theory maintains that many occupational choices represent the sublimation of deep-seated or frustrated needs that are not expressed in more direct ways. Psychoanalysts also recognize the importance of another mechanism—identification—in the development of interests.

Evidence for associations between interests and personality traits exists in research findings that the frequency of psychoneurotic problems is greater in people with high aesthetic and literary interests, that introversion is more common among people with strong scientific interests, and that aggressive people are more likely to be interested in sales work (Darley & Hagenah, 1955; Osipow, 1983; Super & Bohn, 1970). An investigation by Siegelman and Peck (1960) found that curiosity, imagination, intellectuality, creativity, relationship to objects, and emotional involvement in work were characteristic of chemists. Ministers, conversely, tended to be nurturant, personally insecure, and more likely to feel vocationally inadequate. Military officers valued security and variety in living quarters and associations, were acceptant of responsibility and authority, concerned with honesty and loyalty, and dedicated to country.

Stages in the Development of Vocational Interests

Much of the research and theorizing concerned with the relationships between interests and personality has been unsystematic. Developmental theorists, such as Eli Ginzberg and Donald Super, maintained that there are three or four stages in the development of vocational interests.

Ginzberg's Theory

Ginzberg, Ginsburg, Axelrad, and Herma (1951) found evidence for three stages: a *fantasy stage* during early and middle childhood, when interests are arbitrary and unrealistic; a *tentative stage* from ages 11 to 18, during which adolescents begin considering possible vocations; and a *realistic stage* from ages 18 to 21, which begins with exploration and culminates in the crystallization of a vocational pattern.

Super's Theory

Another theory concerned with the relationships of interests to personality is Super's (1957, 1963, 1990) multistage conception of changes in self-concept and interests. Emphasizing the importance of identification and role playing in the development of interests, Super viewed the individual's search for identity and vocational maturity as occurring in three stages. The first (*exploratory*) stage consists of a tentative substage, a transition substage, and an uncommitted trial substage. The second (*establishment*) stage consists of a "committed trial substage" and an "advancement substage." During the third (*maintenance*) stage the person's career choices are reinforced and continued. For many people, there is also a final (*disengagement*) stage, in which the career interests of young and middle adulthood gradually weaken.

Super's emphasis on the importance of the self-concept in preferences for particular occupations has been extended by Betz (1992, 1994) in her adaptation of Bandura's (1977a) perceived self-efficacy model to the vocational counseling process. From Betz's (1994) perspective, counseling to enhance career self-efficacy should concentrate on the four sources of self-efficacy information delineated in Bandura's model: "performance accomplishments; vicarious learning, or modeling; verbal persuasion, or encouragement from other people to engage in a specific behavior; degree of emotional arousal with reference to a domain of behavior, such that the higher the arousal (anxiety), the less self-efficacious the individual will feel" (Betz, 1994, p. 34).

Gottfredson's Theory

Another theory of the development of vocational interests and career aspirations was proposed by Gottfredson (1981). Gottfredson applied the term *circumspection* to the elimination and retention of occupational alternatives during career exploration. Circumspection occurs within a certain *zone of acceptable alternatives*, in that the person considers only a limited range of occupations having acceptable prestige levels and self-typing. Circumspection occurs during four developmental stages.

During the first (ages 3–5) stage, which is characterized by an orientation to size and power, the child perceives occupations as adult roles. During the second stage (ages 6–8), which is characterized by an orientation to sex roles, the child eliminates occupations that are inconsistent with his or her sex role preference. During the third stage (ages 9–13), the child's growing awareness of social class differences leads him or her to eliminate from consideration occupations lower than the *tolerable-level prestige boundary* or higher than the *tolerable-effort prestige boundary*. During the fourth and find stage (ages 14+), the adolescent develops a unique sense of self and eliminates occupations that are inconsistent with his or her interests and abilities. As this stage theory indicates, a person's zone of acceptable alternatives narrows with the elimination of occupations over time. According to Gottfredson, the need to compromise among interest, prestige, and sex-role preferences results in interest being sacrificed first, followed by prestige preference, and only last by sex-type preference.

Research stimulated by Gottfredson's theory has failed to support many of its tenets. For example, an empirical study by Leung and Harmon (1990) found that, rather than decreasing, the range of acceptable alternatives increased from early childhood through adolescence. Furthermore, several variables appear to affect the process of circumspection. Research findings indicate, for example, that sex typing limits the career choices of boys more than those of girls (Hannah & Kahn, 1989; Henderson, Hesketh, & Tuffin, 1988); the range of acceptable alternatives also varies with gender role orientation (Leung & Harmon, 1990). Furthermore, ability is more closely related than socioeconomic status to prestige preferences (Henderson et al., 1988).

Gottredson's (1981) postulate concerning compromise has also failed to receive consistent support (Holt, 1989). When compromise is necessary, sex-type preference appears to be less important—and, hence, *more* likely to be sacrificed—than interest or prestige. In addition, prestige is more likely to be eliminated than interest (Holt, 1989; Hesketh, Durant, & Pryor, 1990; Hesketh, Elmslie, & Kaldor, 1990).

Interest Inventories As Personality Measures

The first personality inventory consisting of items designed expressly to measure interests was constructed by Forer (1948). Arguing that interests are dynamic characteristics and reflections of an individual's self-concept, Forer demonstrated that his inventory could differentiate between various medical and psychiatric groups ranging from asthmatics to schizophrenics. The idea that interest inventories are actually measures of personality was also emphasized by Darley and Hagenah

(1955) and Super (1972). The relationship between interests and personality traits is documented by the many statistically significant correlations between scores on interest inventories and scores on personality inventories (Utz & Korben, 1976).

Roe's Person–Environment Theory

Two sets of interest inventories that are based on theories relating interests to personality are Anne Roe's person–environment theory of career choice and John Holland's vocational personalities–work environments theory. From the findings of her research on the personalities of physical, biological, and social scientists, Roe concluded that an important dimension of career choice is the degree of orientation to personal relations ("people") versus orientation to natural phenomena ("things"). She maintained that entry into more person-oriented vocational environments, such as general cultural, arts, entertainment, and business contact occupations, is associated with a strong interest in *people*. Entry into more nonperson-oriented vocations (scientific, outdoor, technological, etc.), conversely, is associated with a strong interest in *things*.

Roe thought that the extent to which a person is oriented toward people or things is determined by the rewards and punishments administered for various activities in childhood and the psychological climate of the home (warm or accepting versus cold or avoiding). A strong interest in people is presumably encouraged by a warm family environment, whereas a greater interest in things is promoted by a cold environment. However, there is also evidence for the role of genetic makeup in the development of interests (Bouchard, Maloney, & Segal, 1989; Grotevant, Scarr, & Weinberg, 1978).

A second dimension in Roe's three-dimensional conception of interested is orientation to resource use versus orientation to purposeful communication. A third dimension—low level versus high level—consists of the skill level required by the occupation (unskilled, skilled, professional). The first two dimensions are represented by the horizontal and vertical axes of the circular diagram in Figure 7.1, and the third dimension by the distance from the center of the diagram.

Roe's model has been applied to the construction of several interest inventories, foremost among which is the COPS Interest Inventory (by L. Knapp-Lee, R. R. Knapp, & L. F. Knapp; EdITS). Designed for high school, college, and adult examinees, the Likert-type items on the COPS can be answered in 20 to 30 minutes. Scores are obtained on the eight major clusters represented by the segments of the circle in Figure 7.1. The 1995 edition of the COPS contains new job activity items reflecting

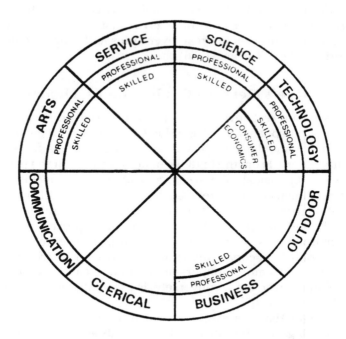

FIGURE 7.1. Model of Variables Measured by the COPS Interest Inventory. The horizontal axis corresponds to the "people vs. things" dimension, the vertical axis corresponds to the "orientation" dimension, and distance from the center of the circle corresponds to the "level" dimension of Anne Roe's person-environment model of vocational interests. (From *COPSystem Technical Manual* [p. 4] by R. R. Knapp, L. Knapp, & L. Knapp-Lee, 1990, San Diego, CA: EdITS. Copyright 1990 EdITS. Reprinted with permission.)

the increased use of computers and other trends. Also provided are occupational preference scores related to choice of job and curriculum and occupational clusters for professionally and vocationally oriented individuals.

Bauerfeind's (1986) review of the previous edition of the COPS is fairly positive, although some problems regarding the clarity of the manual, weaknesses in the norms, and questions concerning the predictive validities of the instrument are noted. Unfortunately, Roe's three-dimensional model of interests, on which the COPS is based, has not been well supported by research. People within the same profession may have different orientations, and the differences in interests between people in low-level occupations are as great in some instances as those between people in high-level occupations. Even the notions that individuals are either person or thing oriented in their interests and that interest-orientation affects vocational choice have not been completely supported by research (Osipow, 1983).

Holland's Theory of Vocational Personalities

A major premise of J. L. Holland's (1985) theory of vocational personalities and work environments is that behavior is determined by the interaction between the personality and the psychological environment of the person. The *psychological environment* is not necessarily the same as the actual environment, but rather it is the environment as it is perceived by the individual. According to Holland, people tend to seek and remain in environments that are congruent with their personalities. They are happier, more satisfied, and more productive in such places than in environments that are incongruent with their personalities. If a person obtains sufficient reinforcement and satisfaction in a particular environment, he or she will remain there. Otherwise, either the person or the environment must change, or the person must seek an environment that is more compatible with his or her personality.

Holland's model consists of six vocational personalities and six work environments (see Figure 7.2). Descriptions of the six personality types are given in Table 7.1. The six types of environment are labeled in the same way as the personality types: (R)ealistic, (I)nvestigative, (A)rtistic, (I)ntegrative, (E)nterprising, and (C)onventional. The six personalities and six environments are idealizations; any individual personality or environment is a composite of two or more ideal types.

There are 15 possible pairings of the six (RIASEC) themes, some of the pairs being more closely related, or consistent, than other pairs. The *consistency* of the interest pattern of a person is indicated by the extent to which he or she has high scores on interests that are close to each other in the model. As seen in Figure 7.2, the investigative and conventional types are adjacent to the realistic type—and, hence, more consistent with it than they are with each other or with the social type.

Four other important concepts in Holland's theory are differentiation, identity, congruence, and calculus. Greater *differentiation* of interests is seen in a person who has only one or two high-type scores. A combination of high consistency and high differentiation is, according to Holland, characteristic of people who deal effectively with their vocational problems.

Identity, another concept in Holland's theory, may be either personal or environmental. People with a keen sense of *personal identity* have a

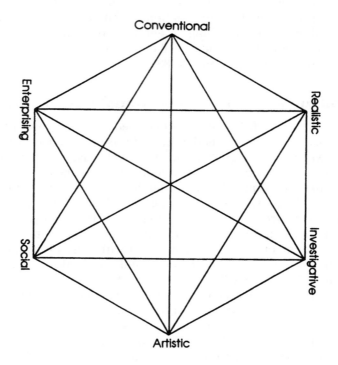

FIGURE 7.2. Holland's Hexagonal (RIASEC) Model of Vocational Person-alities. A corresponding set of six themes is used to describe work environments.

clear, stable picture of their goals, interests, and talents, a condition that is associated with having a few vocational goals in a few major categories. When the goals, tasks, and rewards of a particular environment are stable over time, a state of *environmental identity* exists.

Congruence, a third concept in Holland's theory, occurs when there is a match between personality and environmental types. When the opportunities and rewards provided by the environment are congruent with the person's abilities and preferences, a state of congruence exists. The final concept in the theory, that of *calculus*, is concerned with whether the types of personalities and environments can be ordered according to a hexagonal model in which the distances between types are consistent with their theoretical relationships.

Many self-report inventories have incorporated Holland's six RIASEC themes into their scoring, but the major instrument constructed by

TABLE 7.1 Descriptions of Holland's Six Vocational Personalities

---

Realistic Type

Likes to manipulate tools, machines, and other objects; likes being outdoors; likes working with plants and animals; dislikes educational and therapeutic activities.

Tends to have athletic, mechanical, and technical competencies; is deficient in social and educational skills.

Characterized as practical, conforming, and natural.

Avoids situations requiring verbal and interpersonal skills; seeks jobs such as automobile mechanic, farmer, or electrician.

Investigative Type

Prefers activities that demand a great deal of thinking and understanding (e.g., scientific enterprises).

Likes to observe, learn, investigate, analyze, evaluate, and solve problems.

Characterized as rational, cautious, curious, independent, and introversive.

More likely to be found in fields, such as chemistry, physics, biology, geology, and other sciences. Tends to avoid situations requiring interpersonal and persuasive skills.

Artistic Type

Tends to prefer unstructured situations in which creativity or imagination can be expressed.

Characterized as imaginative, introspective, complicated, emotional, expressive, impulsive, nonconforming, and disorderly.

Jobs, such as actor, musician, or writer, are likely to appeal to people in this category.

Social Type

Is verbally and interpersonally skilled; likes to work with people—developing, enlightening, informing, training, curing, and helping or supporting them in various ways.

Humanistic and empathic; tends to have teaching abilities, but minimal mechanical and scientific abilities. Viewed as cooperative, friendly, helpful, persuasive, tactful, and understanding.

Likely to be found in clinical or counseling psychology, speech therapy, teaching, and related fields.

Enterprising Type

Described as aggressive, ambitious, energetic, domineering, pleasure seeking, self-confident, and sociable.

Tends to have high verbal and leadership abilities.

Likely to influence and persuade others, and to manage organizations for economic gain. Jobs, such as manager, business executive, or salesperson, are preferred by these individuals.

(Continued)

TABLE 7.1 *(Continued)*

Conventional Type

Described as conscientious, efficient, inflexible, obedient, orderly, persistent, and self-controlled.

Tends to have good arithmetic and clerical abilities, and thereby adept at filing, record keeping, and data processing. Skills are congruent with an emphasis on business and economic achievement, leading to jobs such as bander, bookkeeper, and tax expert.

Holland to measure the six themes is the Self-Directed Search (SDS). Available from Psychological Assessment Resources and The Psychological Corporation, Form R of the 1994 edition of the SDS was designed to assess the career interests of high school students, college students, and adults in 35 to 45 minutes. The items on the SDS consist of questions concerning aspirations, activities, competencies, occupations, and self-estimates. Responses are scored on the six RIASEC themes, and scores are then converted to a three-letter code designating the three personality types that the examinee resembles most closely. Referring the coded scores to an Occupations Finder reveals the matches between the examinee's personality and more than 1,300 occupations. The 1994 revision of the SDS was standardized on 1,600 women and 1,002 men, consisting of students and working adults between the ages of 17 and 65 years.

Dolliver's (1985) review of a previous edition of the SDS was positive. Similarly, Osipow (1983) awarded high marks to Holland's research program, but concluded that the ability of the RIASEC model to explain the process of personality development and its role in vocational selection is limited.

In addition to interest inventories being measures of personality, personality inventories, such as the 16 PF Questionnaire and the Self-Descriptive Inventory (by C. B. Johannson; NCS Assessments), can serve as measures of interests. For example, the latter instrument provides scores on 11 personal description scales as well as scores on six vocationally oriented scales based on Holland's RIASEC themes.

ATTITUDES, VALUES, AND PERSONAL ORIENTATIONS

Associated with but not identical to interests are attitudes, opinions, beliefs, values, and personal orientations. Of these concepts, the greatest attention in measurement and research has been given to attitudes.

Attitudes, which may be defined as "learned predispositions to respond positively or negatively to certain objects, situations, institutions, concepts, or persons" (Aiken, 1980, p. 2), have both cognitive and affective components. *Opinions* are similar to, but less generalized and more cognitive than attitudes. Both *beliefs* and opinions constitute judgments or acceptances of propositions or facts, but the factual support for an opinion is substantially weaker than that for a belief. *Values*—the importance or worth attached to particular activities and objects—are also closely related to interests, attitudes, opinions, and beliefs. Furthermore, all of these concepts are associated with personality traits.

Although there is a danger of overgeneralizing from attitudes and beliefs to personality traits, research on concepts such as the achievement motive, the authoritarian personality, and Machiavellianism has revealed many connections between attitudes, beliefs, and personality. One must be careful not to expect a person to express the same attitudes or personality characteristics in all situations. So-called political conservatives are not necessarily conservative in other respects, nor are political liberals necessarily liberal in everything. It is possible to be a social liberal, an economic conservative, and a political middle-of-the-roader at the same time.

To overgeneralize from one context to another without sufficient rational justification can lead to stereotyping, which promotes prejudice and discrimination. Nevertheless, a representative sample of information about a person's attitudes, opinions, and beliefs can provide fruitful hypotheses about the kind of personality with which one is dealing and what sort of reactions or behaviors might be expected from that person in certain situations.

Measures of Values

Interest measurement has generally occurred in vocational counseling and selection contexts, whereas attitudes, values, opinions, and beliefs have been assessed mostly in social psychological, sociological, and other social science research contexts. Two of the most time-honored measures of values are Rokeach's Value Survey and Allport, Vernon, and Lindzey's Study of Values. Rokeach differentiated between *instrumental values*, which are concerned with modes of conduct, and *terminal values*, which are concerned with end states. Instrumental values are subdivided into *moral values* and *competence values,* and terminal values into *personal values* and *social values.* Many of the 36 values in these categories are close to what have traditionally been designated as personality variables.

The six values (theoretical, economic, aesthetic, social, political, and religious) measured by Allport's Study of Values and based on Eduard Spranger's "types of men," are also closely related to personality variables and significantly correlated with scores on personality inventories. Furthermore, measures of values have sometimes been used, like interest inventories, to identify the vocational or career orientations of people. Examples of instruments employed in this fashion are the Work Values Inventory, The Values Scale, and the Temperament and Values Scale.

Gender Roles

Perhaps even more closely related to personality than interests, attitudes, and values are gender roles and other personal orientations. Sex differences in response to all kinds of psychometric instruments—both cognitive and affective—have been studied extensively. In recent years, increased attention has been paid to gender differences in scores on many of these instruments and to potential gender bias in what they measure. A great deal of effort is now being expended by Educational Testing Service, the American College Testing Program, and other commercial test publishers to make certain that their psychometric products are not biased toward a particular gender, ethnic, or social group.

Despite careful screening of test items and attention to test administration procedures for possible gender bias, test scores obtained by male subjects are still often significantly different from those of female subjects. How can these differences be explained? Are they caused by genetic differences between the sexes, by differences in the psychological or physical environment, by some combination of these, or what? Although there is ample evidence for genetic differences between the sexes in both cognitive and affective characteristics, environmental factors have received the greatest attention from psychologists (see Ashmore, 1990). An environmentalist explanation emphasizes the origin of gender differences in differential social expectations and reinforcements for gender-appropriate behavior in the two sexes.

Several self-report inventories, such as the Bem Sex-Role Inventory (BSRI) (Bem, 1974) and the Personal Attributes Questionnaire (PAQ) (Spence & Helmreich, 1978), have been designed to measure and analyze differences in gender roles. Research with both of these instruments supports a dualistic conception of gender roles, in which masculinity and femininity are viewed as different dimensions rather than the bipolar conception in which they are seen as opposite ends of a continuum. Furthermore, scores on both the BSRI and the PAQ have been found to be significantly related to various measures of personality adjustment (Payne, 1985).

Personal Orientation Inventory

Paper-and-pencil inventories and scales designed to assess gender role are actually measures of one kind of *personal orientation*. Another example of a personal orientation is *self-actualization*—the extent to which a person fulfills his potential and becomes all that he or she can be. An instrument designed to measure values and behaviors that are important in the development of self-actualizers—people who develop and use all their potentials and are free of the emotional turmoil and inhibitions that characterize non–self-actualizers—is the Personal Orientation Inventory (POI) (E. L. Shostrum; EdITS). The 150 forced-choice items on the POI are scored first for two major orientation ratios: Time Ratio (Time Incompetence/Time Competence) and Support Ratio (Other Support/Inner Support). The Time Ratio indicates whether the respondent's time orientation is primarily in the present, in the past, or in the future. The Support Ratio indicates whether the respondent's reactivity orientation is basically toward other people or the self. After the two ratios have been computed, scores on the following 10 scales are obtained:

Self-Actualizing Value. Affirmation of primary values of self-actualizing people

Existentiality. Ability to situationally or existentially react

Feeling Reactivity. Sensitivity of responsiveness to one's own needs and feelings

Spontaneity. Freedom to react spontaneously to be oneself

Self Regard. Affirmation of self because of worth

Self Acceptance. Affirmation of self or acceptance of self despite weaknesses or deficiencies

Nature of Man. Degree of the constructive view of the nature of man, masculinity, and femininity

Synergy. Ability to be synergistic, to transcend dichotomies

Acceptance of Aggression. Ability to accept one's natural aggressiveness as opposed to defensiveness, denial, and repression of aggression

Capacity for Intimate Contact. Ability to develop contactful intimate relationships with other human beings, unencumbered by expectations and obligations

Mean scores, standard deviations, and score profiles from clinically nominated "self-actualized" and "non–self-actualized" groups of adults, in addition to several other clinical and industrial samples, are presented in the POI manual. Despite the fact that the norms are dated and probably not adequately representative of the target population and that the reliability and validity coefficients only borderline in acceptability, the POI remains a widely used inventory. Tosi and Linamood (1975) recommended that it be used in counseling and psychotherapeutic situations as a point of departure for greater client self-awareness and self-exploration.

COGNITIVE VARIABLES AND PERSONALITY

Although there is such a thing as a "happy idiot," like poor health and poverty low levels of mental ability are generally associated with greater maladjustment. Despite some notable exceptions, as a rule health, wealth, and wisdom all contribute to feeling good about oneself and life in general. It is just as likely that a pleasing, well-adjusted personality contributes to being healthy, wealthy, and wise, and that wisdom influences health and wealth. Wiser, or more intelligent, people have a greater repository of knowledge and are usually better predictors, planners, and problem solvers. Consequently, they are more likely to possess the financial resources and other capabilities needed to avoid and cope with potential physical and mental difficulties.

To theorists such as R. B. Cattell mental (cognitive) abilities not only contribute to personality, they are a part of it. As a kind of demonstration of this belief, Cattell and J. M. Schuerger constructed the Objective-Analytic Test Battery. This test measures a combination of affective and cognitive traits, such as perceptual-motor rigidity, picture perception, endurance of difficulty, criticalness of judgment, humor appreciation, and musical preferences. The integration of cognitive and affective measures into a single instrument should not, however, be construed as demonstrating that these variables are highly related or that they measure a single factor. For example, scores on the 20 folk concept and the three structural scales on the revised version of the CPI have fairly low correlations with a variety of cognitive measures. A few correlations in the .30s and .40s were found between scores on ability tests and scores on the Achievement via Independence and Intellectual Efficiency scales of the CPI, but these were the highest correlations obtained (Gough, 1987). After reviewing empirical studies linking personality to intelligence, Brebner and Stough (1995) concluded that the results provide support only for a rather weak relationship between intelligence and speed-related personality measures and a negative relationship between intelligence and impulsivity. It is possible that these relationships are mediated through the biological variable of arousal level.

Wechsler Adult Intelligence Scale–Revised

Like most individual intelligence tests, in addition to being a measure of intellectual potential, the Wechsler Adult Intelligence Scale (WAIS-R) provides opportunities for obtaining observational and interview information on the examinee's personality. Anyone who has administered an individual intelligence test has observed significant differences in the ways in which different people approach intellectual problems, how anxious or motivated they are, how they evaluate their own abilities, how they respond to success and failure, and how they behave on an interpersonal level. Squirming, scowling, sighing, trembling, hesitating, avoiding eye contact, and changing the volume and tone of voice are some of the nonverbal behaviors that provide clues to personality characteristics and problems. Reacting slowly and deprecating one's performance may suggest depression, whereas hesitations and suspiciousness are consonant with a diagnosis of paranoia (Matarazzo, 1972). In responding to particular items, inclusion of irrelevant details (overelaboration), responding too generally (overinclusion), being evasive, making frequent references to oneself, and giving idiosyncratic or bizarre answers are indicative of various types of psychopathology. Personalizing responses is characteristic of paranoid thinking, whereas bizarre, overinclusive responses point to schizophrenia.

Cattell (1965) viewed intelligence as a part of personality, but, in a sense, David Wechsler turned it around and emphasized that personality affects intelligence. Wechsler (1975) realized that the ability to cope with the environment—which was his definition of intelligence—depends not only on cognitive abilities but also on affective (emotional) and conative (striving) factors. In sum, Wechsler viewed intelligence as a multifaceted, holistic index of cognitive, affective, and conative behaviors, and thereby a function of the entire personality.

According to Wechsler, if scores on intelligence tests are affected by personality as a whole, then differences between scores on the various subtests of which a test, such as the WAIS-R, is composed should contribute to the analysis of personality and the diagnosis of personality disorders. Schizophrenics, for example, should have a different pattern of subtest scores than depressives and organics. Unfortunately, research provides little support for this assumption. Different patterns of subtest-scaled scores on the WAIS-R are not reliably associated with different psychodiagnostic groups. Large differences between Verbal and Performance IQs may point to organic brain damage, language deficits, or socioeducational differences, but a strong case cannot be made even here.

Despite the failure of subtest score differences (subtest scatter analysis) to provide significant diagnostic information, in addition to noting qualitatively distinct responses an analysis of errors and correct responses to questions on the WAIS-R or other intelligence tests can provide information on the problem-solving approaches and cognitive styles of examinees.

Schemas and Attributions

Cognitive theories of personality assume the existence of internal mental (cognitive) structures that determine how people evaluate, interpret, and organize information about themselves and others. These cognitive structures, which are designated as "schemas," "plans," "scripts," and the like, are abstract representations and organizers of events, objects, and relationships in the external world that determine the behavior, affect, and experience of the individual (Abelson, 1981). Of particular interest to cognitive personality theorists are *self-schemas*, which organize experience, feelings, judgments, and perceptions of the self (Markus & Nurius, 1986).

With respect to how the individual comes to know and understand the world, cognitive theorists have conducted research on attributions, social judgment, person perception, and cognitive styles. Considerable research has been stimulated by *attribution theory*, which seeks to explain how people decide, on the basis of samples of an individual's behavior, what the specific causes of that behavior are (Abramson, Garber, & Seligman, 1980). Attributions may be *internal*, in which case one's behavior is attributed to ability, personality, or other internal forces. Alternatively, attributions may be *external*, in which case a person's behavior is attributed to "bad luck" or the difficulty of the task. The *fundamental attribution error* occurs when one's own behavior is attributed to situational influences, but the behavior of other people is attributed to their personality characteristics or dispositions (Weary, 1978). However, the tendency to attribute success and failure to forces within or outside oneself varies with the individual and, therefore, qualifies as a personality variable. Two examples of instruments for assessing attributions in the domain of personal health are the Attributional Styles Questionnaire (Peterson et al., 1982) and the Health Attribution Test (J. Achterberg & G. F. Lawlis, IPAT).

Cognitive Styles

A *cognitive style* is a strategy or approach to perceiving, remembering, and thinking that one prefers in attempting to understand and cope with the world. Descriptions of nine types of cognitive styles are given in Table 7.2. Of these, the greatest amount of research has been conducted on the field independence/field dependence, reflective/impulsive, and internal/external locus of control styles.

Field-Independence/Dependence

Herman Witkin and his colleagues (Witkin et al., 1974; Witkin & Goodenough, 1977) devised three tests—the Body Adjustment Test, the Rod and Frame Test, and the Embedded Figures Test—to study and classify individuals as field independents or field dependents. On the Body Adjustment Test, the examinee is seated in a tilted chair placed in a tilted room and told to adjust the chair to the true vertical position. On the Rod and Frame Test, the examinee is taken into a darkened room, seated in front of a luminous rod placed inside a luminous square frame, and told to adjust the rod to the true vertical. On the Embedded Figures Test, the examinee is told to locate simple figures within a series of complex forms as quickly as possible. Witkin maintained that these three tests are measures of the same thing—the ability to differentiate aspects or parts of a complex confusing whole. Rather than relying exclusively on visual cues, high scorers on the Body Adjustment Test and the Rod and Frame Test make use of the gravitational sense to find the true vertical position. High scorers are designated as field independents, and low scorers as field dependents.

Several differences between the personalities of field independents and field dependents were found by Witkin and his coworkers. Field independents tended to be secure, independent, controlled, psychologically more mature, and self-accepting persons who were active in dealing with the environment, preferred intellectualization as a defense mechanism, and were more aware of their inner experiences. They did better than field dependents in engineering, the sciences, and mathematics, and were more likely to be boys. Field dependents, conversely, were more likely to be females, and to be tense, less secure, psychologically immature, passive, less attuned to their inner experiences, and less self-insightful; they also tended to have greater feelings of inferiority, a low evaluation of the physical self, and were more likely to employ primitive defense mechanisms such as repression and denial. With respect to college major, field dependents tended to do better in counseling, the social sciences, teaching, and other people-oriented professions. Also of interest is that the parents of field-independent children tend to be less restrictive and less authoritarian than the parents of field-dependent children (Witkin & Berry, 1975; Witkin & Goodenough, 1977).

TABLE 7.2 Nine Cognitive Style Variables

Broad vs. narrow categorizing. Broad categorizers prefer a few categories containing many items; narrow categorizers prefer many categories containing a few items.

Constricted vs. flexible control. People with constricted control are susceptible to distraction by irrelevant information; people with flexible control are resistant to distraction by irrelevant stimuli.

Field independents vs. dependents. Field independent perceivers depend primarily on kinesthetic (gravitational) cues rather than visual cues from the surrounding environment; field-dependent perceivers rely primarily on cues from the surrounding visual environment rather than on kinesthetic (gravitational) cues.

Impulsive vs. reflective. Impulsives are quick and inaccurate in solving problems, reflectives are slow and accurate.

Internal vs. external locus of control. People having an internal locus of control believe that rewards are the consequences of their own behavior; people having an external locus of control believe that their success and failure is controlled by forces outside themselves.

Leveling vs. sharpening. Levelers fit new stimuli into previously developed memory categories; sharpeners differentiate new instances from old ones.

Risk taking vs. caution. Risk takers take risks associated with low probabilities of high payoff; cautioners prefer low risks with high probabilities of low payoff.

Scanning vs. focusing strategies. Scanners identify relevant information in a problem by proceeding in a broad to narrow fashion; focusers proceed in a trial-and-error fashion.

Tolerance vs. intolerance (for incongruous or unrealistic experiences). Tolerants readily adapt to unusual experiences; intolerants demand more information before accepting unusual experiences.

Internal/External Locus of Control

Two tests for measuring the reflective/impulsive and locus of control styles are the Matching Familiar Figures Test (Kagan et al., 1964) and the I-E Scale (Rotter, 1966). The former test is designed for children, so no more will be said about it here. The I-E Scale consists of a series of paired statements, such as the following (Rotter, 1966. Copyright 1966 by the American Psychological Association. Reprinted by permission.):

1A Many of the unhappy things in people's lives are partly due to bad luck.

1B People's misfortunes result from the mistakes they make.

2A No matter how hard you try, some people just don't like you.

2B People who can't get others to like them don't understand how to get along with others.

3A In the case of the well-prepared student, there is rarely if ever such a thing as an unfair test.

3B Many times exam questions tend to be so unrelated to course work that studying is really useless.

4A Becoming a success is a matter of hard work; luck has little or nothing to do with it.

4B Getting a good job depends mainly on being in the right place at the right time.

5A The average citizen can have an influence in government decisions.

5B This world is run by the few people in power, and there is not much the little guy can do about it.

The B statement in statement-pairs 1 and 2 and the A statement in statement-pairs 3 to 5 are associated with the belief that a person can control his or her own life (*internal locus of control*); the remaining statements are associated with the belief that a person's life is controlled by fate or luck (*external locus of control*).

Research has found that an internal locus of control, which increases with age, is fostered by warm, responsive, supportive parents who encourage independence. Many other findings with the I-E Scale have been obtained from results comparing the characteristics of persons high and low on internal and external locus of control. However, the notion that locus of control is a general trait has been criticized (Levenson, 1981; Paulhus, 1983), and other self-report inventories have been designed to measure locus of control in specific contexts (Miller, Lefcourt, & Ware, 1983; Wallston & Wallston, 1981).

Interpersonal Trust Scale

Rotter also constructed an Interpersonal Trust Scale to measure the expectancy on the part of a person or group "that the word, promise, verbal or written statement of another individual or group can be relied upon" (Rotter, 1967, p. 651). Summarizing the results of research findings with this scale, he concluded that people who score high on interpersonal trust tend to have higher socioeconomic status; had strong parental support as children; are happier and less conflicted; have more friends; are less likely to lie; and, although not gullible, are more willing to give people a second chance (Rotter, 1980).

Also related to the topic of cognitive styles is Sternberg's (1988, 1989) concept of *intellectual styles*, the ways in which the types of intelligence—componential, experiential, and contextual—delineated by his triarchic theory of intelligence are brought to bear in solving problems. In the concept of intellectual styles, Sternberg attempted to combine the concept of intelligence with that of personality. He maintained that a particular intellectual style works for an individual to the extent that it matches his or her intellectual ability, preferred style, and the nature of the problem to be solved.

Personalities of Mentally Gifted and Creative Individuals

The first systematic, longitudinal study of mentally gifted individuals was initiated by Lewis Terman in 1921 and continued for more than a half-century (Oden, 1968; Sears, 1977). Among the many findings of this study were that, as adults, these individuals were equal or superior in personal and social adjustment and that they had a lower incidence of mental disorder than a comparison group of average intelligence. Later research conducted by Julian Stanley and his colleagues and students (Keating, 1976; Stanley, Keating, & Fox, 1974) with mathematically talented children appeared to confirm Terman's findings: These children tended to be personally well adjusted and highly motivated. However, the mentally gifted children studied by Webb and Meckstroth's (1982) were described not only as inquisitive, active, and energetic, but also as more obnoxious, unruly, strong-willed, mischievous, unmanageable, and rebellious than average. Similarly, studies of highly creative adults (Andreasen, 1987; Jamison, 1984) have found a higher frequency of personality problems in these individuals. Jamison (Goodwin & Jamison, 1990) reported that the prominent British artists (novelists, painters, playwrights, poets, and sculptors) whom she studied were significantly more likely than less creative individuals to have been treated for mania or depression. Likewise, in Andreasen's (1987) study, 80% of the 30 faculty members in a writers' workshop exhibited depression or some other form of mood disorder, and 43% were diagnosed as suffering from bipolar (manic-depressive) disorder. So it would seem that the time-worn stereotype of genius as being related to mental disorder cannot be dismissed as easily as Lewis Terman may have thought.

BIOLOGICAL FOUNDATIONS OF PERSONALITY

It is a truism that the seat of personality lies in the biology of the organism. The structure and dynamics of the human nervous system and endocrine glands determine how people characteristically behave and think. So far, however, efforts to find close correspondences between the neurophysiology or biochemistry of the organism and the emotions, motives, abilities, and other variables that make up what is referred to as "personality" have not been very successful. Observations of animal breeding programs and research in experimental and population genetics has shown that hereditary plays an important role in both temperament and abilities (Hall, 1938; Tryon, 1940; Bouchard & McGue, 1981; Bouchard et al., 1990), but the physiological substrates of most personality variables have not been discovered. For example, decades of research on the somatic bases of emotion have failed to reveal distinct bodily patterns associated with specific emotions. Several studies indicate that there is a relationship between depression and damage to the left anterior region of the brain (Robinson, Kubos, Starr, Rao, & Price, 1984; Sackeim et al., 1982).[1] Research findings have also implicated the right anterior region of the brain with more negative emotions and the left anterior region of the brain with more positive emotions (Ahern & Schwartz, 1985; Davidson, 1991). Despite these and other positive research findings (Levenson, 1992), the case for an association between specific emotions and different physiological responses patterns is weak.

Proponents of physiological measures of personality may feel that, unlike personality inventories and projectives, such measures are more basic and reliable. Unfortunately, even the polygraph ("lie detector") test can be notoriously unreliable, falsely identifying the innocent as guilty and the guilty as innocent (Steinbrook, 1992). Tensing certain muscle groups, biting the tongue, or thinking about something else during a polygraph examination can defeat it. Though most people become more autonomically aroused when lying—which is what is indicated by changes in respiration rate, heart rate, skin resistance, and blood pressure measured by means of a polygraph, some people can lie not only with a straight face but with a stable nervous system as well.

The novice liar or any other person who is under stress may show other physiological reactions in addition to those measured by a polygraph. Changes in the voice produced by microtremors of the vocal muscles and changes in the frequency spectrum of the voice can be measured by various *voice stress analyzers*. Changes in the blood supply to the finger, the forearm, the penis, or some other body organ can be measured by a *plethysmograph*, and changes in the diameter of the pupils of the eye can be measured by a *pupillometer*. Advances in the technology of microelectronics have increased the sophistication and mobility of such devices. For example, a subject in an experiment or a patient in therapy may wear a wristwatch-type device that detects movements of the arm and keeps a record of the time when they occurred. Or another subject may swallow a capsule containing a detector/transmitter that reports on the motility and chemistry of his or her digestive tract.

Studies of the relationships between personality and physiology have also not been resoundingly successful, though some interesting results have been obtained. Among these are the discovery of lower heart rates in depressed patients (Henriques & Davidson, 1980), higher heart rates and faster acquisition of conditioned fears in neurotic patients (Hodes, Cook, & Lang, 1985), and a slower speed of habituation of the galvanic skin response in anxious and neurotic individuals (Coles, Gale, & Kline, 1971; review by O'Gorman, 1983). Studies comparing shy children with more socially outgoing children have also found faster heart rates, more widely dilated pupils, greater tension in the voice muscles, and other indicators of sympathetic nervous system activity in shy children when they are confronted with a new situation or unfamiliar people (Kagan, 1994; Kagan, Reznick, & Snidman, 1988).

Physiology of Introversion and Extraversion

The personality trait of shyness is related to introversion/extroversion, and the biological correlates and causes of this variable have been most extensively studied by researchers. Taking a cue from Ivan Pavlov's observations on dogs, Hans Eysenck (1967, 1990) argued that human extroverts condition less quickly than human introverts because they have lower cortical excitation levels and higher sensory thresholds. Extroverts are more likely to seek external stimulation to elevate their lower cortical excitation levels. But activation of the autonomic nervous system is not related to introversion and extroversion in the same way as cortical activation level. The autonomic nervous systems of neurotics are presumably more arousable than those of normals, but the level of activation of the cerebral cortex in normals and neurotics is different for introverts and extroverts. According to Eysenck, neurotic introverts (anxiety, phobic, and obsessive-compulsive neurotics) have higher cortical excitation levels than normal introverts. The cortical excitation levels of neurotic extroverts, however, are higher than those of normal extroverts but lower than those of normal introverts. The result, says Eysenck, is that neurotic extroverts, e.g., psychopaths or antisocial personalities, do not experience sufficient fear to inhibit the expression of their impulses and, hence, are more likely to act them out in behavior.

Research designed to test Eysenck's theory concerning introversion and extroversion has employed various behavioral and physiological measures. One of the simplest tests of the hypothesis that introverts are internally overaroused and, therefore, avoid external sources of arousal, whereas extroverts are internally underaroused and, hence, seek external sources of arousal, is the *lemon juice test*: When drops of natural lemon juice are placed on the tongue, introverts tend to salivate more than extroverts (Deary et al., 1988). Introverts are also more easily aroused than extroverts by caffeine and other stimulants but less easily aroused by alcohol and other depressants (Stelmack, 1990). Also consistent with the Eysenck's theory is the finding that introverts exhibit greater cortical arousal to simple auditory and visual stimuli than extroverts (De Pascalis & Montirosso, 1988; Stelmack, Achorn, & Michaud, 1977; Stelmack & Michaud-Achorn, 1985; Stenberg, Rosen, & Risberg, 1988, 1990).

Sensation Seeking and the P300 Wave

Scores on Zuckerman's Social Disinhibition Scale (SDS) (see Figure 7.3) are positively correlation with extroversion and also related to *event-related cortical potentials (ERPs)*: High SDS scores are associated with increases in the amplitude of ERPs with increasing stimulus intensity, whereas SDS low scores are associated with constant or decreasing ERP amplitude with more intense stimulation (Zuckerman, 1983, 1989). The SDS is part of the Sensation-Seeking Scale, on which extroverts score higher than introverts. In comparison with low scorers on the SDS, high scorers tend to have lower blood levels of monamine oxidase (MAO). This enzyme, which regulates the concentration of two neurotransmitters considered to be important in emotion and motivation, is thought to be affected by heredity and may point to a hereditary basis for sensation seeking.

Other measures of cortical arousal are related to the introversion/extroversion personality dimension. One of these is the P300 wave, the electrically positive brain wave that occurs approximately 300 milliseconds after a momentary stimulus that has considerable meaning for the person. For example, larger P300 waves in response to novel stimuli have been observed in introverts than in extroverts (Polich & Martin, 1992; Wilson & Languis, 1990). The P300 wave is also related to mental disorders: smaller P300 amplitudes have been found in psychotics than in normals (Stelmack, Houlihan, & McGarry-Roberts, 1993), and shorter P300 latencies have been found in neurotics than in normals when the groups are matched on extroversion (Pritchard, 1989). Finally, there is some evidence that the latencies of brainstem-evoked auditory potentials are shorter in introverts than in extroverts (Stelmack & Houlihan, 1995).

SUMMARY

Interests, values, and personal orientations qualify as personality variables to the extent that they refer to behavioral inclinations that are

1.	A.	I like "wild," uninhibited parties.
	B.	I prefer quiet parties with good conversation.
2.	A.	I dislike "swingers" (people who are uninhibited and free about sex).
	B.	I enjoy the company of real "swingers."
3.	A.	I find that stimulants make me uncomfortable.
	B.	I often like to get high (drinking liquor or smoking marijuana).
4.	A.	I am not interested in experience for its own sake.
	B.	I like to have new and exciting experiences and sensations even if they are a little frightening, unconventional, or illegal.
5.	A.	I like to date members of the opposite sex who are physically exciting.
	B.	I like to date members of the opposite sex who share my values.
6.	A.	Heavy drinking usually ruins a party because some people get loud and boisterous.
	B.	Keeping the drinks full is the key to a good party.
7.	A.	A person should have considerable sexual experience before marriage.
	B.	It's better if two married persons begin their sexual experience with each other.
8.	A.	Even if I had the money I would not care to associate with flighty rich persons like those in the "jet set."
	B.	I could conceive of myself seeking pleasures around the world with the "jet set."
9.	A.	There is altogether too much portrayal of sex in movies.
	B.	I enjoy watching many of the sexy scenes in movies.
10.	A.	I feel best after taking a couple of drinks.
	B.	Something is wrong with people who need liquor to feel good.

(From Zuckerman, M. [1994]. *Behavioral expressions and biosocial bases of sensation seeking.* New York: Cambridge University Press. Reprinted by permission of M. Zuckerman.)

FIGURE 7.3. Items on the Social Disinhibition Scale (SID). This constitutes one of the four subscales on Zuckerman's 40-item Sensation Seeking Scale. Scores on responses to the SID items are computed by assigning one point to each response corresponding to the following key: 1-A, 2-B, 3-B, 4-B, 5-A, 6-B, 7-A, 8-B, 9-B, 10-A.

generalizable across a variety of situations. This appears to be less true of attitudes and opinions, which are not as transsituational as interests and values.

Various theories of the development of vocational interests, including those of Ginzburg, Super, and Gottfredson, have been proposed. The importance of the self-concept to interest development is underscored by both Super and Betz; the latter has also applied Bandura's self-efficacy theory to career counseling.

Holland's Self-Directed Search instrument is based on his RIASEC theory of vocational personalities and work environments, but the theory has also had a widespread influence on the scoring and interpretation of many other interest inventories. In addition to the fact that interest inventories are measures of personality, certain personality inventories can be scored for vocational interests.

Rokeach's Value Survey, which is scored for instrumental and terminal values, and Allport's Study of Values, which is scored for six values based on Spranger's theory of types, are similar to personality inventories. Certain values inventories are also measures of vocational interests and job satisfaction. Inventories of personal orientation, such as the Bem Sex Role Inventory and Shostrum's Personal Orientation Inventory measure of self-actualization, also qualify as measures of personality characteristics.

According to a holistic conception of personality, variables measured by tests of cognitive abilities constitute a part of personality. It is certainly true that emotions, motives, and other affective variables have an influence on cognitive functioning, and vice versa. However, attempts to identify particular personality traits or to diagnose specific mental disorders from the pattern of scores on different subtests constituting tests of intelligence or special aptitudes have not been successful. Scores on measures of cognitive styles, such as field independence/dependence and internal/external locus of control, have significant correlations with personality measures and can be construed as personality characteristics in their own right. The same is true of measures of attributions and self-concept.

According to a monistic body-mind theory, all affective, behavioral, and cognitive variables have biological substrates. However, efforts to identify specific somatic response patterns corresponding to particular emotions or personality traits have not been very successful. The most impressive findings concerning neurophysiological correlates of personality have been obtained from research based on Eysenck's hypothesis that introverts have higher cortical excitation levels than extroverts. Compared with extroverts, introverts show greater cortical arousal to sensory stimuli. Larger P300 brain wave amplitudes to novel stimuli have also been found in introverts than in extroverts, and smaller P300 amplitudes have been found in psychotics than in normals. Shorter P300 latencies but longer reaction times to novel stimuli have been observed in neurotics than in normals. Furthermore, high scorers on Zuckerman's Social Disinhibition Scale tend to have lower blood levels of MAO, an enzyme that regulates the concentration of two neurotransmitters involved in emotion and motivation.

NOTES

1. The *dexamethasone suppression test (DST)* reveals the biological basis of many types of depression. This test is based on the fact that dexamethasone

suppresses the production of cortisol, a hormone found in the cerebral cortex. However, the effects of a DST are not always valid and should be interpreted with caution (Carroll, 1985).

SUGGESTED READINGS

Ashmore, R. D. (1990). Sex, gender, and the individual. In L. A. Pervin (Ed.), *Handbook of personality theory and research* (pp. 486–526). New York: Guilford Press.

Betz, N. E. (1994). Self-concept theory in career development and counseling. *Career Development Quarterly, 43*, 32–42.

Brebner, J., & Stough, C. (1995). Theoretical and empirical relationships between personality and intelligence. In D. H. Saklofske & M. Zeidner (Eds.), *International handbook of personality and intelligence* (pp. 321–347). New York: Plenum.

Eysenck, H. J. (1990). Biological dimensions of personality. In L. A. Pervin (Ed.), *Handbook of personality theory and research* (pp. 244–276). New York: Guilford Press.

Maciel, A. G., Heckhausen, J., & Baltes, P. B. (1995). A life-span perspective on the interface between personality and intelligence. In R. J. Sternberg & P. Ruzgis (Eds.), *Personality and intelligence* (pp. 61–103). New York: Cambridge University Press.

Stelmack, R. M., & Houlihan, M. (1995). Event-related potentials, personality, and intelligence: Concepts, issues, and evidence. In D. H. Saklofske & M. Zeidner (Eds.), *International handbook of personality and intelligence* (pp. 349–365). New York: Plenum.

Weinrach, S. G., & Srebalus, D. J. (1990). Holland's theory of careers. In D. Brown & L. Brooks (Eds.), *Career choice and development: Applying contemporary theories to practice* (2nd ed., pp. 37–67). San Francisco: Jossey-Bass.

Zeidner, M. (1995). Personality trait correlates of intelligence. In D. H. Saklofske & M. Zeidner (Eds.), *International handbook of personality and intelligence* (pp. 299–319). New York: Plenum.

8

Issues and Applications of Personality Assessment

It has been emphasized repeatedly throughout this book that the reliability, validity, and standardization data available on many personality assessment instruments do not justify the use of these instruments for anything other than research purposes. Even then, it would probably be better if the research were conducted to determine the characteristics of the particular instrument rather than assuming that it is a valid measure of the dependent variable. In any event, a typical research study is concerned with drawing conclusions about *groups* rather than *individuals*, and comparisons between groups requires lower reliability coefficients than comparisons between or within individuals.

In some instances, efforts are not even made to determine the reliability of an instrument by diverse means and in various situations, to estimate the validity of an instrument as a measure of whatever it is supposed to measure, and to obtain norms from samples of people who are representative of the individuals with whom the instrument will be used. Even when investigations of the psychometric characteristics of a particular instrument have been conducted, the findings may not be sufficiently encouraging to warrant using it to make decisions about people's lives. These decisions may involve educational or career selections, marriage or divorce, placement of a minor in someone's custody, competency to stand trial or handle one's own affairs, recommendation for psychological or medical treatment of a health problem or disorder, prediction of violent offenses, or even institutionalization, incarceration, parole, or discharge.

The correctness of decisions made on the basis of psychological assessment data is limited not only by the tests and other assessment procedures but also by the training and judgment of the professionals who administer and interpret the results. Such training should include a thorough grounding in the theory, principles, and techniques on which psychological assessment is based as well as the limitations, biases, and potential misuse of these methods. In addition, complete familiarity with the administration, scoring, and interpretation of the particular instruments and procedures to be employed, which can only be acquired by repeated study and supervised practice, is critical. Classroom instruction is necessary but insufficient. Closely supervised experience "in the field"—in the work, educational, or clinical situation in which the assessment instruments and procedures will actually be used—is essential. The training supervisor should be aware of the theoretical orientation and bias (cultural, gender, social class, etc.) of the examiner/ trainee and discuss them with him or her. It is important for the psychological examiner to possess a firm belief, and to engage in behavior consistent with the belief, that psychological assessment should be an ethical enterprise based on truth and designed to help people rather than to manipulate, exploit, or deceive them. The importance of obtaining the informed consent of examinees or their legal representatives and maintaining confidentiality of test results, sharing them only with people who have a legal right to know and then only on a "need-to-know" basis, were discussed in chapter 1. Psychological assessment information, like information shared by doctor and patient or lawyer and client, is privileged communication and should be treated as such.

ISSUES IN PERSONALITY ASSESSMENT

The validity and gender/ethnic bias of personality assessment instruments and the ethics of assessment are important issues regarding these measures. Efforts to design tests that are not biased toward either sex, for example, are represented in the development of the MMPI-2 and the latest edition of the Strong Interest Inventory. However, anyone who decides to employ personality assessment instruments and procedures in research or for some practical purpose should be concerned not only with the psychometric shortcomings of these methods but also with what the results mean and how they should be applied.

There are numerous persisting controversies regarding the determinants of personality and personality test scores, the meaning and utility of the scores, and the social implications of using personality tests to make decisions about people. In this section we shall consider four of them: heredity versus environment, traits versus situations, clinical versus statistical prediction, and idiographic versus nomothetic assessment.

Heredity and Environment

It is generally agreed that personality is shaped by both heredity and environment, but the question concerning which is more important persists. To an interactionist, this is not necessarily an appropriate question because both heredity and environment—nature and nurture—are essential determinants of behavior.

Studies of the personalities of people of different degrees of kinship have yielded results pointing to a significant genetic component in personality characteristics, such as introversion-extroversion, activity level, anxiety, dependence, dominance, emotionality, and sociability (Buss & Plomin, 1984, 1986; Floderus-Myrhed et al., 1980; Riese, 1988; Royce & Powell, 1983; Thomas & Chess, 1977; Torgerson, 1985; Worobey, 1986). Evidence for the importance of heredity in mental disorders, such as schizophrenia and bipolar (manic-depressive) disorder is also impressive (Gottesman & Shields, 1972, 1982; Kallmann & Jarvik, 1959). Nevertheless, the findings of such studies vary with the age, sex, and other characteristics of the samples studied, and the way in which heredity affects personality is far from clear. Furthermore, the findings of many of these same studies attest to the importance of environment, particularly the nonshared environment that is unique to an individual within a family, in determining temperament and personality.

Traits and Situations

As indicated in the discussion of theories of personality in chapter 2, trait theorists assume that human behavior is directed by a constellation of personality traits that are expressed in a variety of situations. The environment, or situation, is regarded as a significant factor in determining behavior, but even more important than the specific situation are the relatively stable traits that make up an individual's personality. This has been the position favored by Gordon Allport, Raymond Cattell, Hans Eysenck, and many other psychologists of a more statistical, psychometric persuasion.

In a now classic book published in 1968, Walter Mischel took issue with the assumption that traits contribute more than situations to the determination of behavior. Citing the results of studies conducted in a wide range of situations and with many different personality variables, Mischel concluded that information concerning the relative standing of individuals on several personality traits is less useful than knowledge of the specific situation in predicting how those individuals will behave in that situation. In place of a traditional trait-factor conception of personality, Mischel advocated a social learning approach in which behavior in a specific situation is predictable from the person's learning history in that situation.

Norms, roles, and other group-related conditions are important in determining how people act, and these factors frequently exert a greater influence on behavior than do personal dispositions. Nevertheless, research conducted during the 1970s and 1980s has yielded mixed evidence concerning the relative importance of traits and situations as determinants of behavior. For example, some people are more consistent than others in terms of friendliness, conscientiousness, etc. across different situations, so cross-situational consistency of behavior may itself constitute a trait of personality. In addition, certain behaviors are more consistent than others across different situations. Some behaviors are narrowly situation specific, requiring specific eliciting stimuli, whereas other behaviors occur in a wider range of situations and are presumably reflective of broader personality traits (Funder & Colvin, 1991).

When all the evidence pertaining to the trait-situation debate is considered, it turns out that there is little support for a strict situationist viewpoint. Behavior appears, rather, to be a product of personality and situational variables acting together. Some situations have a stronger influence and some a weaker influence on behavior than others. The same is true of personality dispositions or traits: depending on the person, some traits appear to have stronger transsituational effects than others. Disagreements between trait and situation theorists remain, but the conflict appears much closer to a resolution than it did in the late 1960s and 1970s. What remains to be accomplished is to develop a true interactional, or transactional, procedure for assessing the effects of personality and situations on behavior.

Clinical and Statistical Prediction

As reiterated throughout this book, the validities of single personality assessment instruments tend to be rather low in comparison with those of cognitive measures. Predictive validities can sometimes be improved by weighting the scores on several measures of personality according to their perceived importance and then combining them. But who or what should decide on the weights and how they are to be combined? In a strategy referred to as the *statistical* or *actuarial* approach to personality assessment, behavioral data are weighted and combined by means of a statistical formula, a set of logical rules, or an actuarial table.

The more traditional approach to personality assessment is to have an experienced clinician collect behavioral data by various means (observations, interviews, projective tests, etc.) and then make decisions and predictions by studying the results. This *clinical* or *impressionistic* approach has been favored by clinical psychologists in the past.

Comparisons of the accuracy of predictions made by using the clinical and statistical approaches have yielded consistent evidence in favor of the latter (Meehl, 1954, 1965). Behavioral data may be collected by either a clinical approach (uncontrolled observations, interviews, projective techniques, etc.) or a statistical approach (objective tests, etc.) or the predictions made by either the clinical (subjective judgments from data) or statistical (regression analysis, discriminant analysis, etc.) procedures. There is no doubt that formulas and computers are generally more accurate than people in making predictions, but the superiority of the statistical approach is less clear-cut regarding data collection. Korchin and Schuldberg (1981) found evidence that clinicians are superior to standardized assessment instruments in collecting information on personality and behavior, but that statistical procedures are more accurate in combining and integrating the data to predict behavior. Clinicians can also make important contributions to the assessment process in deciding what kind of information to look for and where to seek it (Arkes, 1994). In sum, a combination of clinical and statistical procedures appears to work best for collecting personality assessment information and making decisions and predictions based on it.

Idiographic and Nomothetic Assessment

Related to the clinical versus statistical prediction issue is the idiographic versus nomothetic debate. This distinction, formulated originally by Gordon Allport (1937), contrasts the traditional viewpoints of clinical and experimental psychologists. The *idiographic approach* views each person as a lawful, integrated system worthy of analysis in his or her own right. The *nomothetic approach*, conversely, searches for general laws of behavior that apply to everyone. Allport (1961) recognized the usefulness of the nomothetic approach, but he was concerned that it "may lead to a dismemberment of personality in such a way that each fragment is related to the corresponding fragments in other people, and

not to the personal system within which they are embedded" (p. 572).
For this reason, Allport preferred that personality be assessed by means
of personal records (biographies, diaries, etc.), case studies, observations, and other nonstandardized, individualized procedures rather
than by means of tests, inventories, rating scales, and similar norm-
based instruments.

Allport would probably be pleased that the practice of clinical assessment today continues to be more idiographic than nomothetic. Clinical
psychologists still rely greatly on personal interviews, projective techniques, and other impressionistic evaluation procedures. Be that as it
may, clinicians have become less reluctant to combine their impressions
and subjective judgments with ratings and scores based on standardized
instruments and to depend to some degree on statistics, formulas, and
computers in making interpretations, diagnoses, and predictions.

PERSONALITY ASSESSMENT AT WORK AND PLAY

The problem of predicting how productive and proficient candidates for
employment and training will be is an important task for the personnel
department of any business organization. Profit and loss is the bottom
line of most businesses, and unproductive, ineffective employees contribute to the loss side more than the profit side of the ledger. The
possession of job-related skills, or at least the ability to learn them, is
a central component of any job-performance prediction equation, but
by itself it is insufficient. Effective job performance depends not only
on cognitive and psychomotor skills, but also on the ability to work
with other employees and management and, especially in sales and
management occupations, how well the employee can deal with customers, suppliers, and other non-employees with whom he or she comes
in contact in job-related activities.

Depending on the nature and level of the job and the organization,
personnel departments have traditionally screened prospective employees by examining their reported education and training; work histories;
and, for jobs requiring specific skills, performance on one or more trade
or aptitude tests. In addition, a personal interview, which is considered
particularly important for management-level jobs, is conducted as a final
step before making a hiring decision. In some cases, this information is
weighted and entered into a prediction (regression) equation; applicants who attain predicted scores above a certain minimum (cutoff)
score are hired, whereas those whose scores fall below the cutoff are
rejected.

The preceding description constitutes only one of several procedures for selecting applicants for employment, educational programs, or other positions. In many instances, recommendations from powerful or prestigious persons, being related to another employee, or having made oneself visible by some community service or other action can contribute to a positive selection decision. Negative features, even when they are of minor importance, frequently have a greater effect than positive features in determining whether or not one is selected. This is particularly true in the case of personality—as communicated by what other people say about the applicant in a letter, over the telephone, or in person. Such information can have a significant effect, perhaps even more than ability and recommendations, in the decision of whether to accept or reject the applicant.

It is recognized that whether a person adapts and succeeds or becomes maladjusted and fails on a job, as in other walks of life, depends not only on his or her abilities but also on motivation, interests, and temperament. Thus, what makes a person suitable for certain jobs is not primarily youth, education, previous experience, gender, or ethnicity, but rather the dynamics within the person. If one has the "right" internal dynamics, on-the-job training may well make him or her as effective as someone with more education and experience. This is probably more likely to be the case in management, sales, and related jobs, where contacts with other people and the candidate's ability to cooperate; persuade; and, in general, get along are crucial.

Personal interviews have traditionally been used to evaluate personality characteristics, but interviewees can "role play" or react in such a way as to please the interviewer for a short period. Such role playing may misrepresent the former's long-term, on-the-job interpersonal behavior. Because of the low reliabilities and validities of many preemployment interviews, the need to assess personality factors important for effective job performance has led to the use of personality tests as employee selection devices.

Illustrative Selection Tests of Personality

Personality tests have been used for employee selection purposes for more than a half-century, though not for all jobs or by all organizations. During that time, personality assessment has become increasingly popular in business and industrial organizations, ranging from accounting firms to manufacturing plants (Schmidt, Ones, & Hunter, 1992).

Brief descriptions of illustrative personality assessment instruments that have been used for employee selection purposes are listed in Table 8.1. Several of these instruments, such as the Comprehensive Personal-

**TABLE 8.1 Some Personality Assessment Instruments for Employee
Selection**

Comprehensive Personality Profile (Wonderlic Personnel Test, & L. L. Craft;
  adults; scored on 27 management, sales, and administration factors; to identify individuals with personality traits that are compatible with both occupational and organizational demands)
Employee Reliability Inventory (G. L. Borofsky; Wonderlic Personnel Test; prospective employees; seven scores; designed as preemployment instrument
  to assess several dimensions of reliable and productive work behavior; reviewed in MMYB 12:137)
Inwald Personality Inventory–Revised (R. Inwald; Hilson; public safety, security,
  and law enforcement applications [police, correction, fire, security]; 26
  scores; to aid public safety/law enforcement and security agencies in selecting
  new officers; reviewed in MMYB 11:183 & 12:194)
Meyer-Kendall Assessment Survey (H. D. Meyer & E. L. Kendall; Western Psychological Services; business employees and job applicants; scored on 12 scales;
  self-report measure of 10 personal attributes thought to be important for
  success in business management; reviewed in MMYB 12:234)
Occupational Personality Questionnaire (Saville & Holdsworth Ltd.; business or
  industry; self-report measure of personality and motivational characteristics
  particularly relevant to the world of work; 31 scores; reviewed in MMYB
  11:267)
Sales Achievement Predictor (J. Friedland, S. Marcus, & H. Mandel; Western
  Psychological Services; adults; scored on 18 scales)
Sales Personality Questionnaire (Saville & Holdsworth Ltd.; sales applicants; to
  assess personality characteristics necessary for sales success; 12 scores;
  reviewed in MMYB 12:337)
Work Adjustment Inventory (J. E. Gilliam; pro.ed.; ages 12–22; six scales for
  measuring work-related temperament traits; designed to evaluate adolescents' and young adults' temperament toward work activities, work environments, other employees, and other aspects of work)

---

ity Profile, the Inwald Personality Inventory, and the Sales Personality
Questionnaire, were designed specifically for use in employee selection.
Other instruments, such as the Adult Personality Inventory, the Eysenck
Personality Inventory, the Guilford-Zimmerman Temperament Survey,
the Myers–Briggs Type Indicator, and the 16 PF Questionnaire, which are
described in Appendix 5.1, were designed for more general assessment
purposes but have also been applied to the task of personnel selection.
As suggested by the listing in Table 8.1, personality assessment instruments have been used more in selecting individuals for personal contact
jobs, such as sales, public safety and security, and management occupations, than for other jobs.

One of the simplest personality assessments for sales personnel is a
measure of introversion/extroversion, such as the Eysenck Personality

Inventory. Most of the instruments listed in Table 8.1, however, provide measures of several other variables. The Comprehensive Personality Profile (CPP), for example, consists of 88 true-false items and can be taken in 15 minutes. Responses to the CPP are scored by computer and evaluated from a job-compatibility perspective to describe an applicant's personality in terms of job-related strengths and weaknesses. The computer-generated Job Factor Compatibility Report describes the candidate's personality on 27 scores grouped in three categories: management, sales, and administration; an extensive narrative and a personality profile description are also provided.

Criticisms of Personality Testing in the Workplace

Because of low reliabilities, fakability, and the lesser importance of personality traits compared with the organizational situation in determining behavior, personality tests have frequently failed to make significant contributions to employee selection or other business/industrial decisions. Stone (1988) concluded that, all things considered, personality assessment instruments contribute little to the selection of managers and probably should not be used at all for this purpose. Golden (1990) maintained that people's personalities may be too complex to be easily categorized, and that many people can adapt to a wide variety of jobs. Furthermore, there is the ethical problem of job-related personality assessment as a possible invasion of an individual's right to privacy.

The right to privacy issue was aired in the case of *Soroka v. Dayton–Hudson Corporation* (1991), a dispute concerned with the administration of a personality inventory (Psychscreen) comprised of items from the MMPI and CPI. This inventory, which had been used previously for screening applicants for positions in law enforcement, air-traffic control, and nuclear power plants in which security was of the utmost importance, was administered by Target Stores to security guard applicants. It was argued by the legal council for the plaintiff in the Target Stores case that Psychscreen items of the following kinds were discriminatory with respect to sexual and religious preference (Hager, 1991; p. A-20):

I believe in the second coming of Christ.
I believe there is a devil and a hell in afterlife.
I am very strongly attracted to members of my own sex.
I have never indulged in any unusual sex practices.

Attorneys for Dayton-Hudson Corporation countered that questions such as these are effective in identifying emotionally unstable applicants, who cannot be expected to perform effectively as security guards. The court ruled in favor of the plaintiff, however, concluding that these kinds of questions violate a job seeker's right to privacy. Although this ruling was appealed by the American Psychological Association, it remains debatable whether items concerned with sexual and religious preferences have any place on employment screening tests.

Despite criticisms of personality testing for employment purposes, there have been some notable successes in their use in selecting applicants for jobs and programs. One such success was the use of the MMPI in selecting applicants for the Peace Corps (Hobbs, 1963; Wiggins, 1973). After reviewing the research literature on personality assessments in business and industry, Tett, Jackson, and Rothstein (1991) maintained that "Contrary to conclusions of certain past reviews, the present findings provide some grounds for optimism concerning the use of personality measures in employee selection" (p. 703). At the end of his book on *Personality at Work* (1992), Furnham concludes that there is sufficient evidence to justify the continued use of personality testing in the workplace. According to Richard Skillinger, president of Smalley Transportation,

> It would be a mistake to think you could give employees a test and instantly find out where they should be and what they should do. But personality assessment, when it is properly conducted and interpreted, can help an organization like ours grow, develop, and produce. It can help us to identify the right people for the right positions. (Rubin, Peplau, & Salovey, 1993, p. 413)

Integrity Testing

Another personnel selection area in which personality assessment has been both successful and contentious is integrity testing. Theft is a serious, costly problem in business and industry, so it is not surprising that corporation executives are interested in methods for detecting potential dishonesty among employees or applicants. In response to this problem, for many years polygraph tests were used by business and industrial organizations to detect dishonesty among employees or applicants. But in 1988 the Employee Polygraph Protection Act, which bans most uses of polygraphs in preemployment interviews in government and the private sector, was passed by the U.S. Congress.

To fill the void created by the discontinuance of polygraph testing, several paper-and-pencil tests of honesty or integrity were introduced. In addition to containing items regarding direct admission and opinions of illegal or questionable behavior, as well as reactions to hypothetical situations that possibly feature dishonest behavior, many of the items on these tests were designed to assess personality traits and thought patterns associated with dishonesty. Although some integrity tests, when used appropriately and in conjunction with additional selection procedures, were found to be valid selection procedures, the practice of integrity testing remains controversial (APA Task Force, 1991; Camara & Schneider, 1994, 1995; O'Bannon, Goldinger, & Appleby, 1989). One of these issues is concerned with an individual's right to privacy, which may very well be compromised by some integrity tests.

In addition to their practical applications in employee selection, personality assessment instruments have been used extensively in research on vocational preference, work motivation, productivity, job satisfaction, absenteeism, turnover, accidents, and consumer behavior. Two of these topics—accidents and consumer behavior—will be considered briefly.

Accident-Prone Personalities

Perhaps equal in costliness to theft in business and industry is the occurrence of accidents on the job. The popular notion that there is an *accident-prone* personality, characterized by workers who have accidents at a significantly higher rate than others, has been the topic of a great deal of research in industrial/organizational psychology. Although the results of many initial studies in this area suggested that there is such a syndrome as an accident-prone personality, interest in the topic has waned in recent years. Some authorities have even concluded that the concept of accident proneness is largely a statistical artifact rather than a genuine phenomenon (Schultz & Schultz, 1990).

It is true that temporary emotional problems stemming from the stress of an unhappy home life can make a person more distractible and thereby increase the probability of an accident. It has been found that frustrated, worried, and angry workers tend to have more accidents than happy, contented workers. Shaw and Sichel (1971) reported, for example, that, compared with nonrepeaters, accident repeaters are less emotionally stable, more hostile toward authority, and higher in anxiety. Repeaters also have more problems in getting along with other people, and their work histories are less stable than those of nonrepeaters. In another study (Niemcryk, Jenkins, Rose, & Hurst, 1987), it was found that air-traffic controllers who displayed type A behavior were more likely than those showing type B behavior to experience injuries on the job.[1]

A more recent, and more comprehensive, study of the relationships of biodata, personality, and cognitive variables to accidents was conducted by Hansen (1989) on 363 chemical industrial workers. A social maladjustment scale constructed from the MMPI and a measure of neurotic distractibility both made significant and independent contributions to the prediction of accident rate. Although the notion of an accident-prone personality is a nonuseful overgeneralization, Furnham (1992) concluded from the results of Hansen's (1989) study and those of other investigations (Arnett, 1990; Montag & Comrey, 1987; Perry, 1986) that there is sufficient evidence that personality variables are related to all sorts of accidents in all sorts of populations.[2]

Psychographics

The analysis of attitudes, interests, opinions, values, personality traits, and lifestyles of consumers that are associated with expressed preferences for and the purchase of specific products or services is a part of the marketing mix. Segmentation of a potential market in terms of the patterns of temperament, cognition, and behavior that differentiate among demographic or other groups of people and then designing advertising, packaging, and promotional messages and materials to appeal to and motivate these particular market segments is considered an efficient marketing strategy. This is the approach of *psychographics*, two examples of which are AIO (activities, interests, opinions) inventories and SRI Consulting's Consumer Segmentation System, VALS™2 (values and lifestyles).

AIO inventories are composed of a series of statements concerning the activities, interests, and opinions of specified groups of people. A typical AIO inventory is designed with a particular product and market in mind, and responses to it can distinguish a particular segment of the product market from another segment.

More theoretically based than an AIO inventory is VALS™2. As illustrated in Figure 8.1, this model is based on two dimensions: resources and self-orientations. *Resources* may be high or low, and *self-orientations* are divided into principle, status, and action orientations. Consumers who are classified as *principle oriented* are guided in their product and service choices by abstract, idealized criteria rather than by feelings, events or the behaviors and opinions of other people. *Status-oriented* consumers are interested primarily in products and services that indicate success to their peers, whereas *action-oriented* consumers are motivated toward social or physical activity, variety, and risk taking.

The resources dimension of the VALS™2 model refers to the psychological, physical, demographic, and material means and capacities that are available to consumers. These resources consist of education, income, self-confidence, health, eagerness to buy, and energy level. Re-

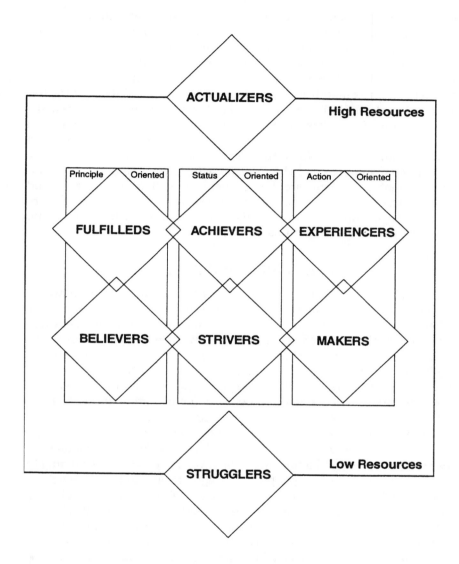

FIGURE 8.1. VALS™2 two-dimensional psychographics model. (Copyright 1996 SRI Consulting. All rights reserved. Unauthorized reproduction prohibited.)

sources are on a continuum from minimal to abundant; they generally decrease in old age, at which time depression, financial reverses, and physical or psychological impairment are more likely to occur.

As depicted in Figure 8.1, the self-orientation and resources dimensions are divided into eight segments of adult behavior. These segments consist of approximately equal proportions of the population. At the top are the *Actualizers*, individuals with abundant resources who represent a combination of the three orientations. The two principle-orientation segments are the *Fulfilleds*, with more resources, and the *Believers*, with fewer resources. The two status-oriented segments are the *Achievers*, with more resources, and the *Strivers*, with fewer resources. The two action-oriented segments are the *Experiencers*, with more resources, and the *Makers*, with fewer resources. At the very bottom of the hierarchy are the *Strugglers*, individuals who have minimal resources, constricted and difficult lives, and are cautious consumers.

Personality and Sports

The initial impetus for using personality assessment devices in sports was concern with enhancing athletic performance. In these efforts, clinical psychologists worked with athletic coaches and as advisers and psychotherapists to professional athletes who were trying to optimize their performance and achieve a winning edge. Sports psychologists applied a variety of techniques and, with the establishment of a separate division in the American Psychological Association (the Division of Exercise and Sport Psychology), began communicating and coordinating their procedures and findings more efficiently.

Although sport psychologists are still concerned with maximizing the performance of elite athletes, the field has broadened to encompass research, theories, and applications on a variety of topics pertaining to the physical activities of people in all age groups and at all levels of athletic ability (Butt, 1987; LeUnes & Nation, 1980). Sports psychologists have conducted numerous studies concerned with methods of selecting potentially winning athletes, using personality assessment instruments, such as the Athletic Motivation Inventory, the MMPI, the 16 PF Questionnaire, the Eysenck Personality Inventory, and the Edwards Personality Inventory. Though none of these instruments is a valid predictor of athletic performance, somewhat better results have been obtained with the POMS. For example, in a comparison of Olympic rowers, wrestlers, and distance runners with unsuccessful candidates in these sports, it was found that successful candidates scored lower than unsuccessful candidates on certain POMS scales (Morgan, 1980). In all three sports, successful candidates scored below average on the tension, depression, anger, fatigue, and confusion scales, but above average on the vigor scale. This is the so-called *iceberg profile*, which has been reported by other investigators as well (Joesting, 1981; Ungerleiter & Golding, 1989).

Other studies in sport psychology have been concerned with the relationships of personality variables to exercise. The results of studies of the effects of exercise on mood and other affective variables indicate that physical exercise has a significant effect on anxiety, depression, self-esteem, and other measures of self-esteem (Greist, 1984; Sonstroem, 1984). Exercise has also been found to act as a buffer against psychological stress (Roth & Holmes, 1985).

PERSONALITY ASSESSMENT IN CLINICS AND COURTROOMS

Clinical psychology is concerned with the diagnosis, treatment, and prevention of emotional and behavior disorders of all kinds and all degrees of severity. The activities of practitioners of this largest of all psychological specialties include personality assessment, diagnosis, counseling, and psychotherapy with mentally disturbed people and research on personality and mental disorders. *Counseling psychologists* do many of the same things as clinical psychologists, but are concerned with less severe problems of adjustment and interpersonal relations. Clinical psychology is also closely related to psychiatry, but, unlike psychiatrists, clinical psychologists do not prescribe drugs or apply other kinds of physical treatments.

In their role as personality assessors, clinical psychologists may be called on to conduct psychological evaluations in mental health, medical, educational, legal, and other settings. They may conduct clinical interviews, make detailed observations under diverse conditions, and administer a variety of personality assessment instruments. The data and information obtained from these activities, it is hoped, contribute to decisions regarding psychodiagnosis, treatment, residential placement, determination of the effectiveness of psychotherapy and chemotherapy, educational intervention or remediation, judicial rulings, rehabilitation, and financial compensation awards.

Clinical assessment specialists receive referrals from psychiatrists, judges, attorneys, and other sources in the form of a referral question. The referral question should provide a brief description of the patient (client), some information on the nature of the problem, and what additional information the referral source wishes the psychologist to obtain. The referral question may be fairly short and specific, such as the following:

Is the patient mentally retarded?
Is the patient mentally gifted?
Is the patient organically impaired (brain damaged)?
Is the patient neurotic or psychotic?
Is the patient likely to commit suicide?
Is the patient competent to stand trial?
Is the patient likely to commit rape (or other violent behavior) again?

The referral question may also be much broader, or more comprehensive, such as the following:

What is the nature and extent of the organic impairment in this patient?
How effective is the patient functioning cognitively and to what extent does any impairment interfere with his or her behavioral competency?
What sort of counseling or psychotherapy can be recommended for the patient, and what outcomes can be expected from such treatment or intervention?

After reading the referral question(s) and studying the accompanying background material, the psychologist must decide what assessment methods and procedures to use to provide useful answers. Furthermore, the referral source may request that certain tests or procedures, such as the WAIS-R, the Rorschach, or the MMPI-2, be administered. A common request is for a *mental status evaluation* to obtain in-depth information concerning the patient's:

Emotional state (affect and mood)
Intellectual and perceptual functioning (attention, concentration, memory, intelligence, and judgment)
Style and content of thought processes and speech
Level of insight into mental status and personality problems, and psychomotor activity
General appearance, behavior, and attitudes

The report of a mental status examination is helpful not only in decisions regarding treatment but also in legal judgments concerning mental competency, insanity, and so on.

Case Study

In general, the goals of clinical assessment are to provide an accurate description of the patient's problem(s), what interpersonal and environmental factors precipitated and are sustaining the problem(s), and what is likely to happen to the patient with and without treatment. Such information cannot be obtained in a single assessment session or by means of one or two tests, but requires a more thorough case study. A *case study* involves obtaining information not only from the patient himself or herself, but also from family, friends, coworkers, and other people who know the patient fairly well. Data concerning the patient's family, culture, health history, developmental history, educational history, economic history, and legal history, as well as test scores, activities, and thoughts may be elicited.

After all the data have been collected, the psychologist attempts to integrate it by looking for consistencies, contradictions, and other generalizations in the light of various theories of personality and behavior and personal experience with similar cases. A report summarizing the findings and explanatory hypotheses or conclusions is then prepared. In addition to describing the procedures and findings of the case study, the report includes statements regarding the presence of any serious adjustment problem or mental disorder, predictions or prognoses concerning it, and recommendations for treatments or other interventions. The report may then be presented, and its findings discussed, at a case conference or staff meeting with other professionals who are involved with the case. The conferring professionals may include a clinical psychologist, a psychiatrist, a social worker, a psychiatric nurse, and perhaps other mental health personnel. In both the written report and during the conference discussion, the causes of the patient's problems and suggestions for treatment are usually made, with the recommendation that the effectiveness of the therapeutic interventions be reevaluated periodically.

Case conferences are also held with the relatives or other persons who are legally responsible for the patient. At these conferences, the purpose and nature of the evaluation (tests administered, etc.) are described, in addition to why these instruments were used, their limitations, and what the findings were. Descriptive statements and score ranges rather than exact scores are communicated. Rather than focusing on numbers and diagnostic labels, options, and decisions for treatment, remediation, rehabilitation, or other interventions are emphasized. The patient and those who are legally responsible for him or her are provided with ample opportunity to ask questions, discuss concerns, and volunteer further pertinent information.

Psychodiagnosis

In the traditional medical model, both physical and mental illnesses are identified by certain symptoms or syndromes (symptom clusters).

Following this model, the psychodiagnostician observes, interviews, and tests the patient to ascertain the presence of pathological (physical and mental) symptoms. By comparing the patient's symptoms with those incorporated in standard descriptions of a particular syndrome or disorder, a diagnosis of the patient's condition is made, and the patient is labeled as having that condition. The most popular reference for descriptive details pertaining to various mental disorders is the *Diagnostic and Statistical Manual of Mental Disorders-IV* (DSM-IV) (American Psychiatric Association, 1994). Approximately 300 mental disorders, grouped into 16 categories, are described in DSM-IV (see Table 8.2).

The DSM-IV system is multiaxial, in that diagnoses are made with respect to the following five axes referring to different kinds of information about the patient:

    Axis I.   Clinical Disorders
               Other Conditions That May Be a Focus of Clinical Attention
    Axis II. Personality Disorders
               Mental Retardation
    Axis III. General Medical Conditions
    Axis IV. Psychosocial and Environmental Problems
    Axis V. · Global Assessment of Functioning

Each disorder is labeled and numbered with a five-digit code on Axes I and II, and the severity of the condition is designed as "mild, moderate, or severe." Multiple diagnoses are permissible on these two axes. Patients previously diagnosed as having a particular disorder but no longer meeting the criteria for that disorder are designated as "in partial remission" or "in full remission," as the case may be. Accompanying physical disorders and conditions are classified on Axis III, the severity of psychosocial stressors is classified on Axis IV, and a global assessment of functioning (GAF) is designated by means of a numerical index on Axis V.

Although DSM-IV appears to be more reliable than many other systems for diagnosing mental disorders, critics have argued that the diagnostic criteria are too rigid to apply to all patients. Other authorities have warned of the inappropriateness and danger of any kind of psychiatric labeling and the inconsistency with which diagnostic labels, such as schizophrenia and depression, are applied (Rosenhan, 1973; Ziskin & Faust, 1988). Furthermore, labels, such as "psychotic," "neurotic," and "psychopathic personality," may encourage a self-fulfilling prophecy in which the patient is viewed as having the disorder with which he or she is labeled. When one expects a person to behave in a certain way, for whatever reason that person may actually change his or her behavior and begin to act in the expected fashion.

TABLE 8.2 Major Diagnostic Categories of DSM-IV

Delirium, Dementia, and Amnestic and Other Cognitive Disorders
Mental Disorders Due to a General Medical Condition
Substance-Related Disorders
Schizophrenia and Other Psychotic Disorders
Mood Disorders
Anxiety Disorders
Somatoform Disorders
Factitious Disorder
Dissociative Disorders
Sexual and Gender Identity Disorders
Eating Disorders
Sleep Disorders
Impulse-Control Disorders Not Elsewhere Classified
Adjustment Disorder
Personality Disorders
Disorders Usually First Diagnosed in Infancy, Childhood, or Adolescence

Another criticism of psychodiagnosis is that diagnoses vary with the interests, concerns, and theoretical orientation of the diagnostician, the demographic characteristics (sex, socioeconomic status, and ethnicity) of the patient, and with the institution, the community, and the country in which the diagnosis is made. The frequencies with which certain conditions are diagnosed are also influenced by the amount of monetary compensation awarded to patients who are diagnosed as having those conditions. If the government or insurance companies pay for the care and treatment of patients diagnosed as having a psychotic or organic condition, a higher frequency of those diagnoses may be observed. Conversely, if patients lose many of their legal rights when diagnosed as psychotic, for example, diagnosticians may be reluctant to assign that label. In support of psychodiagnosis are those who maintain that it reduces long-winded explanations, increases communication between mental health professionals, contributes to making diagnostic predictions, and facilitates research on abnormal behavior (Spitzer, 1976; Woodruff, Goodwin, & Guze, 1974).

Pitfalls in Clinical Judgment

It has been noted repeatedly throughout this book that clinical judgments are seldom completely accurate. In fact, experienced clinicians are often less effective psychodiagnosticians and psychotherapists than nonprofessionals who have essentially no training or experience in diagnosis (Garb, 1989). Several factors detract from the judgments and predictions made by clinicians, and, in fact, people in general (Arkes, 1994; Murphy & Davidshofer, 1994; Tversky & Kahneman, 1981). One of these—the *self-fulfilling prophecy*—was referred to earlier. Another factor that interferes with sound clinical judgment is *preconceived notions*, such as forming a hypothesis to explain the behavior of a patient and then actively searching for information to confirm the hypothesis. A fairly common preconceived notion is the *illusory correlation* error of basing a judgment on the number of times a symptom and a disorder have occurred together while overlooking the number of times they have not occurred together. An illustration is the widely publicized "personality portrait" of a serial killer or the "Unabomber."

Other pitfalls to good clinical judgment are (a) the *availability heuristic* of basing judgments on the availability of information in our memories; (b) the *hindsight bias* of maintaining, after an event has occurred, that one could have predicted it if he or she had been asked to do so beforehand; (c) *overconfidence*, or the tendency of those who judge least accurately to be most confident in their judgments; (d) the *conjunction fallacy* of assuming that the conjunction of two events is more likely than either event alone; and (e) *belief perseverance*, or clinging to one's beliefs in the face of contrary evidence. Failure to consider the *base rate*—the proportion of people in a population having the characteristic or condition—also makes it more difficult to identify or diagnose a pathological condition by means of available assessment methods. These sources of error in clinical judgments persist not only because they save time and enhance one's self-esteem, but because they often work in real life. Unfortunately, by failing to follow up on the results of their judgments, clinicians frequently remain unaware of the many mistakes they make in diagnosis and behavior prediction.

Psychological Report

Whatever the purposes of a psychological examination or case study may be, the results are typically summarized and communicated in the form of a written report. The outline, length, and language of such a report vary with the purposes of the examination, but the outline shown in Figure 8.2 is representative. In preparing a report of a psychological examination, the writer should include information on the following:

1. The reason why the examinee was referred for or sought psychological evaluation

2. The bearing that the findings have on the referral question(s) and the potential solutions to the examinee's needs and problems
3. The examinee's mental, emotional, physical, and socioeconomic capacities to deal with his or her situation
4. The probable future or outcomes (prognosis) for the examinee

The physical, cognitive, and affective characteristics of the examinee should be described fully and specifically. Then the various sources of information should be compared and integrated, and an overall picture drawn and defensible diagnostic conclusions presented.

A variety of writing styles—literary, clinical, scientific, etc. (Groth-Marnat, 1990)—may be found in a psychological report. Of foremost importance, however, is for the results be presented meaningfully and in a style that can be understood by people who will read the report. Realizing that the report of a psychological examination is of little value if it cannot be understood by those who are in a position to use the information it contains to make decisions concerning the examinee's welfare, the report writer employs simple, objective behavioral language rather than abstract, technical terminology. This does not mean that interpretations and conclusions should not be based on psychological theory or expressed in terms of hypotheses. However, the assumptions of the theory and the data on which the hypotheses are based should be made clear.

Health Psychology

Psychologists have always been interested in mental health, but in recent years many psychologists have also devoted a great deal of attention to the role of personality in physical health. To help identify psychological conditions and states that affect health and disease and to assist in formulating plans for treating health problems, many new health-related personality inventories have been devised. Representative inventories of this type for evaluating alcoholism or the abuse of other substances, eating disorders, and type A personality are described in Table 8.3. These kinds of paper-and-pencil instruments have been used extensively in research on psychological factors in coronary heart disease, anorexia and bulimia, alcohol dependency, drug addiction, and many other disorders. Measures of pain perception and control (e.g., TMJ Scale) and imagery in cancer (e.g., Imagery and Disease, and Imagery of Cancer) are also available.

In addition to narrow-band instruments for identifying psychological factors in specific health problems, instruments such as the Millon Behavioral Health Inventory (from NCS Assessments) have been de-

---

Psychological Assessment Report

Name of Examinee _____

Age _____ Birth Date _____ Education _____

Examiner _____

Place of Examination _____ Date _____

Tests Administered. List the names, including forms and levels, of all tests and inventories that were administered.

Referral Questions and Relevant Background Data. Why was the examinee referred for psychological testing? What was the purpose of the referral, and what person or facility made it? What background information relevant to the case was obtained from other sources (school, work, medical, military or other records, interviews, etc.)? Give the examinee's own story, as well as that of other observers if available. Describe the examinee's physical and psychological history and characteristics, and educational and employment situation. Serious sensory or psychomotor handicaps, as well as the presence of emotional disorder should also be noted.

Observations of Appearance and Behavior. Describe the appearance and behavior of the examinee during the examination. Describe the examinee's characteristics, his or her approach to the tasks, level of motivation and emotionality, and any other factors that might have influenced the results. What behaviors on the part of the examinee were symptomatic of particular physical, cognitive, or affective conditions or characteristics?

Test Results and Interpretations. Give a detailed description of the results of the tests or other instruments administered and how they may be interpreted. If the examiner is interpreting the results according to a particular theory of personality or behavior, make certain that the reader understands the language and assumptions of that theory. Be as specific and individualized as possible in interpreting the results.

Conclusions and Recommendations. Describe the conclusions stemming from the observational, interview and standardized or unstandardized test data. What recommendations are warranted by the results? Include appropriate interpretative cautions, but do not "hedge" or deal in generalities. Additional psychological assessment, neurological or other medical examinations, counseling or psychotherapy, special class placement and training, and vocational rehabilitation and institutionalization are among the recommendations that might be made. Provide information on specific referral sources is possible.

_____

Signature and Printed Name of Examiner

_____

Position

FIGURE 8.2. Outline of a Psychological Assessment Report.

TABLE 8.3 Illustrative Health-Related Personality Inventories

Alcoholism and Other Substance Abuse

Alcohol Use Inventory (J. L. Horn, K. W. Weinberg, & F. M. Foster; NCS Assessments; adolescents and adults, 16 years and older; to assess the nature of an individual's alcohol use pattern, and problems associated with that pattern)

Substance Abuse Subtle Screening Inventory (G. A. Miller; The Psychological Corporation; adolescents and adults; to identify alcohol and drug dependent individuals and differentiate them from social users and general psychiatric clients; reviewed in MMYB 12:381)

The Western Personality Inventory (M. P. Manson; Western Psychological Services; adults; to identify alcoholics and potential alcoholics and measures the extent of alcohol addiction; reviewed in TC II:826)

Eating Disorders

Eating Disorder Inventory-2 (D. M. Garner; Psychological Assessment Resources; ages 12 and older; self-report measure of psychological features commonly associated with anorexia nervosa and bulimia nervosa; reviewed in MMYB 12:130; TC X:226)

Eating Inventory (A. J. Stunkard & S. Messick; The Psychological Corporation; 17 years and older; to assess 3 dimensions of eating behavior found to be important in recognizing and treating eating-related disorders: cognitive control of eating, disinhibition, and hunger; reviewed in TC VIII:158)

Type A Behavior

Jenkins Activity Survey (C. D. Jenkins, S. J. Zyzanski, & R. H. Rosenman; The Psychological Corporation; employed adults ages 25–65; measure of Type A behavior, coronary prone behavior pattern; reviewed in MMYB 9:545; TC VII:264)

---

signed to assess the psychological correlates of a wide range of physical health problems. Various instruments are also available to study the types, causes, and consequences of psychological stress and methods of coping with stress (see Appendix 5.2). Among the psychological constructs that have been investigated for their role in physical disorders are anxiety, depression, locus of control, attributions, and feelings of helplessness and personal efficacy. Several of these constructs are concerned with the sense of predictability and control over outcomes and the feelings of responsibility that individuals have over their own lives. Being able to forecast personally significant events and to control for their occurrence are helpful in avoiding stress or at least moderating its effects.

Related to the variable of personal efficacy and control are *attributions*, explanations that people give for the causes (internal or external) of their behavior. Two instruments designed to study the role of attributions, and the related concept of *locus of control*, in determining behavior are the Health Attribution Test (by J. Achterberg & G. F. Lawlis; Institute of Personality and Ability Testing) and the Health Locus of Control Scale (Wallston & Wallston, 1981). However, as defined by certain instruments, the concept of *health* has a broader connotation than the absence of disease: It means *positive wellness* and the attainment of a good *quality of life*.

Forensic Psychology

Psychologists who are employed in law enforcement contexts perform a variety of tasks, including the following:

- Serving as human relations experts and staff developers
- Using tests, questionnaires, and interviews to assist in selecting personnel and evaluating staff development programs
- Counseling police officers and their families in crisis situations
- Conducting research on the training and treatment of law enforcement personnel
- Evaluating defendants in court cases to determine if they are competent to stand trial, responsible for their behavior, and dangerous or likely to be repeat offenders

As most forensic psychologists and psychiatrists are quick to learn, the legal arena is not a place where psychological and medical science necessarily have the last word. A criminal court case is a kind of theatrical drama where two adversaries present and debate the merits of the evidence pertaining to a crime. Because scientific truth is rarely absolute, the "reasonable doubt" that exists in most cases requires that the defendant be found not guilty.

Two legal matters in which personality assessment frequently plays a role are decisions involving competency and sanity. A person is legally determined to possess *competency* when he or she has sound judgment and can manage his or her own property and affairs, enter into contracts, and so on. The question of competency may arise in the case of a person who, because of physical or mental infirmity, is experiencing problems in taking care of his or her property and other matters. If the person is found legally incompetent, the court will appoint a guardian to manage the person's property and situation.

The concept of competency is also used, in a second sense, regarding an accused's person's "competency" to stand trial. To be judged competent to stand trial, a defendant must understand the charges against him or her and be able to consult with attorneys in a rational manner and thereby assist in his or her own defense (*Dusky v. United States*, 1960). Incompetency is not synonymous with insanity; the legal concept of *insanity* pertains to the defendant's state at the time the crime was committed, whereas incompetency is a continuing condition. In addition to competency and insanity, the legal concepts of *diminished capacity* and *responsibility* (for one's actions) come into play in court cases involving insanity pleas. In any event, because insanity is more difficult to prove than incompetency, in a court trial it is more likely that a defendant will be found incompetent than insane.

The concept of *legal insanity*, as applied in the United States, stems from the M'Naghten Rule, the Durham Decision, and the Model Penal Code (*Durham v. United States*, 1960; Smith & Meyer, 1987). The standard for insanity applied in most states is described in the Model Penal Code of the American Law Institute (ALI) (1956):

> A person is not responsible for criminal conduct, i.e., insane if, at the time of such conduct, as a result of mental disease or defect, he lacks substantial capacity either to appreciate the criminality (wrongfulness) of his conduct, or to conform his conduct to the requirement of the law.

Several procedures and instruments may be used by psychologists to assess competency, several of which are listed in Table 8.4. Regarding the role of the psychologist in insanity determinations, in addition to in-depth interviews and detailed observations of the defendant, two tests that are commonly administered are the MMPI and the Rorschach. Other psychometric instruments, such as the Rogers Criminal Responsibility Assessment Scales (RCRAS), may also be used. Measures on five scales of the RCRAS—Patient Reliability, Organicity, Psychopathology, Cognitive Control, and Behavioral Control—provide data on the examinee's degree of impairment at the time he or she is alleged to have committed the crime. The quantified degree of impairment is then related to the ALI legal standard, and an opinion with respect to the standard is presented by the examiner.

Psychologists often serve as expert witnesses in court cases involving sexual or violent offenses, and special psychometric instruments have also been constructed to enhance the validity of such testimony. The Clarke Sex History Questionnaire for Males, for example, may be of help to the forensic psychologist in determining the kinds and strengths of sexually anomalous behavior engaged in by the defendant. Although violent behavior cannot be predicted from a single instrument, the MMPI, combined with observational, interview, and personal history data, can improve the prediction. Among the behavioral predictors of violence are a recent history of violence, substance abuse, breakup of

TABLE 8.4 Illustrative Instruments and Procedures for Forensic Psychological Assessment

---

Carlson Psychological Survey (CPS) (K. A. Carlson; Psychological Assessment Resources; adolescent and adult criminal offenders; assesses behavior or substance abuse problems in criminal offender populations; reviewed in MMYB 9:203; TC IV:144)

Clarke Sex History Questionnaire for Males (Langevin, 1983)

Competency Screening Test (Lipsitt, Lelos, & McGarry, 1971; sentence completion test consisting of 22 items, each related to a legal criterion to stand trial)

The Custody Quotient (R. Gordon & L. A. Peck; The Wilmington Institute; parents or other adults seeking access or custody; provides relevant information about the knowledge, attributes, and skills of adults involved in custody disputes; reviewed in MMYB 11:98; TC IX:145)

Georgetown Screening Interview for Competency to Stand Trial (Bukatman, Foy, & De Grazia, 1971; Georgetown University Law School; enumerates 13 criteria of competency to stand trial and specific questions for a competency screening interview)

Georgia Court Competency Test (Wildman et al., 1980)

The Hare Psychopathy Checklist-Revised (PCL-R) (R. D. Hare; Psychological Assessment Resources; adult prison inmates; consists of 20 items designed to assess psychopathic (antisocial) personality disorders in forensic populations; based on H. Cleckley's (1976) profile of psychopaths as callous, impulsive, nonempathic, etc.; reviewed in MMYB 12:177)

Lifestyle Criminality Screening Form (Walters, Revella, & Baltrusaitis, 1990; 14-item questionnaire scored on information from offender's presentence investigation report on self-indulgence, interpersonal intrusiveness, social rule breaking, and irresponsibility; high scorers have high rates of parole and probation violations)

Rogers Criminal Responsibility Assessment Scales (R. Rogers; Psychological Assessment Resources; adults; 25 items scored on reliability (including malingering), organic factors, psychopathology, cognitive control, and behavioral control to assess criminal responsibility; reviewed in MMYB 10:316; TC VI:643)

Structured Interview of Reported Symptoms (SIRS) (R. Rogers; Psychological Assessment Resources; ages 18 and older; to detect malingering and feigning of psychiatric symptoms)

Uniform Child Custody Evaluation System (UCCES) (H. L. Munsinger & K. W. Karlson; Psychological Assessment Resources; parent and child forms; designed to meet the need for a uniform custody evaluation procedure for mental health professionals)

---

a marital or love relationship, being disciplined or terminated on a job, and having access to guns or other weapons (Hall, 1987).

Recidivism is common in both sexual and violent crimes, so parole boards, personnel departments, and other organizations or persons with whom such offenders come into contact require the best information they can obtain regarding the probability of repeat offenses. This is particularly true in cases of child abuse or mistreatment. In child custody cases, it is important to evaluate both the child and the caretakers. A comprehensive system for evaluating parents and children in such cases is the Uniform Child Custody Evaluation System. A complete evaluation with this system entails the completion of 25 forms, including 10 general data and administrative forms, 9 parent forms, and 6 child forms. The parent forms involve a complete family/personal history, an interview with the parent, a parenting abilities checklist, an interview of the parent's suitability for joint custody, a form for behavioral observations of the interaction between the parent and child, a home visit observation form, and forms for the analysis of response validity, agreement between parent and evaluation, and explanation of custody evaluation procedures for parents and attorneys.

FORWARD TO THE FUTURE

The major applications of personality assessment have traditionally been in the prediction of performance and the diagnosis of adjustment problems and behavior disorders. Because the practice of personality assessment began in clinical contexts, the identification and diagnosis of maladjustment have been emphasized more than adaptation, coping behavior, and the fulfillment of potential.

By identifying certain common features among cases, it is reasonable to expect that one case in a group of cases will turn out much the same way as another. In other words, similar diagnoses should lead to similar prognoses. Unfortunately, this Aristotelian reasoning, which is basic to the medical model of illness, does not appear to fit mental disorders as well as it does physical ones. In fact, over a decade ago Ziskin (1986) concluded that what he perceived as the unhealthy state of clinical assessment was due, in large measure, to an inadequate system of classifying mental disorders. Other contributing factors, according to Ziskin, were contamination of data by situational effects, difficulties in differentiating between normal and psychopathological behavior, problems with computer interpretation of data, and the failure of clinical skills to improve with practice.

Computer-Based Assessment

Regarding the use of computer-based interpretations and diagnoses, initial enthusiasm in that sphere has dampened somewhat over the years. Despite the aspirations of some computer-oriented psychologists, computers are still only complex machines that can be programmed by human beings, and their output is no better than either the machines or the programmers. Be that as it may, computers have become faster, more versatile, and more convenient to use, and, for the most part, they seem to be holding up their end of the person-machine system. Recent research on applying item-response theory and adaptive testing procedures to personality assessment, in particular, have yielded promising results (Holden, Fekken, & Cotton, 1991; Roper, Ben-Porath, & Butcher, 1995).

But what of the human clinician? Is he or she capable of contributing anything of value to the assessment process as either a data collector, or a data interpreter and integrator? This question should be easy to answer in the affirmative, but it is not. Perhaps the best answer is "sometimes." One reason why a unequivocal "yes" cannot be given is because graduate students no longer receive adequate training in the theory and practice of psychological assessment. Certainly, most psychology majors are not equipped by nature with a special empathic ability that enables them to understand and predict the behavior of other people. The ability to understand both oneself and others has to be learned—by the hard work of studying concepts and cases, observing expert clinicians, and undertaking extensive personal practice.

Managed Care

The skyrocketing costs of health care, including mental health care, during recent years and the emphasis on fiscal responsibility, third-party payers, and managed care have increased concern as to whether psychodiagnosis, and the contributions of psychological tests to that process, is justifiable and defensible. Not only have health care reimbursement and the managed care revolution affected the practice of clinical assessment but also the values that underlie it (Acklin, 1996). Changes made in diagnostic procedures, including "refinements" in the *Diagnostic and Statistical Manual of Mental Disorders* and the requirement that all diagnostic and therapeutic procedures be defended both fiscally and in terms of real changes in behavior and health, have led to a decreased liberality in ordering and implementing appropriate psychodiagnostic procedures.

What Acklin (1996) calls the "remedicalization of psychiatry," that is, the reassertion of the "medicality" of psychotherapeutic psychiatry, has had the effect of requiring that the "medical necessity" of mental health services, including psychological assessment, be demonstrated to case managers and third-party payers. As a consequence, the suitability for reimbursement of personality disorders and other conditions without demonstrable "medical" causes is being questioned.

The impact of the managed care revolution on traditional psychological assessment in applied fields, such as clinical and health psychology, will undoubtedly continue to be felt. Assessment certainly has a future, but psychological assessors will have to make changes in what they do if they wish to continue practicing. According to Acklin (1996), the language in which psychological assessors talk to case managers who make decisions regarding medical necessity needs to become more medicalized. The assessment of adults, in particular, requires focusing on the acuteness, risk, and potential destructiveness of psychological problems, such as mood disorders, psychosis, and anger control, to both the patient and other people. In addition, psychological assessment will, of necessity, involve rapid, more problem-oriented strategies with an emphasis on symptoms and problem areas rather than comprehensive personality assessment.

An Optimistic Outlook

There are many questions and misgivings concerning the future of personality assessment, but leaders in professional psychology continue to forecast a bright future for this field (Butcher & Rouse, 1996; Matarazzo, 1992; Megargee & Spielberger, 1992; Weiner, 1983; Ziskin, 1986). If the past is any guide to the future, new theories and techniques will go hand in hand with new assessment methods—one driving the other. More sophisticated statistical procedures for evaluating what new instruments measure, and how well they predict and explain behavior, are continually being developed. This does not mean that we will be strangers in a strange land where nothing is recognizable. The MMPI, the Rorschach, and many other seemingly timeless instruments will still be there, at least for a while.

Some 40 years ago, when I was a graduate student, we were told that because psychology was a young science it lacked the vast array of facts and principles that characterize the natural sciences. We were assured, however, that it was only a matter of time before psychology attained the same level of understanding, prediction, and control as physics and chemistry. Surely relatively few, if any, students today would subscribe to that optimistic, idealistic viewpoint. Psychology has not, and may never, attain the scientific status of physics, chemistry, or even biology. Nevertheless, if we cannot do everything, we can, at least, do something. To many of us the future remains interesting, exciting, and full of promise for psychological assessment, and consequently well worth waiting for and working.

SUMMARY

After more than three quarters of a century of activity, personality assessment remains a controversial area. Still, the prevalence of personal and social problems in our society demands continuing efforts to understand, predict, treat, and control human behavior. Valid diagnostic and prognostic instruments designed to measure both cognitive (achievement and aptitude) and affective (personality, preferences, etc.) variables can contribute to the attainment of these goals.

The success of personality assessment instruments in industrial/organizational, clinical/counseling, and educational situations has, until now, been somewhat middling. In general, tests of achievement, general intelligence, and special abilities are better predictors than personality inventories, rating scales, and projective techniques. The modest reliabilities and validities of most personality assessment instruments can be attributed to several factors, including their fakability, the fact that the behaviors being measured may change as a result of experience and intervention, and the impact of the situation on behavior.

Research has shown that the statistical (actuarial) approach to predicting behavior, and in many cases collecting and integrating assessment information, is more accurate than the clinical (impressionistic) approach. Despite advances in computer-based test scoring and interpretation, however, most clinical psychologists continue to rely more on their impressions than on formulas, cookbooks, or computers.

Personality assessment instruments and procedures have been employed for more than a half-century for employee selection and placement purposes, but the results are mixed, and there have been many critics and detractors. Personality tests are also employed to some extent in marketing to analyze and predict consumer behavior and in sports psychology.

Workhorses, such as the MMPI and the Rorschach, continue to be used extensively for psychodiagnosis in clinical, health, and legal contexts. Clinical psychologists and psychiatrists still rely greatly on the medical model of mental disorders and the associated diagnostic system of the *Diagnostic and Statistical Manual of Mental Disorders (DSM-IV)*. Several personality inventories are keyed to this system, which has been criticized as inaccurate and misleading. Be that as it may, there are many defenders of psychiatric classification, who see it as facilitating treatment, record keeping, the processing of insurance claims, and research on mental disorders.

Personality assessments have been used extensively in forensic contexts to determine a defendant's competency to stand trial and his or her mental state at the time the crime was committed. Assessment results also contribute to the prediction of repeat offenses of a sexual or violent nature, as well as to decisions in custody cases and in other court-related matters. In addition to psychometric instruments, such as the Rorschach and the MMPI, several specially designed questionnaires and inventories can contribute to these determinations.

As the end of the 20th century approaches, it can be predicted that, although personality assessment may have an unstable past, it has a promising future. The level of accuracy in prediction achieved by the natural sciences and engineering should not be expected of psychological assessment, but measures of personality and ability are improving and will continue to make important contributions to the understanding of human behavior and the attainment of human welfare.

NOTES

1. A type A behavior pattern, which is associated with a higher incidence of coronary heart disease, consists of a combination of aggressiveness, competitiveness, hostility, quick actions, and constant striving. A type B behavior pattern, which is associated with a lower incidence of coronary heart disease, consists of a relaxed, easygoing, patient, noncompetitive lifestyle.
2. The results of a meta-analysis conducted by Friedman and Booth-Kewley (1987) of research concerned with the causal role of personality in the development of physical illness indicate that there is a generic *disease-prone personality* involving depression, anger/hostility, anxiety, and perhaps other personality variables. Except in the case of coronary heart disease, however, the connections between personality and disease appear to be weak. Furthermore, it is likely that the connections are multifactorial, interacting with social factors, genetic factors, and health-risk factors such as smoking in their effects on disease. It is suggested that, rather than affecting the functioning of particular organs, personality imbalance and psychological disturbances have systemic effects on the immune system and metabolic processes (see Friedman, 1990).

SUGGESTED READINGS

Butcher, J. N. (1995). How to use computer-based reports. In J. N. Butcher (Ed.), *Clinical personality assessment: Practical approaches* (pp. 78–94). New York: Oxford University Press.

Butcher, J. N., & Rouse, S. V. (1996). Personality: Individual differences and clinical assessment. *Annual Review of Psychology, 47,* 87–111.

Eyde, L. D., & Quaintance, M. K. (1988). Ethical issues and cases in the practice of personnel psychology. *Professional Psychology: Research and Practice, 19,* 148–154.

Hogan, R., Hogan, J., & Roberts, B. W. (1996). Personality measurement and employment decisions. *American Psychologist, 51*, 469–477.

Matarazzo, J. D. (1992). Psychological testing and assessment in the 21st century. *American Psychologist, 47*, 1007–1018.

McReynolds, P. (1989). Diagnosis and clinical assessment: Current status and major issues. *Annual Review of Psychology, 40*, 83–108.

Megargee, E. I., & Spielberger, C. D. (1992). Reflections on fifty years of personality assessment and future directions for the field. In *Personality assessment in America* (pp. 170–190). Hillsdale, NJ: Erlbaum.

Moreland, K. L. (1992). Computer-assisted psychological assessment. In M. Zeidner & R. Most (Eds.), *Psychological testing: An inside view* (pp. 363–376). Palo Alto, CA: Consulting Psychologists Press.

Rubenezer, G. (1991). Computerized testing and clinical judgment: Cause for concern. *The Clinical Psychologist, 44*, 63–66.

Stone, R. (1988). Personality tests in management selection. *Human Resources Journal, 3*, 51–55.

Tett, R., Jackson, D., & Rothstein, M. (1991). Personality measures as predictors of job performance: A meta-analytic review. *Personnel Psychology, 44*, 703–735.

Wittenborn, J. R. (1990). Psychological assessment in treatment. In G. Goldstein & M. Hersen (Eds.), *Handbook of psychological assessment* (2nd ed., pp. 467–485). New York: Pergamon.

Glossary

ABC approach. Behavioral assessment approach, involving the identification of the antecedent events (A) and consequences (C) of the behavior (B). The behavior is modified by controlling for A and changing C.

Accident proneness. Now largely discredited theory of a particular personality type associated with a greater tendency to have accidents.

Acquiescence response set. Tendency of a person to answer affirmatively ("yes" or "true") on personality test items and in other alternative response situations.

Affective assessment. Measurement of noncognitive (nonintellective) variables or characteristics. Affective variables include temperament, emotion, interests, attitudes, personal style, and other behaviors, traits, or processes that are typical of a person.

Altruism. Unselfish concern for or devotion to the welfare of other people at the cost of some sacrifice to oneself.

Anecdotal record. A written record of behavioral observations of a specified individual. Care must be taken to differentiate between observation and interpretation if the record is to be objective.

Anxiety. Vague feeling of uneasiness or apprehension, not necessarily directed toward a specific object or situation.

Assessment. Appraising the presence or magnitude of one or more personal characteristics. The assessment of human behavior and mental processes includes such procedures as observations, interviews, rating scales, checklists, inventories, projectives, and tests.

Assessment center approach. Technique, used primarily in the selection of executive personnel, for assessing the personality characteristics and behavior of a small group of individuals by having them perform a variety of tasks during a period of a few days.

Astrology. Pseudoscience of interpreting an individual's personality and future circumstances from data on the individual's birth and the relative positions of the moon and planets at that time.

225

Attitude.   Tendency to react positively or negatively to some object, person, or circumstance.

Attitude scale.   A paper-and-pencil instrument, consisting of a series of statements concerning an institution, situation, person, event, etc. The examinee responds to each statement by endorsing it or indicating his or her degree of agreement or disagreement with it.

Attribution.   Process of interpreting a person's behavior as caused by forces within (*internal attribution* or disposition) or outside (*external attribution* or situation) the person.

Aunt Fanny error.   Accepting as accurate a trivial, highly generalized personality description that could pertain to almost anyone, even one's Aunt Fanny.

Authoritarian personality.   Tendency to view the world in terms of a strict social hierarchy in which a person higher on the hierarchy demands cooperation and deference from those below him or her.

Availability heuristic.   Estimating the likelihood of an event by its availability in memory; events that come readily to mind, perhaps because of their vividness, are perceived as more likely to occur.

Barnum effect.   Accepting as accurate a personality description phrased in generalities, truisms, and other statements that sound specific to a given person but are actually applicable to almost anyone. (Same as *Aunt Fanny error.*)

Base rate.   Proportion of a specified population of people who possess a characteristic of interest. The base rate should be considered when evaluating the effectiveness of a psychometric instrument in identifying and diagnosing people who have that characteristic.

Behavior analysis.   Procedures that focus on objectively describing a particular behavior and identifying the antecedents and consequences of that behavior. Behavior analysis may be conducted for research purposes or to obtain information in planning a behavior modification program.

Behavior modification.   Psychotherapeutic procedures based on learning theory and research and designed to change inappropriate behavior to more personally or socially acceptable behavior. Examples of such procedures are systematic desensitization, counterconditioning, extinction, and implosion.

Belief bias.   The tendency for preexisting beliefs to distort logical reasoning, making invalid conclusions appear valid or valid conclusions appear invalid.

Biographical inventory.   Questionnaire composed of items designed to collect information on an individual's background, interests, and other personal data.

Bipolar disorder.   Condition in which a person's mood fluctuates between euphoric mania and depression.

Cardinal trait.   According to G. W. Allport, a disposition or theme so dominant in a person's life that it is expressed in almost all of his or her behavior (e.g., power striving, self-love).

Case study.   Detailed study of an individual, designed to provide a comprehensive, in-depth understanding of personality. Information for a case study is obtained from biographical, interview, observational, and test data.

Central tendency error. General tendency to avoid extreme judgments in appraising or assessing a person, and to assign ratings in the middle categories of a continuum or scale.

Central trait. According to G. W. Allport, the tendency to behave in a particular way in various situations (sociability, affectionateness), but less general or pervasive than a *cardinal trait.*

Cerebrotonia. In Sheldon's temperament typology, the tendency to be introversive and prefer mental to physical or social activities; most closely related to ectomorphic body build.

Checklist. List of words, phrases, or statements descriptive of personal characteristics; respondents endorse (check) those items characteristic of themselves (self-ratings) or other people (other ratings).

Classification. Assigning individuals to specified groups or categories on the basis of personal data obtained from various sources (observations, interviews, tests, inventories, etc.).

Client-centered therapy. A type of psychotherapy, pioneered by Carl Rogers, in which the client decides what to talk about and when, without direction, judgment, or interpretation on the part of the therapist. Unconditional positive regard, empathy, and congruence characterize the therapist's attitude in this type of therapy.

Clinical (impressionistic) approach. Approach to behavioral prediction and diagnosis in which psychologists assign their own judgmental weights to the predictor variables and then combine them in a subjective manner to make behavioral forecasts or diagnoses.

Clinical psychologist. A psychologist who is trained to assess, diagnose, and treat emotional and behavioral disorders.

Cognitive assessment. Measurement of cognitive processes, such as perception, memory, thinking, judgment, and reasoning. (See *Affective assessment.*)

Cognitive style. Strategy or approach to perceiving, remembering, and thinking that a person seems to prefer in attempting to understand and cope with the world (for example, field independence-dependence, reflectivity-impulsivity, and internal-external locus of control).

Competency. Legal determination that a person's judgment is sound and that he or she is able to manage his or her own property, enter into contracts, and so forth.

Concordance rate. Degree to which other people have the same characteristic as a specific individual (proband or index case). The extent to which the characteristic is genetically based is determined by comparing the concordance rates for the proband's relatives with those of the general population.

Conditions of worth. According to Carl Rogers, the feelings experienced by a person who is evaluated as a totality, and not according to his or her specific actions. The person feels that his or her worth depends on manifesting the right behaviors, attitudes, and values.

Confirmation bias.   Tendency to seek and remember information that is consistent with one's beliefs or preconceptions.

Construct validity.   The extent to which scores on a psychometric instrument designed to measure a certain characteristic are related to measures of behavior in situations in which the characteristic is supposed to be an important determinant of behavior.

Consumer psychology.   Concerned with the identification or segmentation of markets based on the psychological characteristics of consumers; designing, advertising, and selling products and services with respect to consumer characteristics.

Content analysis.   Method of studying and analyzing written (or oral) communications in a systematic, objective, and quantitative manner to assess certain psychological variables.

Contrast error.   In interviewing or rating, the tendency to evaluate a person more positively if an immediately preceding individual was assigned a highly negative evaluation or to evaluate a person more negatively if an immediately preceding individual was given a highly positive evaluation.

Convergent validity.   Situation in which an assessment instrument has high correlations with other measures (or methods of measuring) the same construct. (See *Discriminant validity*.)

Coping.   Controlling, reducing, or learning to tolerate stress-provoking events.

Correlation.   Degree of relationship or association between two variables, such as a test and a criterion measure.

Correlation coefficient.   A numerical index of the degree of relationship between two variables. Correlation coefficients usually range from −1.00 (perfect negative relationship), through .00 (total absence of a relationship) to +1.00 (perfect positive relationship). Two common types of correlation coefficient are the product-moment coefficient and the point-biserial coefficient.

Counseling.   General term for providing advice and guidance to individuals who need assistance with vocational, academic, or personal problems.

Criterion.   A standard or variable with which scores on a psychometric instrument are compared or against which they are evaluated. The validity of a test or other psychometric procedure used in selecting or classifying people is determined by its ability to predict a specified criterion of behavior in the situation for which people are being selected or classified.

Criterion-related validity.   The extent to which a test or other assessment instrument measures what it was designed to measure, as indicated by the correlation of test scores with some criterion measure of behavior.

Critical incident.   A measure of performance, used primarily in industrial-organizational contexts, in which an individual's overall criterion score is determined by the extent to which behavior thought to be critical for effective performance in a given situation occurs.

Defense mechanisms. In psychodynamic theory, psychological techniques that defend the ego against anxiety, guilt, and a loss of self-esteem resulting from awareness of certain impulses or realities.

Depression. Mood disorder characterized by dejection, loss of interest in things, negative thoughts (including suicidal thoughts), and various physical symptoms (e.g., loss of appetite, insomnia, fatigue).

Diagnostic interview. An interview designed to obtain information on a person's thoughts, feelings, perceptions, and behavior; used in making a diagnostic decision about the person.

Discriminant validity. Situation in which a psychometric instrument has low correlations with other measures of (or methods of measuring) different psychological constructs.

Dispositional approach. Includes any one of the many different theories of personality based on the assumption of stable, enduring internal dispositions to feel, think, or act in certain ways. Different dispositions are considered to be characteristic of different individuals and to be expressed across a variety of situations.

Dogmatism. Personality trait characterized by chronic, unfounded assertions of one's opinions as being the truth; may be assessed by Rokeach's Dogmatism Scale.

Ectomorph. In Sheldon's somatotype system, a person with a tall, thin body build; related to the cerebrotonic (thinking, introversive) temperament type.

Ego. In psychoanalytic theory, that part of the personality ("I" or "me") that obeys the reality principle and attempts to mediate the conflict between the id and superego.

Electroencephalograph (EEG). Electronic apparatus designed to detect and record brain waves from the intact scalp.

Electromyograph (EMG). Electronic apparatus designed to measure muscular activity or tension.

Endomorph. In Sheldon's somatotype system, a person having a rotund body shape (fat); related to the viscerotonic (relaxed, sociable) temperament.

Evaluation. To judge the merit or value of an examinee's behavior from a composite of test scores, observations, and reports.

Extrovert. C. G. Jung's term for people who are oriented, in thought or social orientation, toward the external environment and other people rather than toward their own thoughts and feelings.

Factor. A dimension, trait, or characteristic of personality revealed by factor analyzing the matrix of correlations computed from the scores of many people in several different tests or items.

Factor analysis. A mathematical procedure for analyzing a matrix of correlations among measurements to determine what factors (constructs) are sufficient to explain the correlations.

False negative.   Selection error or diagnostic decision error in which an assessment procedure incorrectly predicts a maladaptive outcome (e.g., low achievement, poor performance, or psychopathology).

False positive.   Selection error or diagnostic decision error in which an assessment procedure incorrectly predicts an adaptive outcome (e.g., high achievement, good performance, or absence of psychopathology).

Fantasy stage.   The earliest stage in the development of interests, in which a child's interest orientations are not based on an accurate perception of reality.

Field dependence.   A perceptual style in which the perceiver relies primarily on cues from the surrounding visual environment, rather than kinesthetic (gravitational) cues, to determine the upright position in H. A. Witkin's rod-and-frame test.

Field independence.   A perceptual style in which the perceiver depends primarily on kinesthetic (gravitational) cues, rather than visual cues from the surrounding environment, to determine the upright position in H. A. Witkin's rod-and-frame test.

Forced-choice item.   Item on a personality or interest inventory, arranged as a dyad (two options), a triad (three options), or a tetrad (four options) of terms or phrases. The respondent is required to select an option viewed as most descriptive of the personality, interests, or behavior of the person being evaluated and perhaps another option perceived to be least descriptive of the personality, interests, or behavior of the person being evaluated. Forced-choice items are found on certain personality inventories (e.g., the Edwards Personal Preference Schedule, interest inventories [Kuder General Interest Survey], and rating forms to control for response sets).

Fraternal (dizygotic) twins.   Twins resulting from coincident pregnancies in the same person. Originating from two separately fertilized eggs, fraternal twins are genetically no more alike than ordinary brothers and sisters.

Fundamental attribution error.   Tendency to attribute one's own behavior to situational influences but to attribute the behavior of other people to dispositional causes.

Gender identity.   Inner sense of being male or female, resulting from child-rearing practices combined with genetic and hormonal factors.

Gender role.   Patterns of appearance and behavior associated by a society or culture with being male or female and expected of the appropriate sex.

Graphic rating scale.   A rating scale containing a series of items, each consisting of a line on which the rater places a check mark to indicate the degree of a characteristic that the ratee is perceived as possessing. Typically, at the left extremity of the line is a brief verbal description indicating the lowest degree of the characteristic, and at the right end is a description of the highest degree of the characteristic. Brief descriptions of intermediate degrees of the characteristic may also be located at equidistant points along the line.

Graphology.   The analysis of handwriting to ascertain the character or personality of the writer.

Group test. A test administered simultaneously to a group of examinees by one examiner. (See *Individual test.*)

Halo effect. Rating a person high on one characteristic merely because he or she rates high on other characteristics.

Hardiness. Personality trait characterized by commitment, challenge, and control, and associated with a lower rate of stress-related illness.

Health psychology. Branch of psychology concerned with research and applications directed toward the maintenance of health and the prevention of illness.

Hindsight bias. Tendency to believe, after an event has occurred, that one could have predicted it beforehand.

Ideal self. In Carl Rogers's phenomenological theory, the self that a person would like to be, as contrasted with the person's *real self.*

Identical (monozygotic) twins. Twins produced by a single fertilized egg. Because they are genetically identical, identical twins are often used to investigate the differential effects of heredity and environment on personality and behavior.

Identification. Taking on the personal characteristics of another person, as when a developing child identifies with a significant "other" person. Also, in psychoanalytic theory, an ego defense mechanism for coping with anxiety.

Idiographic approach. Approach to personality assessment and research in which the individual is viewed as a lawful, integrated system in his or her own right. (See *Nomothetic approach.*)

Illusory correlation. Focusing on the number of times that a symptom and a disorder have occurred together and overlooking the number of times they have not occurred together.

In-basket technique. A procedure for evaluating supervisors or executives in which the candidate is required to indicate what action should be taken on a series of memos and other materials of the kind typically found in a supervisor's or executive's in-basket.

Incompetency. Legal determination that a person is suffering from a disorder that causes a defect of judgment such that the person is unable to manage his or her own property, enter into contracts, and take care of his or her other affairs.

Independent variable. The variable whose effects on a dependent variable are being determined in a research investigation.

Individual test. A test administered to one examinee at a time.

Industrial/organizational (I/O) psychologist. A psychologist who contributes to the understanding, prediction, and control of behavior in the workplace. Activities of I/O psychologists include selection and training of employees, the implementation of programs to improve morale and productivity, and the design and evaluation of products and procedures in marketing.

Informed consent. A formal agreement made by an individual, or the individual's guardian or legal representative, with an agency or another person to permit use of the individual's name or personal information (test scores and the like) for a specified purpose.

Insanity.　A legal term for a disorder of judgment or behavior in which a person is unable to tell the difference between right and wrong (McNaghten Rule) or cannot control his or her actions and manage his or her affairs.

Integrity (honesty) testing.　Use of psychometric devices to screen employees for dishonesty and other undesirable characteristics; questions pertaining to attitudes toward theft and the admission of theft and other illegal activities are commonly found on such tests.

Intelligence.　Many definitions of this term have been offered, such as "the ability to judge well, understand well, and reason well" (Binet) and "the capacity for abstract thinking" (Terman). In general, what is measured by intelligence tests is the ability to succeed in school-type tasks.

Interest inventory.　A test or checklist, such as the Strong Interest Inventory or the Kuder General Interest Survey, designed to assess an individual's preferences for certain activities and topics.

Internal consistency.　The extent to which all items on a test measure the same variable or construct. The reliability of a test computed by the Spearman-Brown, Kuder-Richardson, or Cronbach-alpha formulas is a measure of the test's internal consistency.

Interview.　A systematic procedure for obtaining information by asking questions and, in general, verbally interacting with a person (the interviewee).

Introvert.　Carl Jung's term for orientation toward the self; primarily concerned with one's own thoughts and feelings rather than with the external environment or other people; preference for solitary activities.

Inventory.　A set of questions or statements to which the individual responds (e.g., by indicating agreement or disagreement), designed to provide a measure of personality interest, attitude, or behavior.

Ipsative measurement.　Test item format (e.g., forced choice) in which the variables being measured are compared with each other, so that a person's score on one variable is affected by his or her scores on other variables measured by the instrument.

Kuder-Richardson formulas.　Formulas used to compute a measure of internal-consistency reliability from a single administration of a test having 0 to 1 scoring.

L data.　R. B. Cattell's term for personality data (recorded or rated) concerned with the individual's behavior in everyday situations.

Leaderless group discussion (LGD).　Six or so individuals (e.g., candidates for an executive position) are observed while discussing an assigned problem to determine their effectiveness in working with the group and reaching a solution.

Leniency error.　Tendency to rate an individual higher on a positive characteristic and less severely on a negative characteristic than he or she actually should be rated.

Life style.　Composite of habits, attitudes, preferences, socioeconomic status, and other features constituting a person's manner of living.

Likert scale. Attitude scale in which respondents indicate their degree of agreement or disagreement with a particular proposition concerning some object, person, or situation.

Locus of control. J. B. Rotter's term for a cognitive-perceptual style characterized by the typical direction (internal or self versus external or other) from which individuals perceive themselves as being controlled.

M'Naughten rule. Standard of legal insanity stating that "the party accused was laboring under such a defect of reason, from disease of the mind, as not to know the nature and quality of the act he was doing."

Machiavellianism. Personality trait in which the individual is concerned with manipulating other people or using them for his or her own purposes.

Man-to-man scale. Procedure in which ratings on a specific trait (e.g., leadership) are made by comparing each person to be rated with several other people whose standings on the trait have already been determined.

Measurement. Procedures for determining (or indexing) the amount or quantity of some construct or entity; assignment of numbers to objects or events.

Medical model of mental disorders. The concept that mental disorders can be diagnosed on the basis of a pattern of symptoms (syndromes) and cured through physical or psychological therapies.

Mesomorph. W. H. Sheldon's term for a person having an athletic physique; correlated with a somatotonic temperament (active, aggressive, energetic).

Model Penal Code. Standard of legal insanity applied in most states that "A person is not responsible for criminal conduct, i.e., insane if, at the time of such conduct, as a result of mental disease or defect, he lacks substantial capacity either to appreciate the criminality (wrongfulness) of his conduct, or to conform his conduct to the requirement of the law."

Moderator variable. Demographic or personality variable (e.g., age, sex, cognitive style, compulsivity) affecting the correlation between two other variables (e.g, aptitude and achievement).

Multitrait-multimethod matrix. Matrix of correlation coefficients resulting from correlating measures of the same trait by the same method, different traits by the same method, the same trait by different methods, and different traits by different methods. The relative magnitudes of the four types of correlations are compared in evaluating the construct validity of a test.

Need. A physiogenic or psychogenic drive or motive underlying behavior. Henry Murray's need/press theory of personality lists numerous physiogenic and psychogenic needs, several of which (e.g., need for achievement, need for affiliation, need for power) have been extensively investigated in research.

Need achievement. Motive to excel or attain success in some field or endeavor; measured and studied extensively by D. C. McClelland.

Neuropsychological assessment. Measurement of cognitive, perceptual, and motor performance to determine the locus, extent, and effects of neurological damage.

Neurosis (psychoneurosis). Nonpsychotic mental disorder characterized by anxiety, obsessions, compulsions, phobias, or bodily complaints or dysfunctions having no demonstrable physical basis.

Nomothetic approach. A search for general laws of behavior and personality that apply to all individuals.

Nonverbal behavior. Any behavior in which the respondent does not make word sounds or signs. Nonverbal behavior serving a communicative function includes movements of large (macrokinesics) and small (microkinesics) body parts, interpersonal distance or territoriality (proximics), tone and rate of voice sounds (paralinguistics), and communications imparted by culturally prescribed matters relating to time, dress, memberships, and the like (culturics).

Norm group. Sample of people on whom a test is standardized.

Normal distribution. A smooth, bell-shaped frequency distribution of scores, symmetrical about the mean and described by an exact mathematical function. The test scores of a large group of examinees are frequently distributed in an approximately normal manner.

Norms. A list of scores and the corresponding percentile ranks, standard scores, or other transformed scores of a group of examinees on whom a test has been standardized.

Numerology. The study of numbers, such as the figures designating the year of one's birth, to determine their supposed influence on one's life and future.

Objective test. A test scored by comparing the examinee's responses to a list of correct answers (a key) prepared beforehand, in contrast to a subjectively scored test. Examples of objective test items are multiple choice and true-false.

Observation method. Observing behavior in a controlled or uncontrolled situation and making a formal or informal record of the observations.

Palmistry (chiromancy). Telling fortunes and interpreting character from the lines and configurations in the palms of the hand.

Parallel forms. Two tests that are equivalent in the sense that they contain the same kinds of items of equal difficulty and are highly correlated. The scores made by examinees on one form of the test are close to those made by them on the other form.

Parallel forms reliability. An index of reliability determined by correlating the scores of individuals on parallel forms of a test.

Participant observation. A research technique, used mainly by cultural anthropologists, in which an observer attempts to minimize the intrusiveness of his or her person and observational activities by becoming part of the group being observed, for example, by dressing and behaving like the other group members.

Percentile. The pth percentile is the test score at or below which $p\%$ of the examinee's test scores fall.

Percentile norms. A list of raw scores and the corresponding percentages of the test standardization group whose scores fall below the given percentile.

Percentile rank. The percentage of scores falling below a given score in a frequency distribution or group of scores; the percentage corresponding to the given score.

Personal orientation. Generalized personality disposition, such as gender role or self-actualization, that directs behavior in a variety of situations.

Personality. The sum total of all the qualities, traits, and behaviors that characterize the thoughts, feelings, and behaviors of a person and by which, together with his or her physical attributes, the person is recognized as a unique individual.

Personality assessment. The description and analysis of personality by means of various techniques, including personality inventories, observations, interviews, checklists, rating scales, and projective techniques.

Personality disorder. Maladaptive behavioral syndrome originating in childhood but not characterized by psychoneurotic or psychotic symptomatology.

Personality inventory. A self-report inventory or questionnaire consisting of statements concerned with personal characteristics and behaviors. On a true-false inventory, the respondent indicates whether or not each test item or statement is self-descriptive; on a multiple-choice or forced-choice inventory, the respondent selects the statements that are self-descriptive.

Personality profile. Graph of scores on a battery or set of scales of a personality inventory or rating scale. The elevation and scatter of the profile assist in the assessment of personality and mental disorders.

Personality test. Any one of several methods of analyzing personality, such as checklists, personality inventories, and projective techniques.

Phenomenology. Study of objects and events as they appear to the experiencing observer; type of psychotherapy (Rogers, Maslow, etc.) that emphasizes the importance of self-perceptions and impressions of others in determining personality and behavior.

Phenotype. The way in which a genetically determined characteristic is actually manifested in a person's appearance or behavior.

Phrenology. Discredited theory and practice of Gall and Spurzheim relating affective and cognitive characteristics to the configuration (bumps) of the skull.

Physiognomy (anthroposcopy). A pseudoscience that maintains that the personal characteristics of an individual are revealed by the form or features of the body, especially the face.

Polygraph. An apparatus that monitors respiration rate, blood pressure, pulse rate, and the galvanic skin response (GSR); formerly used to detect lying or verify truthfulness in responding to interrogation.

Predictive validity. Extent to which scores on a test are predictive of performance on some criterion measure assessed at a later time; usually expressed as a correlation between the test (predictor variable) and the criterion variable.

Press. As contrasted with *need*, external, environmental pressures influencing behavior. Henry Murray's need/press theory of personality differentiates between press from the objective environment (*alpha press*) and press from the perceived environment (*beta press*).

Profile (psychograph). Graph depicting an individual's scores on several parts of the same test. By examining the profile of scores on a personality inventory such as the MMPI, a psychologist may obtain information useful in personality analysis and the diagnosis of psychopathology.

Projective technique. A relatively unstructured personality assessment technique in which the examinee responds to materials, such as inkblots, ambiguous pictures, incomplete sentences, and other materials, by telling what he or she perceives, making up stories, or constructing and arranging sentences and objects. Theoretically, because the material is fairly unstructured, whatever structure the examinee imposes on it represents a projection of his or her own personality characteristics (needs, conflicts, sources of anxiety, etc.).

Psychoanalysis. Developed by Sigmund Freud and his followers, psychoanalysis is a theory of personality concerned with the dynamic interaction between the conscious and unconscious, a psychotherapeutic method for dealing with personality problems, and a research method for studying personality.

Psychodiagnosis. Examination and evaluation of personality in terms of behavioral, cognitive, and affective characteristics and the interactions among them.

Psychodynamic theory. Theory emphasizing the interaction of conscious and unconscious mental process in determining thoughts, feelings, and behavior.

Psychographics. Study of the relationships of consumer behavior to personality characteristics and lifestyles.

Psychohistory. Biography, such as E. H. Erikson's *Young Man Luther* or *Gandhi's Truth*, written from a psychoanalytic viewpoint.

Psychometrics. Theory and research pertaining to the measurement of psychological (cognitive and affective) characteristics.

Psychosexual stages. Sequence of stages in sexual development (oral, anal, phallic, latency, genital) characterized by a focus on different erogenous zones and associated conflicts.

Psychosis. Severe mental disorder characterized by faulty perception of reality, deficits of language and memory, disturbances in the emotional sphere, and other bizarre symptoms.

Psychosocial stages. Erik Erikson's modification of Freud's theory of psychosexual stages; emphasizes environmental and social problems, as contrasted with biological factors, in the progression of development from infancy through old age.

Pupillometrics. Procedure for measuring pupillary diameter as a measure of pleasure or interest in a specific stimulus.

Q data. R. B. Cattell's term for personality data obtained from questionnaires.

Q technique. A set of procedures, used to conduct research on the individual, which center on sorting decks of cards called Q sorts and correlating the responses of different individuals to the Q sorts.

Questionnaire. A list of questions concerning a particular topic, administered to a group of individuals to obtain information concerning their preferences, beliefs, interests, and behavior.

r. A symbol for the Pearson product-moment correlation coefficient.

Rapport. A warm, friendly relationship between examiner and examinee.

Rating scale. A list of words or statements concerning traits or characteristics, sometimes in the form of a continuous line divided into sections corresponding to degrees of the characteristic, on which the rater indicates judgments of either his or her own behavior and traits or the behavior and traits of another person (ratee).

Real self. In C. R. Rogers' phenomenological theory, a person's perception of what he or she really is, as contrasted with what he or she would like to be (*ideal self*).

Realistic stage. Final stage in the development of vocational interests, usually occurring during late adolescence or early adulthood. At this stage, the individual has a realistic notion about what particular occupations entail, and the vocation he or she would like to pursue.

Reliability. The extent to which a psychological assessment device measures anything consistently. A reliable instrument is relatively free from errors of measurement, so the scores obtained on the instrument are close in numerical value to the true scores of examinees

Reliability coefficient. A numerical index, between .00 and 1.00, of the reliability of an assessment instrument. Methods for determining reliability include test-retest, parallel forms, and internal consistency.

Representativeness heuristic. Judging the likelihood of events in terms of how well they appear to represent or match particular prototypes, possibly leading to the ignoring of other relevant information.

Repression-sensitization. Donald Byrne's conception of a personality continuum representing a person's typical response to threat; information-avoidance behaviors are at one end of the continuum and information-seeking behaviors are at the other end.

Response sets (styles). Tendencies for individuals to respond in relatively fixed or stereotypes ways in situations where there are two or more response choices, such as on personality inventories. Tendencies to guess, to answer true (acquiescence), and to give socially desirable answers are some of the response sets that have been investigated.

RIASEC model. John Holland's model of person-environment interest/personality types consisting of realistic, investigative, artistic, social, enterprising, and conventional themes.

Schema. A cognitive structure that abstractly represents events, objects, or relationships in the external world.

Secondary trait. Less important personality traits, such as preferences or interests, that affect behavior less than central or cardinal traits.

Self.   Perceived identity, individuality, or ego; that which consciously knows and experiences.

Self-actualization.   In C. R. Rogers's phenomenological theory, attaining a state of congruence between one's real and ideal selves; developing one's abilities to the fullest; becoming the kind of person one would ideally like to be.

Self-concept.   An individual's evaluation of her or his self as assessed by various psychometric instruments.

Self-efficacy.   A person's judgment concerning his or her ability to accomplish a particular task in a certain situation successfully.

Self-fulfilling prophecy.   Tendency for a person's expectations and attitudes concerning future events or outcomes to affect their occurrence; the tendency for children to behave in ways in which parents or teachers expect them to behave.

Self-monitoring.   The extent to which people are sensitive to, or monitor, their own behavior according to environmental cues. High self-monitors are more sensitive to what is situationally appropriate and act accordingly. Low self-monitors are less sensitive to external cues and act more in response to their own internal attitudes and feelings.

Self-report inventory.   A paper-and-pencil measure of personality traits or interests comprised of a series of items that the examinee indicates as characteristic (true) or not characteristic (not true) of himself (herself).

Semantic differential.   A rating scale, introduced by C. E. Osgood, for evaluating the connotative meanings that selected concepts have for a person. Each concept is rated on a 7-point, bipolar adjectival scale.

Sentence completion test.   A projective test of personality consisting of a series of incomplete sentences that the examinee is instructed to complete.

Situation(al) test.   A performance test in which the examinee is placed in a realistic but contrived situation and directed to accomplish a specified task. Situation tests are sometimes used to assess personality characteristics, such as honesty and frustration tolerance.

Social desirability response set.   Response set or style affecting scores on personality inventories. It refers to the tendency on the part of an examinee to respond to the assessment materials in a more socially desirable direction rather than responding in a manner that is truly characteristic or descriptive of his or her personality.

Social learning theory.   Conceptualizations of learning that occur by imitation or interactions with other people.

Sociometric technique.   Method of determining and describing the pattern of acceptances and rejections in a group of people.

Somatotonia.   Athletic, aggressive temperament type in W. H. Sheldon's three-component system of personality; most closely correlated with a mesomorphic (muscular) body build.

Somatotype.   Classification of body build (physique) in W. H Sheldon's three-component system (endomorphy, mesomorphy, ectomorphy).

Source traits. R. B. Cattell's term for organizing structures or dimensions of personality that underlie and determine surface traits.

Standard scores. A group of scores, such as z scores, T scores, or stanine scores, having a desired mean and standard deviation. Standard scores are computed by transforming raw scores to z scores, multiplying the z scores by the desired standard deviation, and then adding the desired mean to the product.

Standardization. Administering a carefully constructed test to a large, representative sample of people under standard conditions for the purpose of determining norms.

Standardized test. A test that has been carefully constructed by professionals and administered with standard directions and under standard conditions to a representative sample of people for the purpose of obtaining norms.

State anxiety. A temporary state of anxiety, precipitated by a specific situation.

Statistical (actuarial) approach. Combining quantified clinical information according to empirically established rules, and then making behavioral predictions or diagnoses on the basis of the results.

Stress interview. Interviewing procedure in which the interviewer applies psychologically stressful techniques (critical and hostile questioning, frequent interruptions, prolonged silences, etc.) to break down the interviewee's defenses or determine how the interviewee reacts under pressure.

Structured interview. Interviewing procedure in which the interviewee is asked a planned series of questions.

Sublimation. A defense mechanism in which unacceptable unconscious impulses are expressed in indirect, socially acceptable ways.

Surface traits. Publicly manifested characteristics of personality; observable expressions of source traits.

T scores. Converted, normalized standard scores having a mean of 50 and a standard deviation of 10. Z scores are also standard scores with a mean of 50 and a standard deviation of 10, but in contrast to T scores they are not normalized.

Target behaviors. Specific, objectively defined behaviors observed and measured in behavioral assessments. Of particular interest are the effects on these behaviors of antecedent and consequent events in the environment.

Target population. The population of interest in standardizing a test or other assessment instrument; the norm group (sample) must be representative of the target population if valid interpretations of (norm-referenced) scores are to be made.

Test. Any device used to evaluate the behavior or performance of a person. Psychological tests are of many kinds—cognitive, affective, and psychomotor.

Test anxiety. A feeling of fear or uneasiness that one will not do well on a test.

Trait. A cognitive, affective, or psychomotor characteristic possessed in different amounts by different people.

Trait anxiety.   Generalized level of anxiety expressed in a variety of situations.

Trait theory.   Personality theory that conceptualizes human personality as consisting of a combination of traits.

Transitional stage.   An intermediate stage in the development of interests; falls between the fantasy stage of early childhood and the realistic stage of late adolescence and early adulthood.

Type.   A larger dimension of personality that a *trait*; a combination of traits characterizing a particular kind of personality.

Type A personality.   Personality pattern characterized by a combination of behaviors, including aggressiveness, competitiveness, hostility, quick actions, and constant striving; associated with a high incidence of coronary heart disease.

Type B personality.   Personality pattern characterized by a relaxed, easygoing, patient, noncompetitive lifestyle; associated with a low incidence of coronary heart disease.

Unconditional positive regard.   In client-centered therapy, an accepting, sincere attitude on the part of the therapist, regardless of the feelings or actions revealed by the client.

Unconscious.   In psychoanalytic theory, that part of the personality that is below the level of conscious awareness and is brought into consciousness only in disguised form.

Unobtrusive observations.   Observations made without the awareness of the person whose behavior is being observed.

Unstructured interview.   Interviewing procedure in which the questions asked are not planned but vary with the progress or flow of the interview.

Validity.   The extent to which an assessment instrument measures what it was designed to measure. Validity can be assessed in several ways: by analysis of the instrument's content (*content validity*), by relating scores on the test to a criterion (*predictive* and *concurrent validity*), and by a more thorough study of the extent to which the test is a measure of a certain psychological construct (*construct validity*).

Variability.   The degree of spread or deviation of a group of scores around their average value.

Variable.   In contrast to a **constant**, any quantity that can assume more than one state or numerical value.

Variance.   A measure of variability of test scores, computed as the sum of the squares of the deviations of raw scores from the arithmetic mean, divided by one less than the number of scores; the square of the standard deviation.

Viscerotonia.   Jolly, sociable temperament type in W. H. Sheldon's three-component description of personality; most closely correlated with the endomorphic (rotund) body build.

Word association test.   A list of words that is read aloud to an examinee who has been instructed to respond with the first word that comes to mind.

APPENDIX

Publishers/Distributors of Personality Assessment Materials

American Guidance Service (AGS), 4201 Woodland Road, P.O. Box 99, Circle Pines, MN 55014-1796. Tel. 800-328-2560.

American Orthopsychiatric Association, Inc., 1790 Broadway, New York, NY 10019.

Andrews University Press, Berrien Springs, MI 49104.

Aurora Publishing Co., 213 West Sixth Avenue, Anchorage, AK 99501.

Behaviordyne, Inc., 994 San Antonio Avenue, P.O. Box 10994, Palo Alto, CA 94303-0992.

Martin M. Bruce Publishers, 50 Larchwood Road, P.O. Box 248, Larchmont, NY 10538. Tel. 914-834-1555.

Arnold R. Bruhn, 7910 Woodmont Ave., Suite 1300, Bethesda, MD 20814.

Wilfred A. Cassell, 4045 Lake Otis Parkway, Suite 101, Anchorage, AK 99508.

Consulting Psychologists Press, Inc. (CPP), 3803 East Bayshore Road, P.O. Box 10096, Palo Alto, CA 94303. Tel. 800-624-1765.

CPPC, 4 Conant Square, Brandon, VT 05733. Tel. 800-433-8234.

C.P.S., Inc., P.O. Box 83, Larchmont, NY 10538. Tel. 800-433-8324.

CTB/McGraw-Hill, 20 Ryan Ranch Road, Monterey, CA 93940-5703. Tel. 800-538-9547.

Department of Research Assessment and Training, New York State Psychiatric Institute, 722 West 168th Street, New York, NY 10032.

Diagnostic Specialists Inc., 1170 North 660 West, Orem, UT 84057.

DLM Resources, One DLM Park, Allen, TX 75002. Tel. 800-527-4747.

Educational and Industrial Testing Service (EdITS), P.O. Box 7234, San Diego, CA 92167. Tel. 619-222-1666.

Family Social Science, 290 McNeal Hall, 1985 Buford Avenue, University of Minnesota, St. Paul, MN 55108.

Fels Research Institute, 800 Livermore Street, Yellow Springs, OH 45837.

Grune & Stratton, Inc., 465 South Lincoln Drive, Troy, MO 63379.

Harvard University Press, 79 Garden Street, Cambridge, MA 02138.

Hawthorne Educational Services Inc., 800 Gray Oak Drive, Columbia, MO 65201. Tel. 800-542-1673.

Hilson Research, Inc., P.O. Box 150239, 82-28 Abingdon Road, Kew Gardens, NY 11415-0239. Tel. 800-926-2258.

Hodder & Stoughton Educational, Hodden Headline PLC, 338 Euston Road, London NW1 3BH, England.

Hogan Assessment Systems, P.O. Box 521176, Tulsa, OK 74152.

Integrated Professional Systems, Inc., 5211 Mahoning Avenue, Suite 135, Youngstown, OH 44515.

Institute for Personality and Ability Testing (IPAT), P.O. Box 188, Champaign, IL 61824-1188. Tel. 800-225-4728.

London House, 9701 W. Higgins Rd., Ste. 770, Rosemont, IL 60018. Tel. 708-292-1900.

McCarron-Dial Systems, P.O. Box 45628, Dallas, TX 75245.

MetriTech, Inc., 4106 Fieldstone Road, P.O. Box 6489, Champaign, IL 61826-6479. Tel. 800-747-4868.

Multi-Health Systems, Inc., 908 Niagara Falls Boulevard, North Tonawanda, NY 14120-2060.

NCS Assessments, P.O. Box 1416, Minneapolis, MN 55440. Tel. 800-627-7271.

Organizational Measurement Systems Press, P.O. Box 1656, Buffalo, NY 14221.

Pfeiffer & Company International Publishers, 8517 Production Avenue, San Diego, CA 92121-2280.

pro.ed., 8700 Shoal Creek Boulevard, Austin, TX 78757-6897. Tel. 512-451-3246.

Psychological & Educational Publications, Inc., 1477 Rollins Road, Burlingame, CA 94010-2316. Tel. 800-523-5775.

Psychological Assessment Resources, Inc. (PAR), P.O. Box 998, Odessa, FL 33556-0998. Tel. 800-331-TEST.

Psychological Corporation (The), 555 Academic Court, San Antonio, TX 78204-2498. Tel. 800-228-0752.

Psychological Publications, Inc., 290 Conejo Ridge Avenue, Suite 100, Thousand Oaks, CA 91361-4928. Tel. 800-345-TEST.

Psychological Test Specialists, P.O. Box 9229, Missoula, MT 59807.

Psychologistics, Inc., P.O. Box 3896, Indialantic, FL 32903.

Psychologists and Educators, Inc., P.O. Box 513, Chesterfield, MO 63006.

Publishers Test Service, CTB/McGraw-Hill, 20 Ryan Ranch Road, Monterey, CA 93940. Tel. 800-538-9547.

Research Press, Dept. G, Box 9177, Champaign, IL 61826.

Riverside Publishing Company (The), 8420 Bryn Mawr Avenue, Chicago, IL 60631. Tel. 800-323-9540.

Saville & Holdsworth Ltd. USA, Inc., 575 Boylston Street, Boston, MA 02116.

Scholastic Testing Service, Inc. (STS), 480 Meyer Road, P.O. Box 1056, Bensenville, IL 60106-1617. Tel. 800-642-6STS.

Sigma Assessment Systems, Inc., P.O. Box 610984, Port Huron, MI 48061-0984. Tel. 800-265-1285.

Slosson Educational Publications, Inc., P.O. Box 280, East Aurora, NY 14052-0280. Tel. 800-828-4800.

SOI Systems, P.O. Box D, Vida, OR 97488. Tel. 503-896-3936.

Special Child Publications, P.O. Box 33548, Seattle, WA 98133.

Springer Publishing Co., Inc., 536 Broadway, New York, NY 10012-3955. Tel. 212-431-4370.

SRA/London House, 9701 Higgins Road, Rosemont, IL 60018. Tel. 800-221-8378.

Stoelting, Oakwood Centre: 620 Wheat Lane, Wood Dale, IL 60191. Tel. 708-860-9700.

Swets Test Services, Heereweg 347B, 2161 CA LISSE, The Netherlands.

Timao Foundation for Research and Development, 2828B Alta View Drive, San Diego, CA 92139.

Training House, P.O. Box 3090, Princeton, NJ 08543-3090.

21st Century Assessment, P.O. Box 608, South Pasadena, CA 91031-0608.

University of Minnesota Press, Test Division, 2037 University Avenue, S.E., Minneapolis, MN 55414.

West Virginia Research and Training Center, One Dunbar Plaza, Suite E, Dunbar, WV 25064.

Western Psychological Services (WPS), 12031 Wilshire Boulevard, Los Angeles, CA 90025-1251. Tel. 800-648-8857.

Wide Range, Inc., P.O. Box 3410, Wilmington, DE 19804-0250. Tel. 800-221-WRAT.

Wilmington Institute (The), 13315 Wilmington Drive, Dallas, TX 75234.

Wonderlic Personnel Test, Inc., 1509 N. Milwaukee Avenue, Libertyville, IL 60048-1380. Tel. 800-963-7542.

References

Abelson, R. P. (1981). Psychological status of the script concept. *American Psychologist, 36,* 715–729.

Abramson, L., Garber, J., & Seligman, M. E. P. (1980). Learning helplessness in humans. In J. Garber & M. E. P. Seligman (Eds.), *Human helplessness* (pp. 3–34). New York: Academic.

Acklin, M. W. (1996). Personality assessment and managed care. *Journal of Personality Assessment, 66*(1), 194–201.

Adorno, T. W., Frenkel-Brunswik, E., Levinson, D., & Sanford, N. (1950). *The authoritarian personality.* New York: Harper & Row.

Ahern, G. L., & Schwartz, G. E. (1985). Differential lateralization for positive and negative emotion in the human brain: EEG spectral analysis. *Neuropsychologists, 23,* 745–756.

Aiken, L. R. (1980). Attitude measurement and research. In D. A. Payne (Ed.), *Recent developments in affective measurement* (pp. 1–24). No. 7 of *New directions for testing and measurement.* San Francisco: Jossey-Bass.

Aiken, L. R. (1995). *Personality assessment methods and practices.* Göttingen, Germany: Hogrefe & Huber.

Aiken, L. R., & Zweigenhaft, R. (1978). Signature size, sex and status: A cross-cultural replication. *Journal of Social Psychology, 106,* 273–274.

Albert, S., Fox, H. M., & Kahn, M. W. (1980). Faking psychosis on the Rorschach: Can expert judges detect malingering? *Journal of Personality Assessment, 44,* 115–119.

Allport, G. W. (1937). *Personality: A psychological interpretation.* New York: Holt, Rinehart & Winston.

Allport, G. W. (1942). *The use of personal documents in psychological science.* New York: Social Science Research Council.

Allport, G. W. (1961). *Pattern and growth in personality.* New York: Holt, Rinehart & Winston.

Allport, G. W. (1965). *Letters from Jenny.* New York: Harcourt Brace.

Allport, G. W., & Allport, F. H. (1928). *The A-S Reaction Study.* Boston: Houghton Mifflin.

American Educational Research Association, American Psychological Association, & National Council on Measurement in Education. (1985). *Standards for educational and psychological testing.* Washington, DC: American Psychological Association.

American Law Institute. (1956). *Model penal code.* Tentative Draft (No. 4).

American Psychiatric Association. (1994). *Diagnostic and statistical manual of mental disorders* (4th ed.). Washington, DC: Author.

American Psychological Association. (1992). Ethical principles of psychologists and code of conduct. *American Psychologist, 47,* 1597–1611.

American Psychological Association, Committee on Professional Standards & Committee on Psychological Tests and Assessment. (1993). *Guidelines for computer-based tests and interpretation.* Washington, DC: American Psychological Association.

Andreasen, N. C. (1987). Creativity and mental illness: Prevalence rates in writers and their first-degree relatives. *American Journal of Psychiatry, 144,* 1288–1292.

Angleitner, A., & Ostendorf, F. (1994). Temperament and the Big Five factors in personality. In C. F. Halverson, Jr., G. A. Kohnstamm, & R. P. Martin (Eds.), *The developing structure of temperament and personality from infancy to adulthood* (pp. 69–90). Hillsdale, NJ: Erlbaum.

APA task force releases final report on integrity testing (1991, May–June). *Psychological Science Agenda, 4*(3), 1, 6. Washington, DC: American Psychological Association.

Arkes, H. R. (1994). Clinical judgment. In R. J. Corsini (Ed.), *Concise encyclopedia of psychology* (2nd ed., pp. 237–238). New York: Wiley.

Arnett, J. (1990). Drunk driving, sensation seeking, and egocentrism among adolescents. *Personality and Individual Differences, 11,* 541–546.

Ashmore, R. D. (1990). Sex, gender, and the individual. In L. A. Pervin (Ed.), *Handbook of personality theory and research* (pp. 486–526). New York: Guilford.

Bandura, A. (1977a). Self-efficacy: Toward a unifying theory of behavioral change. *Psychological Review, 84,* 191–215.

Bandura, A. (1977b). *Social learning theory.* Upper Saddle River, NJ: Prentice Hall.

Bandura, A. (1986). *Social foundations of thought and action: A social cognitive theory.* Upper Saddle River, NJ: Prentice Hall.

Barends, A., Westen, D., Leigh, J., Silbert, D., & Byers, S. (1990). Assessing affect-tone of relationship paradigms from TAT and interview data. *Psychological Assessment: A Journal of Consulting & Clinical Psychology, 2,* 329–332.

Bauerfeind, R. H. (1986). COPSystem Interest Inventory. In D. J. Keyser & R. C. Sweetland (Eds.), *Test critiques* (Vol. V, pp. 76–82). Kansas City, MO: Test Corporation of America.

Baum, G. (1994, October 3). Flirting fundamentals. *Los Angeles Times,* pp. E1, E5.

Bech, P. (1993). *Rating scales for psychopathology, health status, and quality of life.* New York: Springer-Verlag.

Bellak, L. (1992). Projective techniques in the computer age. *Journal of Personality Assessment, 58,* 445–453.

Bellak, L. (1993). *The T.A.T., C.A.T., and S.A.T. in clinical use.* Des Moines, IA: Longwood Division, Allyn & Bacon.

Bellak, L., & Bellak, S. (1973). *Manual: Senior Apperception Test*. Larchmont, NY: C.P.S.

Bem, S. L. (1974). The measurement of psychological androgyny. *Journal of Consulting and Clinical Psychology, 42*, 165–172.

Ben-Porath, Y. S., & Waller, N. G. (1992). Five big issues in clinical personality assessment: A rejoinder to Costa and McCrae. *Psychological Assessment, 4*, 23–25.

Benton, A. L., Windle, C. D., & Erdice, F. (1957). *A review of sentence completion techniques* (Project No. NR 151-175). Washington, DC: Office of Naval Research.

Bernard, H. W., & Huckins, W. C. (1978). *Dynamics of personality adjustment* (3rd ed.). Boston: Holbrook.

Berne, E. (1966). *Principles of group treatment*. New York: Oxford.

Betz, N. E. (1992). Counseling uses of career self-efficacy theory. *Career Development Quarterly, 41*, 22–26.

Betz, N. E. (1994). Self-concept theory in career development and counseling. *Career Development Quarterly, 43*, 32–42.

Binion, R. (1976). *Hitler among the Germans*. New York: Elsevier.

Biskin, B. H. (1992). Review of the State-Trait Anger Expression Inventory (res. ed.). In J. J. Kramer & J. C. Conoley (Eds.), *The eleventh mental measurements yearbook* (pp. 868–869). Lincoln: Buros Institute of Mental Measurements of the University of Nebraska–Lincoln.

Blatt, S. J., & Berman, W. H. (1984). A methodology for use of the Rorschach in clinical research. *Journal of Personality Assessment, 48*, 226–239.

Block, J. (1995). A contrarian view of the five-factor approach to personality description. *Psychological Bulletin, 117*(2), 187–215.

Bolton, B. (1992). Review of the California Psychological Inventory (rev. ed.). In J. J. Kramer & J. C. Conoley (Eds.), *The eleventh mental measurements yearbook* (pp. 138–139). Lincoln: Buros Institute of Mental Measurements of the University of Nebraska–Lincoln.

Botwin, M. D. (1995). Review of the Revised NEO Personality Inventory. In J. C. Conoley & J. C. Impara (Eds.), *The twelfth mental measurements yearbook* (pp. 862–863). Lincoln: Buros Institute of Mental Measurements of the University of Nebraska–Lincoln.

Bouchard, T. J., Jr., Lykken, D. T., McGue, M., Segal, N. L., & Tellengen, A. (1990). Sources of human psychological differences: The Minnesota study of twins reared apart. *Science, 250*, 223–228.

Bouchard, T. J., Jr., & McGue, M. (1981). Familial studies of intelligence: A review. *Science, 212*, 1055–1059.

Bouchard, T., Maloney, D., & Segal, N. (1989). *Genetic similarity in vocational interests*. Paper presented at the ISSID meeting, Heidelberg, West Germany.

Boyle, G. J. (1995a). Review of the Rotter Incomplete Sentences Blank. In J. C. Conoley & J. C. Impara (Eds.), *The twelfth mental measurements yearbook* (pp. 880–883). Lincoln: Buros Institute of Mental Measurements of the University of Nebraska–Lincoln.

Boyle, G. J. (1995b). Myers-Briggs Type Indicator (MBTI): Some psychometric limitations. *Australian Psychologist, 30*, 71–74.

Brebner, J., & Stough, C. (1995). Theoretical and empirical relationships between personality and intelligence. In D. H. Saklofske & M. Zeidner (Eds.), *International handbook of personality and intelligence* (pp. 321–347). New York: Plenum.

Brodie, F. M. (1983). *Richard Nixon: The shaping of his character.* Cambridge, MA: Harvard University Press.

Bruhn, A. R. (1992). The Early Memories Procedure: A projective test of autobiographical memory: Part I. *Journal of Personality Assessment, 58,* 1–15.

Bruhn, A. R. (1995). Early memories in personality assessment. In J. N. Butcher (Ed.), *Clinical personality assessment: Practical approaches* (pp. 278–301). New York: Oxford University Press.

Burdock, E. L., Hardesty, A. S., Hakerem, G., Zubin, J., & Beck, Y. M. (1968). *Ward Behavior Inventory.* New York: Springer-Verlag.

Bukatman, B. A., Foy, J. L., & DeGrazia, E. (1971). What is competency to stand trial? *American Journal of Psychiatry, 127,* 1225–1229.

Burisch, M. (1984a). Approaches to personality inventory construction. *American Psychologist, 39,* 214–227.

Burisch, M. (1984b). You don't always get what you pay for measuring depression with short and simple versus long and sophisticated scales. *Journal of Research in Personality, 18,* 81–98.

Burns, R. C. (1987). *Kinetic-house-tree-person drawings (K-H-T-P): An interpretative manual.* New York: Brunner/Mazel.

Burns, R. C., & Kaufman, S. H. (1970). *Actions, styles and symbols in Kinetic Family Drawings (K-F-D): An interpretative manual.* New York: Brunner/Mazel.

Burns, R. C., & Kaufman, S. H. (1972). *Actions, styles, and symbols in Kinetic Family Drawings (K-F-D).* New York: Brunner/Mazel.

Buros, O. K. (Ed.). (1970). *Personality tests and reviews.* Highland Park, NJ: Gryphon Press.

Buros, O. K. (Ed.). (1978). *The eighth measurements yearbook* (Vols. 1 and 2). Highland Park, NJ: Gryphon Press.

Buss, A. H., & Plomin, R. (1984). *Temperament: Early developing personality traits.* Hillsdale, NJ: Erlbaum.

Buss, A. H., & Plomin, R. (1986). The EAS approach to temperament. In R. Plomin & J. Dunn (Eds.), *The study of temperament: Changes, continuities and challenges* (pp. 67–79). Hillsdale, NJ: Erlbaum.

Butcher, J. N. (Ed.). (1995). *Clinical personality assessment.* New York: Oxford.

Butcher, J. N., & Rouse, S. V. (1996). Personality: Individual differences in clinical assessment. In J. T. Spence, J. M. Darley, & D. J. Foss (Eds.), *Annual Review of Psychology, 47,* 87–111.

Butt, D. S. (1987). *Psychology of sport* (2nd ed.). New York: Van Nostrand Reinhold.

Camara, W. J., & Schneider, D. L. (1994). Integrity tests: Facts and unresolved issues. *American Psychologist, 49,* 112–119.

Camara, W. J., & Schneider, D. L. (1995). Questions of construct breadth and openness of research in integrity testing. *American Psychologist, 50,* 459–460.

Carroll, B. J. (1985). Dexamethasone suppression test: A review of contemporary conclusion. *Journal of Clinical Psychiatry, 46,* 13–24.

Caspi, A., & Herbener, E. S. (1989). *Continuity and change: Assortative marriage and the consistency of personality in adulthood.* Unpublished manuscript, Harvard University.

Cattell, R. B. (1965). *The scientific analysis of personality.* New York: Penguin.

Champion, C. H., Green, S. B., & Sauser, W. I. (1988). Development and evaluation of shortcut-derived behaviorally anchored rating scales. *Educational and Psychological Measurement, 48,* 29–41.

Chun, K. T., Cobb, S., & French, J. R. P. (1976). *Measures for psychological assessment.* Ann Arbor: Institute for Social Research, University of Michigan.

Clark, L. A. (1994). *Schedule for Nonadaptive and Adaptive Personality: Manual for administration, scoring, and interpretation.* Minneapolis: University of Minnesota Press.

Cleckley, H. (1976). *The mask of sanity* (5th ed.). St. Louis, MO: Mosby.

Coan, R. W. (1972). Measurable components of openness to experience. *Journal of Consulting Psychology, 39,* 346.

Cocks, G., & Crosby, T. L. (Eds.). (1987). *Psycho/history: Readings in the method of psychology, psychoanalysis, and history.* New Haven, CT: Yale University Press.

Coles, M. G. H., Gale, A., & Kline, P. (1971). Personality and habituation of the orienting reaction: Tonic and response measures of electrodermal activity. *Psychophysiology, 8,* 54–63.

Comrey, A. L., Bacher, T. E., & Glaser, F. M. (1973). *A source book for mental health measures.* Los Angeles: Human Interaction Research Institute.

Conoley, J. C., & Impara, J. C. (Eds.). (1995). *The twelfth mental measurements yearbook.* Lincoln: Buros Institute of Mental Measurements of the University of Nebraska–Lincoln.

Conoley, J. C., & Kramer, J. J. (Eds.). (1989). *The tenth mental measurements yearbook.* Lincoln: Buros Institute of Mental Measurements of the University of Nebraska–Lincoln.

Corcoran, K., & Fischer, J. (1987). *Measures for clinical practice: A sourcebook.* New York: The Free Press.

Corsini, R. J., & Marsella, A. J. (Eds.). (1983). *Personality theory, research, and assessment.* Itasca, IL: F. E. Peacock.

Costa, P. T., Jr., & McCrae, R. R. (1986). Personality stability and its implications for clinical psychology. *Clinical Psychology Review, 5,* 407–423.

Costantino, G., Malgady, R., & Rogler, I. H. (1988). *Tell-Me-a-Story—TEMAS— manual.* Los Angeles: Western Psychological Services.

Craig, R. J., & Horowitz, M. (1990). Current utilization of psychological tests at diagnostic practicum sites. *The Clinical Psychologist, 43,* 29–36.

Cramer, P., & Blatt, S. J. (1990). Use of the TAT to measure change in defense mechanisms following intensive psychotherapy. *Journal of Personality Assessment, 54,* 236–251.

Crandall, E. (1975). A scale for social interests. *Journal of Individual Psychology, 31,* 187–195.

D'Amato, R. C. (1995). Review of the Adult Personality Inventory. In J. C. Conoley & J. C. Impara (Eds.), *The twelfth mental measurements yearbook* (pp. 52–54). Lincoln, NE: Buros Institute of Mental Measurements and the University of Nebraska—Lincoln.

Dana, R. H. (1955). Clinical diagnosis and objective TAT scoring. *Journal of Abnormal and Social Psychology, 50,* 19–25.

Dana, R. H. (1959). Proposal for objective scoring of the TAT. *Perceptual and Motor Skills, 10,* 27–43.

Darley, J. B., & Hagenah, T. (1955). *Vocational interest measurement.* Minneapolis: University of Minnesota Press.

Davidson, R. J. (1991). Biological approaches to the study of personality. In V. J. Derlega, B. A. Winstead, & W. H. Jones (Eds.), *Personality: Contemporary theory and research* (pp. 87–112). Chicago: Nelson-Hall.

Dawes, R. M. (1994). *House of cards.* New York: Free Press.

De Pascalis, V., & Montirosso, R. (1988). Extraversion, neuroticism and individual differences in event-related potentials. *Personality and Individual Differences, 9,* 353–360.

Deary, I. J., Ramsay, H., Wilson, J. A., & Riad, M. (1988). Stimulated salivation: Correlations with personality and time of day effects. *Personality and Individual Differences, 9,* 903–909.

Devito, A. J. (1985) Review of the Myers-Briggs Type Indicator. In J. V. Mitchell, Jr. (Ed.), *The ninth mental measurements yearbook* (pp. 1030–1032). Lincoln: Buros Institute of Mental Measurements of the University of Nebraska–Lincoln.

Dolliver, R. H. (1985). Review of Self-Motivated Career Planning. In J. V. Mitchell, Jr. (Ed.), *The ninth mental measurements yearbook* (Vol. 2, pp. 1247–1248). Lincoln: Buros Institute of Mental Measurements of the University of Nebraska–Lincoln.

Domino, G., & Affonso, D. D. (1990). A personality measure of Erikson's life stages: The Inventory of Psychosocial Balance. *Journal of Personality Assessment, 54*(2 & 4), 576–588.

Dowd, E. T. (1992). Review of the Beck Hopelessness Scale. In J. J. Kramer & J. C. Conoley (Eds.), *The eleventh mental measurements yearbook* (pp. 81–82). Lincoln: Buros Institute of Mental Measurements of the University of Nebraska–Lincoln.

Drake, L. E. (1946). A social I.E. scale for the MMPI. *Journal of Applied Psychology, 30,* 51–54.

Dreger, R. M. (1978). Review of State-Trait Anxiety Inventory. In O. K. Buros (Ed.), *The eighth mental measurements yearbook* (Vol. 1, pp. 1094–1095). Highland Park, NJ: Gryphon Press.

Dubious memories. (1994, May 23). *Time,* p. 51.

Durham v. United States, 214 F.2d 862 (D.C. Cir. 1954).

Dusky v. United States, 362 U.S. 402. (April 18, 1960).

Edmonds, J. M. (Ed. and Trans.). (1920). *The characters of Theophrastus.* Cambridge, MA: Harvard University Press.

Edwards, A. L. (1954). *Manual—Edwards Personal Preference Schedule.* New York: The Psychological Corporation.

Elias, J. Z. (1989). The changing American scene in the use of projective techniques: An overview. *British Journal of Projective Psychology, 34*, 31–39.

Elms, A. (1976). *Personality and politics*. San Diego: Harcourt Brace Jovanovich.

Engelhard, G. Jr. (1992). Review of the California Psychological Inventory (rev. ed.). In J. J. Kramer & J. C. Conoley (Eds.), *The eleventh mental measurements yearbook* (pp. 139–141). Lincoln: Buros Institute of Mental Measurements of the University of Nebraska–Lincoln.

Erikson, E. H. (1963). *Childhood and society* (2nd ed.). New York: Norton.

Erikson, E. H. (1969). *Gandhi's truth: On the origins of militant nonviolence*. New York: Norton.

Eron, L. D. (1950). A normative study of the Thematic Apperception Test. *Psychological Monographs, 64* (9, Whole No. 351).

Eron, L., Terry, D., & Callahan, R. (1950). The use of rating scales for emotional tone of TAT stories. *Journal of Consulting Psychology, 14*, 473–478.

ETS test collection catalog. Vol. 6: Affective measures and personality tests. (1992). Phoenix, AZ: Oryx Press.

Exner, J. E. (1976). Projective techniques. In I. B. Weiner (Ed.), *Clinical methods in psychology*. New York: Wiley.

Exner, J. E. (1993). *The Rorschach: A comprehensive system: Vol. 1. Basic foundations* (3rd ed.). New York: Wiley.

Exner, J. E., Jr., & Andronikof-Sanglade, A. (1992). Rorschach changes following brief and shot-term psychotherapy. *Journal of Personality Assessment, 59*, 59–71.

Eysenck, H. J. (1967). *The biological basis of personality*. Springfield, IL: Charles C Thomas.

Eysenck, H. J., & Eysenck, S. B. G. (1975). *Manual of the Eysenck Personality Questionnaire*. San Diego: Educational and Industrial Testing Service.

Fabiano, E. (1989). *Index to tests used in educational dissertations*. Phoenix, AZ: Oryx Press.

Fadiman, C. (Ed.). (1945). *The short stories of Henry James*. New York: Random House.

Farrell, A. D. (1993). Computers and behavioral assessment: Current applications, future possibilities, and obstacles to routine use. *Behavioral Assessment, 13*, 159–170.

Finn, S. E., & Tonsager, M. E. (1992). Therapeutic effects of providing MMPI-2 test feedback to college students awaiting therapy. *Psychological Assessment, 4*, 278–287.

Floderus-Myrhed, B., Pedersen, N., & Rasmuson, I. (1980). Assessment of heritability for personality based on a short form of the Eysenck Personality Inventory: A study of 12,898 twin pairs. *Behavior Genetics, 10*, 153–162.

Forer, R. B. (1948). A diagnostic interest blank. *Rorschach Research Exchange and Journal of Projective Techniques, 12*, 1–11.

Fowler, O. L. (1890). *Practical phrenology* (rev. ed.). New York: Fowler & Wells.

Frank, L. K. (1948). *Projective methods*. Springfield, IL: Charles C Thomas.

Freud, S. (1905, reprinted 1959). Fragment of an analysis of a case of hysteria. In *Collected papers* (Vol. 3). New York: Basic Books.

Freud, S., & Bullitt, W. C. (1967). *Thomas Woodrow Wilson*. Boston: Houghton-Mifflin.

Friedman, H. S. (Ed.). (1990). *Personality and disease*. New York: Wiley.

Friedman, H. S., & Booth-Kewley, S. (1987). The "disease-prone personality." *American Psychologist, 42*, 539–555.

Funder, D. C., & Colvin, C. R. (1991). Some behaviors are more predictable than others. *The Score* (Newsletter of Division of the American Psychological Association), *13*(4), 3–4.

Furnham, A. (1992). *Psychology at work*. London: Routledge.

Garb, H. N. (1989). Clinical judgment, clinical training, and professional experience. *Psychological Bulletin, 105*, 387–396.

Garwood, J. (1977). A guide to research on the Rorschach Prognostic Rating Scale. *Journal of Personality Assessment, 41*, 117–118.

Gendlin, E. T., & Tomlinson, T. M. (1967). The process conception and its measurement. In C. R. Rogers, E. T. Gendlin, D. J. Kiesler, & C. B. Truax (Eds.), *The therapeutic relationship and its impact: A study of psychotherapy with schizophrenics* (pp. 109–131). Madison: University of Wisconsin Press.

Ginzberg, E., Ginsburg, S. W., Axelrad, S., & Herma, J. L. (1951). *Occupational choice: An approach to a general theory*. New York: Columbia University Press.

Glad, B. (1980). *Jimmy Carter: In search of the great White House*. New York: Norton.

Goldberg, L. R. (1994). Basic research on personality structure: Implications of the emerging consensus for applications to selection and classification. In M. G. Rumsey, C. B. Walker, & J. H. Harris (Eds.), *Personnel selection and classification* (pp. 247–259). Hillsdale, NJ: Erlbaum.

Goldberg, P. (1965). A review of sentence completion methods in personality assessment. *Journal of Projective Techniques and Personality Assessment, 29*, 12–45.

Golden, D. (1990, January 7). Give me an E. Give me an S. *Boston Globe Magazine*, pp. 16, 43–44, 52–59.

Goldfried, M. R., & Zax, M. (1965). The stimulus value of the TAT. *Journal of Projective Techniques, 29*, 46–57.

Goldman, B. A., & Busch, J. C. (Eds.). (1982). *Directory of unpublished experimental mental measures* (Vol. 3). New York: Human Sciences Press.

Goldman, B. A., & Mitchell, D. F. (Eds.). (1990). *Directory of unpublished experimental mental measures* (Vol. 5). Dubuque, IA: William C. Brown.

Goldman, B. A., & Osborne, W. L. (Eds.). (1985). *Directory of unpublished mental measures* (Vol. 4). New York: Human Sciences Press.

Goldman, B. A., & Saunders, J. L. (Eds.). (1974). *Directory of unpublished experimental mental measures* (Vol. 1). New York: Human Sciences Press.

Goodwin, F. K., & Jamison, K. R. (1990). Assessment of manic and depressive states. In *Manic-depressive illness* (pp. 318–331). New York: Oxford.

Gottesman, I. I., & Shields, J. (1973). *Schizophrenia and genetics: A twin study vantage point*. New York: Academic Press.

Gottfredson, L. S. (1981). Circumscription and compromise: A developmental theory of career aspiration. *Journal of Counseling Psychology, 28*, 416–427.

Gough, H. G. (1987). *California Psychological Inventory: Administrator's guide.* Palo Alto, CA: Consulting Psychologists Press.

Gregory, R. J. (1996). *Psychological testing* (2nd ed.). Needham Heights, MA: Allyn & Bacon.

Greist, J. H. (1984). Exercise in the treatment of depression. *Coping with mental stress: The potential and limits of exercise intervention.* Washington, DC: National Institute of Mental Health.

Grigoriadis, S., Fekken, G. C., & Nussbaum, D. (1994). *MMPI-2 or BPI, which to use?* Paper presented at the Annual Meeting of the American Psychological Association, Los Angeles.

Grotevant, H. D., Scarr, S., & Weinberg, R. A. (1978). Are career interests inherited? *Psychology Today, 11,* 88–90.

Groth-Marnat, G. (1990). *Handbook of psychological assessment* (2nd ed.). New York: Wiley.

Hager, P. (1991, October 29). Court bans psychological tests in hiring. *Los Angeles Times,* p. A-20.

Haladyna, T. M. (1992). Review of the Millon Clinical Multiaxial Inventory–II. In J. J. Kramer & J. C. Conoley (Eds.), *The eleventh mental measurements yearbook* (pp. 532–533). Lincoln: Buros Institute of Mental Measurements, The University of Nebraska–Lincoln.

Hall, C. S. (1938). The inheritance of emotionality. *Sigma Xi Quarterly, 26,* 17–27.

Hall, E. T. (1969). *The hidden dimension.* Garden City, NY: Doubleday.

Hall, H. V. (1987). *Violence prediction: Guidelines for the forensic practitioner.* Springfield, IL: Charles C Thomas.

Haller, N., & Exner, J. E. (1985). The reliability of Rorschach variables for inpatients presenting symptoms of depression and/or helplessness. *Journal of Personality Assessment, 49,* 516–521.

Hammill, D. D., Brown, L., & Bryant, B. R. (1992). *A consumer's guide to tests in print* (2nd ed.). Austin, TX: pro.ed.

Hannah, J. S., & Kahn, S. E. (1989). The relationship of socioeconomic status and gender to the occupational choices of grade 12 students. *Journal of Vocational Behavior, 34,* 161–178.

Hansen, C. (1989). A causal model of the relationship among accidents, biodata, personality, and cognitive factors. *Journal of Applied Psychology, 74,* 81–90.

Harkness, A. R., & McNulty, J. L. (1994). The Personality Psychopathology Five (PSY-5): Issue from the pages of a diagnostic manual instead of a dictionary. In S. Strack & M. Lorr (Eds.), *Differentiating normal and abnormal personality* (pp. 291–315). New York: Springer.

Harmon, L. W., Hansen, Jo-Ida C., Borgen, F. H., & Hammer, A. L. (1994). *Strong Interest Inventory: Applications and technical guide.* Palo Alto, CA: Consulting Psychologists Press.

Hathaway, S. R., & McKinley, J. C. (1940). A multiphasic personality schedule (Minnesota): 1. Construction of the schedule. *Journal of Psychology, 10,* 249–254.

Hathaway, S. R., & McKinley, J. C. (1943). *The Minnesota Multiphasic Personality Inventory.* New York: Psychological Corporation.

Hathaway, S. R., & McKinley, J. C. (1989). *MMPI-2*. Minneapolis: University of Minnesota Press.

Henderson, S., Hesketh, B., & Tuffin, K. (1988). A test of Gottfredson's theory of circumscription. *Journal of Vocational Behavior, 32,* 37–48.

Henriques, J. B., & Davidson, R. J. (1980). Affective disorders. In G. Turpin (Ed.), *Handbook of clinical psychophysiology* (pp. 357–392). New York: Wiley.

Hesketh, B., Durant, C., & Pryor, R. (1990). Career compromise: A test of Gottfredson's theory using a policy-capturing procedure. *Journal of Vocational Behavior, 36,* 97–108.

Hesketh, B., Elmslie, S., & Kaldor, W. (1990). Career compromise: An alternative account to Gottfredson's 1981 theory. *Journal of Counseling Psychology, 37,* 49–50.

Heymans, G., & Wiersma, E. (1906). Beitrage zur Speziellen Psychologie auf Grundeiner Massenuntersuchung. *Zeitschrift für Psychologie, 43,* 81–127, 258–301.

Hibbard, S. R., Farmer, L., Wells, C., Difillipo, E., & Barry, W. (1994). Validation of Cramer's defense mechanism manual for the TAT. *Journal of Personality Assessment, 63,* 197–210.

Hobbs, N. (1963). A psychologist in the Peace Corps. *American Psychologist, 18,* 47–55.

Hoch, A., & Amsden, G. S. (1913). A guide to the descriptive study of personality. *Review of Neurology and Psychiatry, 11,* 577–587.

Hodes, R. L., Cook, E. W., & Lang, P. (1985). Individual differences in autonomic response: Conditioned association or conditioned fear? *Psychophysiology, 22,* 545–560.

Holden, R. R., Fekken, G. C., & Cotton, D. H. (1991). Assessing psychopathology using structured test-item responses latencies. *Psychological Assessment, 3,* 111–118.

Holland, J. L. (1985). *Making vocational choices: A theory of careers: A theory of vocational personalities and work environments* (2nd ed.). Upper Saddle River, NJ: Prentice Hall.

Hollingworth, H. L. (1920). *The psychology of functional neuroses.* New York: D. Appleton.

Holmes, T. H., & Rahe, R. H. (1967). The Social Readjustment Scale. *Journal of Psychosomatic Research, 11,* 213–218.

Holt, P. A. (1989). Differential effect of status and interest in the process of compromise. *Journal of Counseling Psychology, 36,* 42–47.

Holtzman, W. H. (1988). Beyond the Rorschach. *Journal of Personality Assessment, 52,* 578–609.

Honigfelt, G., & Klett, C. (1965). The Nurses' Observation Scale for Inpatient Evaluation (NOSIE): A new scale for measuring improvement in schizophrenia. *Journal of Clinical Psychology, 21,* 65–71.

Hurt, S. W., Reznikoff, M., & Clarkin, J. F. (1995). The Rorschach. In L. E. Beutler & M. R. Berren (Eds.), *Integrative assessment of adult personality* (pp. 187–205). New York: Guilford.

Hutt, M. L. (1977). *The Hutt adaptation of the Bender-Gestalt test* (3rd ed.). New York: Grune & Stratton.

Jackson, D. N., Helmes, E., Hoffmann, H., Holden, R. R., Jaffe, P. G., Reddon, J. R., & Smiley, W. C. (1989). *Basic Personality Inventory manual*. Port Huron, MI: Sigma Assessment Systems.

Jamison, K. R. (1984). Manic-depressive illness and accomplishment: Creativity, leadership, and social class. In F. K. Goodwin & K. R. Jamison (Eds.), *Manic-depressive illness*. New York: Oxford University Press.

Joesting, J. (1981). Comparison of personalities of athletes who sail to those who run. *Perceptual and Motor Skills, 52,* 514.

Juni, S. (1995). Review of the Revised NEO Personality Inventory. In J. C. Conoley & J. C. Impara (Eds.), *The twelfth mental measurements yearbook* (pp. 863–868). Lincoln: Buros Institute of Mental Measurements of the University of Nebraska–Lincoln.

Kagan, J. (1966). Reflective-impulsivity: The generality and dynamics of conceptual tempo. *Journal of Abnormal Psychology, 71,* 17–24.

Kagan, J. (1994). *Galen's prophecy*. New York: Basic Books.

Kagan, J., Reznick, J. S., & Snideman, N. (1990). Biological bases of childhood shyness. *Science, 240,* 167–171.

Kagan, J., Rosman, B. L., Day, D., Albert, J., & Phillips, W. (1964). Information processing in the child: Significance of analytic and reflective attitudes. *Psychological Monographs, 78* (Whole No. 578).

Kallman, F. J., & Jarvik, L. (1959). Individual differences in constitution and genetic background. In J. E. Birren (Ed.), *Handbook of aging and the individual* (pp. 216–263). Chicago: University of Chicago Press.

Karon, B. P. (1981). The Thematic Apperception Test (TAT). In A. I. Rabin (Ed.), *Assessment with projective techniques* (pp. 85–120). New York: Springer-Verlag.

Katkin, E. S. (1978). Review of State-Trait Anxiety Inventory. In O. K. Buros (Ed.), *The eighth mental measurements yearbook* (Vol. 1, pp. 1095–1906). Highland Park, NJ: Gryphon Press.

Kearns, D. (1976). *Lyndon Johnson and the American dream*. New York: Wilson.

Keating, D. P. (Ed.). (1976). *Intellectual talent: Research and development*. Baltimore, MD: Johns Hopkins University Press.

Kelleher, K. (1996, August 19). In the world of psychology, the eyebrows surely have it. *Los Angeles Times,* p. E3.

Kelly, E. L. (1987). Graphology. In R. J. Corsini (Ed.), *Concise encyclopedia of psychology* (p. 469). New York: Wiley.

Kelly, E. L., & Fiske, D. W. (1951). *The prediction of performance in clinical psychology*. Ann Arbor, MI: University of Michigan Press.

Keyser, D. J., & Sweetland, R. C. (Eds.). (1984–1994). *Test critiques* (Vols. 1–10). Austin, TX: pro.ed.

Kinicki, A. J., & Bannister, B. D. (1988). A test of the measurement assumptions underlying behaviorally anchored rating scales. *Educational and Psychological Measurement, 48,* 17–27.

Klein, M. H., Benjamin, L. S., Rosenfeld, R., Treece, C., & Greist, J. H. (1993). The Wisconsin Personality Disorder Inventory: 1. Development, reliability, and validity. *Journal of Personality Disorders, 7,* 285–303.

Klopfer, W. G. (1984). Application of the consensus Rorschach to couples. *Journal of Personality Assessment, 48,* 422–440.

Klopfer, W. G., & Taulbee, E. S. (1976). Thematic Apperception Test. *Annual Review of Psychology, 27,* 543–567.

Kohlberg, L. (1974). The development of moral stages: Uses and abuses. *Proceedings of the 1973 Invitational Conference on Testing Problems* (pp. 1–8). Princeton, NJ: Educational Testing Service.

Korchin, S. J., & Schuldberg, D. (1981). The future of clinical assessment. *American Psychologist, 36,* 1147–1158.

Kraiger, K., Hakel, M. D., & Cornelius, E. T. (1984). Exploring fantasies of TAT reliability. *Journal of Personality Assessment, 48,* 365–370.

Kramer, J. J., & Conoley, J. (1992). *The eleventh mental measurements yearbook.* Lincoln: Buros Institute of Mental Measurements of the University of Nebraska–Lincoln.

Krug, S. E. (1993). *Psychware sourcebook* (4th ed.). Champaign, IL: MetriTech.

Lang, W. S. (1992). Review of TEMAS (Tell-Me-a-Story). In J. J. Kramer & J. C. Conoley (Eds.), *The eleventh mental measurements yearbook* (pp. 925–926). Lincoln: Buros Institute of Mental Measurements of the University of Nebraska–Lincoln.

Langer, W. C. (1972). *The mind of Adolf Hitler.* New York: Basic Books.

Langevin, R. (1983). *Sexual strands: Understanding and treating sexual abnormalities in men.* Hillsdale, NJ: Erlbaum.

LeUnes, A. D., & Nation, J. R. (1980). *Sport psychology: An introduction.* Chicago: Nelson-Hall.

Leung, S. A., & Harmon, L. W. (1990). Individual and sex differences in the zone of acceptable alternatives. *Journal of Counseling Psychology, 37,* 158–159.

Levenson, H. (1981). Differentiating among internality, powerful others, and chance. In H. M. Lefcourt (Ed.), *Research with the locus of control construct* (Vol. 1, pp. 15–63). New York: Academic Press.

Levenson, R. W. (1992). Autonomic nervous system differences among emotions. *Psychological Science, 3,* 23–27.

Levinson, D. J. (1978). *The seasons of a man's life.* New York: Knopf.

Liberman, R. P. (Ed.). (1988). *Psychiatric rehabilitation of chronic mental patients.* Washington, DC: American Psychiatric Press.

Lindzey, G. (1959). On the classification of projective techniques. *Psychological Bulletin, 56,* 158–168.

Lippsitt, P. D., Lelos, D., & McGarry, A. L. (1971). Competency for trial: A screening instrument. *American Journal of Psychiatry, 128,* 105–109.

Lorr, M. (1991). An empirical evaluation of the MBTI typology. *Personality and Individual Differences, 12,* 1141–1145.

Lyerly, S. B. (Ed.). (1978). *Handbook of psychiatric rating scales* (2nd ed.). Rockville, MD: National Institute of Mental Health.

MacKinnon, D. W. (1962). The nature and nurture of creative talent. *American Psychologist, 17,* 484–495.

Manaster, G. J., & Perryman, T. B. (1974). Early recollections and occupational choice. *Journal of Individual Psychology, 30,* 232–237.

Markus, H., & Nurius, P. (1986). Possible selves. *American Psychologist, 41*, 954–969.

Martin, R. P. (1988). Basic methods of objective test construction. In *Assessment of personality and behavior problems: Infancy through adolescence* (pp. 43–67). New York: Guilford.

Matarazzo, J. D. (1972). *Wechsler's measurement and appraisal of adult intelligence* (5th ed.). Baltimore: Williams & Wilkins.

Matarazzo, J. D. (1992). Psychological testing and assessment in the 21st century. *American Psychologist, 47*, 1007–1018.

Mazlish, B. (1973). *In search of Nixon.* Baltimore, MD: Penguin.

McClelland, D. C. (1961). *The achieving society.* Princeton, NJ: Van Nostrand.

McCrae, R. R., & Costa, P. T. (1987). Validation of the five-factor model of personality across instruments and observers. *Journal of Personality and Social Psychology, 52*, 138–155.

McGrew, M. W., & Teglasi, H., (1990). Formal characteristics of Thematic Apperception Test stories as indices of emotional disturbance in children. *Journal of Personality Assessment, 54*, 639–655.

McLellan, M. J. (1995). Review of the Sixteen Personality Factor Questionnaire (5th ed.). In J. C. Conoley & J. C. Impara (Eds.), *The twelfth mental measurements yearbook* (pp. 947–948). Lincoln: Buros Institute of Mental Measurements of the University of Nebraska–Lincoln.

Meehl, P. E. (1954). *Clinical versus statistical prediction.* Minneapolis: University of Minnesota Press.

Meehl, P. E. (1965). Seer over sign: The first good example. *Journal of Experimental Research in Personality, 11*, 27–32.

Megargee, E. I., & Spielberger, C. D. (Eds.). (1992). Reflections on fifty years of personality assessment and future directions for the field. In *Personality assessment in America* (pp. 170–186). Hillsdale, NJ: Erlbaum

Mehrabian, A., & Weiner, M. (1967). Decoding of inconsistent communication. *Journal of Personality and Social Psychology, 6*, 109–114.

Miller, P. C., Lefcourt, H. M., & Ware, E. E. (1983). The construction and development of the Miller Marital Locus of Control Scale. *Canadian Journal of Behavioral Science, 15*, 266–279.

Millon, T. (1994). *Millon Index of Personality Styles manual.* San Antonio, TX: The Psychological Corporation.

Millon, T., Millon, C., & Davis, R. (1994). *Manual for the MCMI–III.* Minneapolis: NCS Assessments.

Mischel, W. (1968). *Personality and assessment.* New York: Wiley.

Mitchell, J. V., Jr. (Ed.). (1983). *Tests in print III.* Lincoln: Buros Institute of Mental Measurements of the University of Nebraska–Lincoln.

Mitchell, J. V., Jr. (Ed.). (1985). *The ninth mental measurements yearbook.* Lincoln: Buros Institute of Mental Measures of the University of Nebraska–Lincoln.

Montag, I., & Comrey, A. (1987). Internality and externality as correlates of involvement in fatal driving accidents. *Journal of Applied Psychology, 72*, 339–343.

Morey, L. C. (1991). *Personality Assessment Inventory: Professional manual.* Odessa, FL: Psychological Assessment Resources.

Morgan, W. P. (1980). Test of champions. *Psychology Today, 14,* 92–108.

Morris, D. (1967). *The naked ape.* New York: McGraw-Hill.

Munroe, R. L. (1955). *Schools of psychoanalytic thought.* New York: Holt, Rinehart & Winston.

Murphy, D. L., Beigel, A., Weingartner, H., & Bunney, W. E. (1974). The quantification of manic behavior. *Modern Problems in Pharmacopsychiatry, 7,* 203–220.

Murphy, K. R., & Davidshofer, C. O. (1994). *Psychological testing: Principles and applications* (3rd ed.). Upper Saddle River, NJ: Prentice Hall.

Murphy, L. L., Conoley, J. C., & Impara, J. C. (Eds.). (1994). *Tests in print.* Lincoln, NE: University of Nebraska and Buros Institute of Mental Measurements.

Murray, H. A. (and collaborators). (1938). *Explorations in personality.* New York: Oxford.

Murray, H. A. (1943). *Thematic Apperception Test—Manual.* Cambridge, MA: Harvard University Press.

Murray, J. B. (1990). Review of research on the Myers-Briggs Type Indicator. *Perceptual and Motor Skills, 70,* 1187–1202.

Murstein, I. (1963). *Theory and research in projective techniques.* New York: Wiley.

Museum of Modern Art. (1955). *The family of man.* New York: Maco Magazine Corporation.

Neter, E., & Ben-Shakhar, G. (1980). Predictive validity of graphological inferences: A meta-analytic approach. *Personality and Individual Differences, 10,* 737–745.

Netter, B., & Viglione, D., Jr. (1994). An empirical study of malingering schizophrenia on the Rorschach. *Journal of Personality Assessment, 62,* 45–57.

Niemcryk, S. J., Jenkins, C. D., Rose, R. M., & Hurst, M. W. (1987). The prospective impact of psychosocial variables on rates of illness and injury in professional employees. *Journal of Occupational Medicine, 29*(8), 645–652.

O'Bannon, R. M., Goldinger, L. A., & Appleby, J. D. (1989). *Honesty and integrity testing: A practice guide.* Atlanta: Applied Information Resources.

Oden, M. H. (1968). The fulfillment of promise: 40-year follow-up of the Terman gifted group. *Genetic Psychology Monographs, 77*(1), 3–93.

Office of Strategic Services (OSS) Assessment Staff. (1948). *Assessment of men: Selection of personnel for the Office of Strategic Services.* New York: Rinehart.

O'Gorman, J. G. (1983). Habituation and personality. In A. Gale & J. A. Edwards (Eds.), *Physiological correlates of human behavior: Vol. 3. Individual differences and psychopathology* (pp. 45–61). London: Academic Press.

Ornberg, B., & Zalewski, C. (1994). Assessment of adolescents with the Rorschach: A critical review. *Assessment, 1,* 209–217.

Osipow, S. H. (1983). *Theories of career development* (3rd ed.). Upper Saddle River, NJ: Prentice Hall.

Ostendorf, F., & Angleitner, A. (1994). The five-factor taxonomy: Robust dimensions of personality description. *Psychologica Belgica, 34,* 175–194.

Overall, J. E., & Gorham, D. R. (1962). The Brief Psychiatric Rating Scale. *Psychological Reports, 10,* 799–812.

Owen, S. V. (1992). Review of the Beck Hopelessness Scale. In J. J. Kramer & J. C. Conoley (Eds.), *The eleventh mental measurements yearbook* (pp. 82–83).

Lincoln: Buros Institute of Mental Measurements of the University of Nebraska–Lincoln.

Paulhus, D. L. (1983). Sphere-specific measures of perceived control. *Journal of Personality and Social Psychology, 44*, 1253–1265.

Payne, A. F. (1928). *Sentence completions*. New York: New York Guidance Clinic.

Payne, F. D. (1985). Review of Bem Sex-Role Inventory. In J. V. Mitchell, Jr. (Ed.), *The ninth mental measurements yearbook* (Vol. 1, pp. 137–138). Lincoln: Buros Institute of Mental Measurements of the University of Nebraska–Lincoln.

Perry, A. (1986). Type A behavior pattern and motor vehicle drivers' behavior. *Perceptual and Motor Skills, 63*, 875–878.

Peterson, C., Semmel, A., Von Baeyer, C., Abramson, L. Y., Metalsky, G. I., & Seligman, M. E. P. (1982). The Attributional Style Questionnaire. *Cognitive Therapy and Research, 6*, 287–299.

Peterson, R. A. (1978). Review of the Rorschach. In O. K. Buros (Ed.), *The eighth measurements yearbook* (Vol. 1, p. 661). Highland Park, NJ: Gryphon Press.

Peterson, R. A., & Headen, S. W. (1984). Profile of Mood States. In D. J. Keyser & R. C. Sweetland (Eds.), *Test critiques* (Vol. 1, pp. 522–529). Kansas City, MO: Test Corporation of America.

Piacentini, J. (1993). Checklists and rating scales. In T. H. Ollendick & M. Hersen (Eds.), *Handbook of child and adolescent assessment* (pp. 82–97). Boston: Allyn & Bacon.

Piedmont, R. L., & Weinstein, H. P. (1993). A psychometric evaluation of the new NEO-PIR facet scales for agreeableness and conscientiousness. *Journal of Personality Assessment, 60*(2), 302–318.

Piotrowski, C., & Zalewski, C. (1993). Training in psychodiagnostic testing in APA-approved PsyD and PhD clinical psychology programs. *Journal of Personality Assessment, 61*, 394–405.

Polich, J., & Martin, S. (1992). P300, cognitive capability, and personality: A correlational study of university undergraduates. *Personality and Individual Differences, 13*, 533–543.

Pons, L. (1989). Effects of age and sex upon available of responses on a word-association test. *Perceptual and Motor Skills, 68*, 85–86.

Pressey, S. L., & Pressey, L. W. (1919). Cross-out test, with suggestions as to a group scale of the emotions. *Journal of Applied Psychology, 3*, 138–150.

Pritchard, W. S. (1989). P300 and EPQ/STPI personality traits. *Personality and Individual Differences, 10*, 15–24.

Quirk, M. P., Strosahl, K., Kreilkamp, T., & Erdberg, P. (1995). Personality feedback consultation in a managed mental health care practice. *Professional Psychology: Research and Practice, 26*, 27–32.

Rabin, A. I., & Zlotogorski, Z. (1981). Completion methods: Word association, sentence and story completion. In A. I. Rabin (Ed.), *Assessment with projective techniques: A concise introduction* (pp. 641–647). Kansas City, MO: Test Corporation of America.

Rapaport, D., Gill, M. M., & Schafer, R. (1968). *Diagnostic psychological testing*. Chicago: Year Book.

Reik, T. (1948). *Listening with the third ear*. New York: Grove Press.

Retzlaff, P. (1992). Review of the State-Trait Anger Expression Inventory (res. ed.). In J. J. Kramer & J. C. Conoley (Eds.), *The eleventh mental measurements yearbook* (pp. 869–870). Lincoln: Buros Institute of Mental Measurements of the University of Nebraska–Lincoln.

Reynolds, C. R. (1992). Review of the Millon Clinical Multiaxial Inventory–II. In J. J. Kramer & J. C. Conoley (Eds.), *The eleventh mental measurements yearbook* (pp. 533–535). Lincoln: Buros Institute of Mental Measurements of the University of Nebraska–Lincoln.

Reznikoff, M., Aronow, E., & Rauchway, A. (1982). The reliability of inkblot content scales. In C. D. Spielberger & J. N. Butcher (Eds.), *Advances in personality assessment* (Vol. 1, pp. 83–113). New York: Erlbaum.

Riese, M. (1988). Temperament in full-term and preterm infants: Stability over ages 6–24 months. *Journal of Developmental and Behavioral Pediatrics, 9,* 6–11.

Ritter, A., & Effron, L. D. (1952). The use of the Thematic Apperception Test to differentiate normal from abnormal groups. *Journal of Abnormal and Social Psychology, 47,* 147–158.

Ritzler, B. A., Sharkey, K. J., & Chudy, J. (1980). A comprehensive projective alternative to the TAT. *Journal of Personality Assessment, 44,* 358–362.

Robinson, J. P., Athanasiou, R., & Head, K. B. (1974). *Measures of occupational attitudes and occupational characteristics.* Ann Arbor: Institute for Social Research, University of Michigan.

Robinson, J. P., Rush, J. G., & Head, K. B. (1973). *Measures of political attitudes.* Ann Arbor: Institute for Social Research, University of Michigan.

Robinson, J. P., Shaver, P. R., & Wrightsman, L. S. (1991). *Measures of personality and social psychological attitudes.* New York: Academic Press.

Robinson, R. G., Kubos, K. L., Starr, B., Rao, K., & Price, T. R. (1984). Mood disorders in stroke patients: Importance of location of lesion. *Brain, 97,* 81–93.

Ronan, G. F., Colavito, V., & Hammontree, S. (1993). Personal Problem-Solving System for scoring TAT responses: Preliminary validity and reliability data. *Journal of Personality Assessment, 61,* 28–40.

Ronan, G. F., Date, A. L., & Weisbrod, M. (1995). Personal problem-solving scoring of the TAT: Sensitivity to training. *Journal of Personality Assessment, 64,* 119–131.

Roper, B. L., Ben-Porath, Y. S., & Butcher, J. N. (1995). Comparability and validity of computerized adaptive testing with the MMPI-2. *Journal of Personality Assessment, 65,* 358–371.

Rosenfeld, P., Doherty, L. M., Vincino, S. M., Kantor, J., et al. (1989). Attitudes assessment in organizations: Testing three microcomputer-based survey systems. *Journal of General Psychology, 116,* 145–154.

Rosenhan, D. L. (1973). On being sane in insane places. *Science, 179,* 365–369.

Roth, D. L., & Holmes, D. S. (1985). Influence of physical fitness in deterring the impact of stressful events on physical and psychologic health. *Psychosomatic Medicine, 47,* 164–173.

Rothenberg, M. G. (1990). Graphology. *Encyclopedia Americana* (Vol. 13, pp. 190–191). Danbury, CT: Grolier.

Rotter, J. B. (1966). Generalized expectancies for internal versus external control of reinforcement. *Psychological Monographs, 81* (1, Whole No. 609).

Rotter, J. B. (1967). A new scale for the measurement of interpersonal trust. *Journal of Personality, 35,* 651–655.

Rotto, P. C. (1995). Review of the Sixteen Personality Factor Questionnaire (5th ed.). In J. C. Conoley & J. C. Impara (Eds.), *The twelfth mental measurements yearbook* (pp. 948–950). Lincoln: Buros Institute of Mental Measurements of the University of Nebraska–Lincoln.

Royce, J. R., & Powell, A. (1983). *Theory of personality and individual differences: Factors, systems, and processes.* Upper Saddle River, NJ: Prentice Hall.

Rubin, Z., Peplau, L. A., & Salovey, P. (1993). *Psychology.* Boston: Houghton Mifflin.

Sackeim, H. A., Weinman, A. L., Gur, R. C., Greenberg, M., Hungerbuhler, J. P., & Geschwind, N. (1982). Pathological laughter and crying: Functional brain asymmetry in the expression of positive and negative emotions. *Archives of Neurology, 39,* 210–218.

Sattler, J. M. (1985). Review of the Hutt Adaptation of the Bender-Gestalt Test. In J. V. Mitchell, Jr. (Ed.), *The ninth mental measurements yearbook* (Vol. 1, pp. 184–185). Lincoln: Buros Institute of Mental Measurements of the University of Nebraska–Lincoln.

Schaie, K. W. (1967). Age changes and age differences. *Gerontologist, 7,* 128–132.

Schaie, K. W. (1978). Review of Senior Apperception Technique. In O. K. Buros (Ed.), *The eighth mental measurements yearbook* (Vol. 1, p. 1060). Highland Park, NJ: Gryphon.

Schmidt, F. L., Ones, D. S., & Hunter, J. E. (1992). Personnel selection. *Annual Review of Psychology, 42,* 627–670.

Schultz, D. P., & Schultz, S. E. (1990). *Psychology and work today* (6th ed.). New York: Macmillan.

Sears, R. R. (1977). Sources of life satisfactions of the Terman gifted men. *American Psychologist, 32,* 119–128.

Sharkey, K. J., & Ritzler, B. A. (1985). Comparing diagnostic validity of the TAT and a new Picture Projective Test. *Journal of Personality Assessment, 49,* 406–412.

Shaw, L., & Sichel, H. S. (1971). *Accident proneness: Research on the occurrence, causation, and prevention of road accidents.* New York: Pergamon.

Shields, R. B. (1978). The usefulness of the Rorschach Prognostic Rating Scale: A rebuttal. *Journal of Personality Assessment, 42,* 579–582.

Shostrom, E. L. (1974). *Manual for the Personal Orientation Inventory.* San Diego: Educational and Industrial Testing Service.

Siegelman, M., & Peck, R. F. (1960). Personality patterns related to occupational roles. *Genetic Psychology Monographs, 61,* 291–349.

Siipola, E. M. (1987). House-Tree-Person Test. In R. J. Corsini (Ed.), *Concise encyclopedia of psychology* (p. 531). New York: Wiley.

Siipola, E. M., Walker, W., & Kolb, D. (1985). Task attitudes in word association. *Journal of Personality, 23,* 441–459.

Singh, L. (1986). Standardization of n-power measuring instrument (T.A.T). *Journal of Psychological Researches, 28,* 14–20.

Smith, S. R., & Meyer, R. G. (1987). *Law, behavior, and mental health.* New York: New York University Press.

Snyder, M. (1974). Self-monitoring of expressive behavior. *Journal of Personality and Social Psychology, 30,* 526–537.

Snyder, M. (1979). Self-monitoring processes. *Advances in Experimental Social Psychology, 12,* 85–128.

Sonstroem, R. J. (1984). Exercise and self-esteem. *Exercise and Sport Sciences Reviews, 12,* 123–155.

Soroka v. Dayton-Hudson Corp. 91. L.A. Daily Journal D.A.R. 13204 (Cal. Ct. App. 1991).

Spence, J. T., & Helmreich, R. (1978). *Masculinity and femininity: Theory psychological dimensions, correlates, and antecedents.* Austin, TX: University of Texas Press.

Spitzer, R. L. (1976). More on pseudoscience in science and the case for psychiatric diagnosis: A critique of D. L. Rosenhan's "On Being Sane in Insane Place" and "The Contextual Nature of Psychiatric Diagnosis." *Archives of General Psychiatry, 49,* 624–629.

Stanley, J. C., Keating, D. P., & Fox, I. H. (Eds.). (1974). *Mathematical talent: Discovery, description, and development.* Baltimore: Johns Hopkins University Press.

Steinbrook, R. (1992). The polygraph test—a flawed diagnostic method. *The New England Journal of Medicine, 327,* 122–123.

Stelmack, R. M. (1990). Biological bases of extraversion: Psychophysiological evidence. *Journal of Personality, 58,* 293–311.

Stelmack, R. M., Achorn, E., & Michaud, A. (1977). Extraversion and individual differences in auditory evoked response. *Psychophysiology, 14,* 368–374.

Stelmack, R. M., & Houlihan, M. (1995). Event-related potentials, personality, and intelligence: Concepts, issues, and evidence. In D. H. Saklofske & M. Zeidner (Eds.), *International handbook of personality and intelligence* (pp. 349–365). New York: Plenum.

Stelmack, R. M., Houlihan, M., & McGarry-Roberts, P. S. (1993). Personality, reaction time, and event-related potentials. *Journal of Personality and Social Psychology, 65,* 399–409.

Stelmack, R. M., & Michaud-Achorn, A. (1985). Extraversion, attention, and habituation of the auditory evoked response. *Journal of Research in Personality, 19,* 416–428.

Stenberg, G., Rosen, I., & Risberg, J. (1988). Personality and augmenting/reducing in visual and auditory evoked potentials. *Personality and Individual Differences, 9,* 571–580.

Stenberg, G., Rosen, I., & Risberg, J. (1990). Attention and personality in augmenting/reducing of visual evoked potentials. *Personality and Individual Differences, 11,* 1243–1254.

Stephenson, W. (1953). *The study of behavior: Q-technique and its methodology.* Chicago: University of Chicago Press.

Sternberg, R. J. (1988). Mental self-government: A theory of intellectual styles and their development. *Human Development, 31,* 197–224.

Sternberg, R. J. (1989). Domain-generality versus domain specificity: The life and impending death of a false dichotomy. *Merrill-Palmer Quarterly, 35*, 115–130.

Stokes, G. S., Mumford, M. D., & Owens, W. A. (1994). *Biodata handbook: Theory, research, and use of biographical information in selection and performance prediction.* Palo Alto, CA: CPP Books.

Stone, R. (1988). Personality tests in management selection. *Human Resources Journal, 3*, 51–55.

Sundberg, N. D. (1992). Review of the Beck Depression Inventory. In J. J. Kramer & J. C. Conoley (Eds.), *The eleventh mental measurements yearbook* (pp. 79–80). Lincoln: Buros Institute of Mental Measurements of the University of Nebraska–Lincoln.

Super, D. E. (1957). *The psychology of careers.* New York: Harper & Row.

Super, D. E. (1963). Self-concepts in vocational development. In D. E. Super (Ed.), *Career development: Self-concept theory* (pp. 1–16). New York: College Entrance Examination Board.

Super, D. E. (1972). Vocational development theory: Persons, positions, processes. In J. M. Whiteley & A. Resnikoff (Eds.), *Perspectives on vocational development* (pp. 13–33). Washington, DC: American Personnel and Guidance Association.

Super, D. E. (1990). A life-span space approach to career development. In D. Brown & L. Brooks & Associates (Eds.), *Career choice and development* (2nd ed., pp. 197–261). Hillsdale, NJ: Erlbaum.

Super, D. E., & Bohn, M. J., Jr. (1970). *Occupational psychology.* Belmont, CA: Wadsworth.

Sutherland, J. D., & Gill, H. S. (1970). *Language and psychodynamic appraisal.* London: Research Publication Services.

Swartz, J. D. (1978). Review of the TAT. In O. K. Buros (Ed.), *The eighth mental measurements yearbook* (pp. 1127–1130). Highland Park, NJ: Gryphon.

Sweetland, R. C., & Keyser, D. J. (Eds.). (1991). *Tests* (3rd ed.). Austin, TX: pro.ed.

Swiercinsky, D. P. (Ed.). (1985). *Testing adults.* Kansas City, MO: Test Corporation of America.

Teeter, P. A. (1985). Review of Adjective Check List. In J. V. Mitchell, Jr. (Ed.), *The ninth mental measurements yearbook* (Vol. 1, pp. 50–52). Lincoln: Buros Institute of Mental Measurements of the University of Nebraska–Lincoln.

Templer, D. I. (1985). Multiple Affect Adjective Check List–Revised. In D. J. Keyser & R. C. Sweetland (Eds.), *Test critiques* (Vol. 4, pp. 449–452). Kansas City, MO: Test Corporation of America.

Tendler, A. D. (1930). A preliminary report on a test for educational insight. *Journal of Applied Psychology, 14*, 123–126.

Tett, R., Jackson, D., & Rothstein, M. (1991). Personality measures as predictors of job performance: A meta-analytic review. *Personnel Psychology, 44*, 703–735.

Thomas, A., & Chess, S. (1977). *Temperament and development.* New York: Brunner/Mazel.

Thomas, E. E., Alinsky, D., & Exner, J. E. (1982). *The stability of some Rorschach variables in 9-year-olds as compared with non-patient adults* (Rorschach Workshops Study No. 441). Unpublished manuscript.

Thompson, C. (1949). The Thompson modification of the Thematic Apperception Test. *Journal of Projective Techniques, 13*, 469–478.

Tinsley, H. E. A. (1985). Personality Research Form. In D. J. Keyser & R. C. Sweetland (Eds.), *Test critiques* (Vol. 3, pp. 499–509). Kansas City, MO: Test Corporation of America.

Tolor, A., & Schulberg, H. (1963). *Evaluation of the Bender-Gestalt test.* Springfield, IL: Charles C Thomas.

Torgerson, A. M. (1985). Temperamental differences in infants and 6-year-old children: A follow-up study of twins. In J. Strelau, F. Farley, & A. Gales (Eds.), *The biological bases of personality and behavior* (Vol. 1, pp. 227–239). New York: Hemisphere.

Tosi, J., & Lindamood, C. A. (1975). Review of the Personal Orientation Inventory. *Journal of Personality Assessment, 39*(3), 215–224.

Tryon, R. C. (1940). Genetic differences in maze learning in rats. *Yearbook of the National Society for Studies in Education, 39*, 111–119.

Tversky, A., & Kahneman, D. (1981). The framing of decisions and the psychology of choice. *Science, 211*, 453–458.

Ungerleiter, S., & Golding, J. M. (1989). Mood profiles of masters track and field athletes. *Perceptual and Motor Skills, 68*, 607–617.

Urbina, S. (1995). Review of the Basic Personality Inventory. In J. C. Conoley & J. C. Impara (Eds.), *The twelfth mental measurements yearbook* (pp. 105–106). Lincoln: Buros Institute of Mental Measurements of the University of Nebraska–Lincoln.

Utz, P., & Korben, D. (1976). The construct validity of the occupational themes on the Strong-Campbell Inventory. *Journal of Vocational Behavior, 9*, 31–42.

Wagner, E. E. (1985). Review of the Rosenzweig Picture-Frustration Study. In J. V. Mitchell, Jr. (Ed.), *The ninth mental measurements yearbook* (Vol. 2, pp. 1297–1298). Lincoln: Buros Institute of Mental Measurements of the University of Nebraska–Lincoln.

Wallston, K. A., & Wallston, B. S. (1981). Health locus of control scales. In H. M. Lefcourt (Ed.), *Research with the locus of control construct* (Vol. 1, pp. 189–243). New York: Academic Press.

Walters, G. D., Revella, L., & Baltrusaitis, W. J. (1990). Predicting parole/probation outcome with the aid of the Lifestyle Criminality Screening Form. *Psychological Assessment: A Journal of Consulting and Clinical Psychology, 2*, 313–316.

Watkins, C. E., Campbell, V. L., Nieberding, R., & Hallmark, R. (1995). Contemporary practice of psychological assessment by clinical psychologists. *Professional Psychology: Research and Practice, 26*, 54–60.

Weary, G. B. (1978). Self-serving biases in the attribution process: A re-examination of the fact or fiction question. *Journal of Personality and Social Psychology, 36*, 56–71.

Webb, E. (1915). Character and intelligence. *British Journal of Psychology Monograph Supplement, III*.

Webb, J. T., & Meckstroth, B. (1982). *Guiding the gifted child.* Columbus: Ohio Psychology.

Wechsler, D. (1975). Intelligence defined and undefined. *American Psychologist*, *30*, 135–139.

Weiner, I. B. (1983). The future of psychodiagnosis revisited. *Journal of Personality Assessment*, *47*, 451–461.

Wells, R. L. (1914). The systematic observation of the personality—in its relation to the hygiene of the mind. *Psychological Review*, *21*, 295–333.

Welsh, G. S. (1977). Personality correlates of intelligence and creativity in gifted adolescents. In J. C. Stanley, W. C. George, & C. H. Solano (Eds.), *The gifted and the creative: A fifty-year perspective*. Baltimore, MD: Johns Hopkins University Press.

Wewers, M. E., & Lowe, N. K. (1990). A critical review of visual analogue scales in the measurement of clinical phenomena. *Research in Nursing & Health*, *13*(4), 227–236.

Wiggins, J. (1973). *Personality and prediction: Principles of personality assessment*. Reading, MA: Addison-Wesley.

Wildman, R. et al. (1980). The Georgia Court Competency Test: *An attempt to develop a rapid, quantitative measure of fitness for trial*. Unpublished manuscript, Forensic Services Division, Center State Hospital, Milledgeville, GA.

Wilson, M. A., & Languis, M. L. (1990). A topographic study of differences in the P300 between introverts and extraverts. *Brain Topography*, *2*, 269–274.

Winter, D. G., & Stewart, A. J. (1977). Power motive reliability as a function of retest instructions. *Journal of Consulting and Clinical Psychology*, *45*, 436–440.

Witkin, H. A., & Berry, J. W. (1975). Psychological differentiation in cross-cultural perspective. *Journal of Cross-Cultural Psychology*, *6*, 4–87.

Witkin, H. A., Dyk, R. B., Faterson, H. F., Goodenough, D. R., & Karp, S. A. (1974). *Psychological differentiation*. Potomac, MD: Erlbaum.

Witkin, H. A., & Goodenough, D. R. (1977). Field dependence and interpersonal behavior. *Psychological Bulletin*, *84*, 661–689.

Witt, J. C., Heffer, R. W., & Pfeiffer, J. (1990). Structured rating scales: A review of self-report and informant rating processes, procedures, and issues. In C. R. Reynolds & R. W. Kamphaus (Eds.), *Handbook of psychological & educational assessment of children: Personality, behavior, & context* (pp. 364–394). New York: Guilford.

Woodruff, R. A., Goodwin, D. W., & Guze, S. B. (1974). *Psychiatric diagnosis*. London: Oxford University Press.

Worchel, F. F., & Dupree, J. L. (1990). Projective story-telling techniques. In C. B. Reynolds & R. W. Kamphaus (Eds.), *Handbook of psychological and educational assessment of children: Personality behavior, and context* (pp. 70–88). New York: Guilford Press.

Worobey, J. (1986). Convergence among assessments of temperament in the first month. *Child Development*, *57*, 47–55.

Wrightsman, L. S. (1994a). *Adult personality development. Vol. 1. Theories and concepts*. Thousand Oaks, CA: Sage.

Wrightsman, L. S. (1994b). *Adult personality development. Vol. 2. Applications*. Thousand Oaks, CA: Sage.

Yelland, T. (1995). Review of the Basic Personality Inventory. In J. C. Conoley & J. C. Impara (Eds.), *The twelfth mental measurements yearbook* (pp. 106–107). Lincoln: Buros Institute of Mental Measurements of the University of Nebraska–Lincoln.

Zarske, J. A. (1985). Review of Adjective Check List. In J. V. Mitchell, Jr. (Ed.), *The ninth mental measurements yearbook* (Vol. 1, pp. 52–53). Lincoln: Buros Institute of Mental Measurements of the University of Nebraska–Lincoln.

Ziskin, J. (1986). The future of clinical assessment. In B. S. Plake & J. C. Witt (Eds), *The future of testing* (pp. 185–201). Hillsdale, NJ: Erlbaum.

Ziskin, J., & Faust, D. (1988). *Coping with psychiatric and psychological testimony* (3rd ed.). Marina del Rey, CA: Law and Psychology Press.

Zubin, J., Eron, I. D., & Schumer, F. (1965). *An experimental approach to projective techniques*. New York: Wiley.

Zuckerman, M. (1983). *Biological basis of sensation seeking, impulsivity, and anxiety*. Hillsdale, NJ: Erlbaum.

Zuckerman, M. (1989). Personality in the third dimension: A psychobiological approach. *Personality and Individual Differences, 10*, 391–418.

Zuckerman, M. (1994). *Behavioral expressions and biosocial bases of sensation seeking*. New York: Cambridge University Press.

Zuckerman, M., & Lubin, B. (1985). *Manual for the Multiple Affect Adjective Check List–Revised*. San Diego, CA: EdITS.

Author Index

Subject Index

Test Index

$ Springer Publishing Company

Behavior and Personality
Psychological Behaviorism
Arthur W. Staats, PhD

In this capstone work, Arthur Staats synthesizes more than four decades of research, theory, and study to offer a unified theory called Psychological Behaviorism. Drawing upon the study of abnormal behavior, psychological measurement, personality, and child development, he provides an overarching theoretical framework that accounts for all aspects of human behavior. He also develops a theory of personality to show how

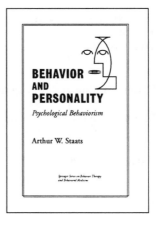

his unifying theory is derived from these various approaches. This book is useful for professionals, researchers, and students interested in a unified approach to psychology, behavior therapy, abnormal behavior, psychological measurement and personality.

Contents:
- Behaviorizing Psychology and Psychologizing Behaviorism: A New Unified Approach
- The Basic Learning / Behavior Therapy
- The Human Learning Theory
- The Child Development and Social Interaction Theories
- The Psychological Behaviorism Theory of Personality
- The Content of Personality: Behaviorizing Psychological Testing
- The PB Theory of Abnormal Behavior
- Psychological Behavior Therapy
- A Theory of Theories, Heuristic, with a Plan and Program

Springer Series: Behavior Therapy and Behavioral Medicine
1996   420pp   0-8261-9311-0   hardcover

536 Broadway, New York, NY 10012-3955 • (212) 431-4370 • Fax (212) 941-7842